Few people in my life have modeled the ___ 119 more than Mark Twombly. In the formative days of my spiritual growth, the Lord blessed me with the godly example of a man who found the Word of God sweeter than honey, better than thousands of gold and silver pieces. He read it, meditated on it, memorized it, taught it, and rejoiced in it as one who finds great spoil. To this day, I recognize that I've memorized portions of Psalm 119 because of how many times I heard Mark quote them to me in conversation.

Those are just some of the reasons why it is a joy for me to commend this volume to you. It represents a faithful disciple's lifelong pursuit of glorifying God by treasuring His Word. It is birthed out of daily walking with Jesus through the trials and triumphs of ordinary life. With helpful insights drawn from other sound teachers, this devotional has the aroma of Christ—bearing plentiful evidence that its author has been with the Lord. The benefits of that communion will prove an immense service to fellow students of the Word.

Michael Riccardi, PhD
Assistant Professor of Theology, The Master's Seminary
Pastor, Local Outreach Ministries, Grace Community Church

Mark Twombly's love for the Word of God is compelling and contagious. Mark's encouragement to me and others to dwell deeply with God through his Word was invaluable to us as a young church plant in New Jersey. His desire is for people to delight in God and to drink deeply from the true source of living water. Mark's example has me hungry to engage the 119th Psalm afresh through this new book.

Reid S. Monaghan
Founder and President, The Gospel Underground

Mark Twombly has a heart for the Bible because he has a heart that desires to know God. This book overflows with a passion for the God who has spoken. Mark's fervent love for the Scriptures and for the God who wrote the Scriptures is evident throughout. I have known Mark for a number of years and I know something of the depth of his love for the Word of God and for the God who inspired it. I know of no one better to write a devotional book on Psalm 119.

Anyone who desires to have a greater fervency for the God of the Bible will profit from Mark's devotional thoughts. Read this book—it is contagious.

Dennis M. Cahill D. Min.
Founding Pastor of Christ Community Church,
Piscataway, NJ, author of *The Shape of Preaching*

"God and His Word" delves into the beauty and power of God's Word with a profound and accessible approach. Mark's insightful commentary on Psalm 119 provides spiritual nourishment for the hungry soul and challenges us to take God's Word more seriously. As readers journey through the book, they will resonate with the psalmist's own cry, "Open my eyes, that I may behold Wonderful things from Your law!"

Omar Villacres M. Div
Lead Pastor, Garwood Church, Garwood, NJ

The hours Mark Twombly has invested in reading and reflection shine through with honesty and transparency. Reading this volume was especially interesting to me because I know Mark. The objective of Psalm 119 is the same, taking us past the words and principles to a relationship with the Author. Many people read Scripture for the sake of reading it; others stop merely at the principles of living without truly knowing the Lord Himself. Mark calls his readers not just to the beauty of the psalm, or the guidance for living, but to join with him into a more intimate relationship with the God who wrote it.

In addition to the devotional benefit made to the reader, Mark has done a great service to the reader by drawing from voluminous commentaries to provide any student or teacher with excellent quotes about each verse. In addition, he connects the patterns of words and phrases from the original Hebrew in a way that is helpful to both those who are familiar with the language, as well as to those who have never studied it. Mark captures in one volume an aid in both spiritual growth and biblical scholarship, yet in a readable and enjoyable manner.

Pastor James G. Miller D. Min
First Baptist Church of Metuchen, NJ

God and His Word

A Devotional Commentary in Psalm 119

James -
May God use the truths of this book to expand your delight in and love for God and His Word.

Blessings,
Mark

MARK DANIEL TWOMBLY

Mark D. Twombly

LUCIDBOOKS

Table of Contents

Dedication

This volume is dedicated to my wife, Betty, who has faithfully loved me in Christ these past 34 years and encouraged me to write and publish, to our children and spouses Lauren, Luke, Seth and Esther Twombly, Noel and Joe Riccardi, Lee, and Jackson, to our grandchildren Nolan, Ella, Micah, and Hailey and

> *"That the generation to come might know,*
> *even the children yet to be born,*
> *That they may arise and recount them to their children,*
> *That they should set their confidence in God*
> *And not forget the deeds of God,*
> *But observe His commandments,"*

—Psalms 78:6-7, LSB

Finally, this volume is dedicated to the one and only triune God whose
Perfect law restores the soul
Sure testimony makes wise the simple
Right precepts rejoice the heart, and
Pure commandments enlighten the eyes.
(from Psalm 19:7-8)

Soli Deo Gloria

Special Thanks

To the parents, pastors, elders, and teachers who have taught and lived the word of God before me:

Lee and Janet Twombly, Pastor Norm Swenson, Mrs. Childers, Chuck and Barbara Lloyd, Peter and Debbie Udall, Pastor Paul Shadle, Peter Blackburn, Larry and Brenda Bauer, Joe Brookman, Wayne Polzin, Pastor Peter Pendell, Reverend David Morgan, Pastor Jim Miller, Pastor Paul Decker, Art Peersen, Carl Smith, Jerry and Dorothy Lee, Pastor Dennis Cahill, Pastor Rick Ravis, Pastor Reid Monaghan, Pastor James Fields, Pastor Mike Riccardi, Pastor Omar Villacres, Pastor Joseph Babij, Pastor David Capoccia, and others unknown.

INTRODUCTION
God and His Word

"For I proclaim the name of the LORD;
Ascribe greatness to our God!
"The Rock! His work is perfect,
For all His ways are just;
A God of faithfulness and without injustice,
Righteous and upright is He."

—Deuteronomy 32:3-4

"I will bow down toward Your holy temple
And give thanks to Your name for
Your lovingkindness and Your truth;
For You have magnified Your word
according to all Your name."

—Psalm 138:2

"The law of the LORD is perfect, restoring the soul;

—Psalm 19:7a

"How blessed are those whose way is blameless,
Who walk in the law of the LORD.
How blessed are those who observe His testimonies,
Who seek Him with all their heart."

—Psalm 119:1-2

1

Approach

As I introduce this devotional commentary, I encourage you to approach it with two key principles in mind: *perfection* and *presence*. Surely we worship a God of infinite perfection, One whose thoughts, words, and ways are infinitely above ours (Isaiah 55:8-11). Surely in light of that perfection, we stand in speechless awe (Psalm 33:8-9, Ecclesiastes 5:2). Yet in that perfection, He is not aloof. He draws near to us through His word (Psalm 119:102, 151), reviving our souls and perfecting our ways. The word for 'perfect' in Deuteronomy 32:4 and Psalm 19:7 and 'blameless' in Psalm 119:1 is the Hebrew תָּמִים, tāmiym, an adjective the sense of which is blameless, complete, integrity, undefiled truth, sound, healthful, and unimpaired. Think about this. The infinitely perfect God of the universe draws near to perfect those who walk in His law, observe His testimonies, and seek Him with all their heart. How does He do this? He provides the knowledge, understanding, desire, ability, and delight; He initiates and sustains it all. For such they are blessed, that is, in an indescribable state of bliss.

Purpose

> 'All Scripture is God-breathed and profitable for teaching, for reproof, for correction, for training in righteousness, so that the man of God may be equipped, having been thoroughly equipped for every good work.'
>
> —2 Timothy 3:16 LSB

Psalm 119 accomplishes these purposes in myriad ways. I trust that by now, even reading this short introduction, your heart is stirred with curiosity, if not with deep hunger.

A Warning

Throughout my life I have been accused of some form of bibliolatry, that is, a worship of the Bible. I have promoted the truth of the Bible in ways that were impatient or angry, not reflecting the character of its Author. I have memorized and studied to impress people more than to please God. I am guilty as charged. Yet, looking back, I see the reality of Psalm 119:176 in my life:

> *"I have gone astray like a lost sheep; seek Your servant,*
> *For I do not forget Your commandments."*

God in His kindness continues to pursue and transform me! In spite of my prideful motivations, God through His word has taught, reproved, corrected, and trained me (2 Timothy 3:16), and continues to do so.

The biblical basis for the accusation of bibliolatry comes from John 5:38-40. How confusing it must have been for the people of Jesus' day to observe those who apparently knew God's word the best reflect God's character the least. They knew the book of life but refused to draw near to its Author. How could this be? Much could be said here, but suffice it to say that the Pharisees' focus was not on God's word, but on their own man-made traditions by which they invalidated it (see Matthew 15:3-9). They worshiped not God, but themselves. They loved God and His word not too much, but too little.

Is there an epidemic of bibliolatry? Is there a growing trend of those who think too highly of the Bible and have no real relationship with the Living God? I trust that as you meditate on the words of Psalm 119, you will see nothing of such a sentiment, but a growing realization of the incalculable treasure that God in His mercy has placed before you. You will be blessed beyond measure as you experience God's presence as He speaks personally and powerfully to you by His perfect Word.

> *"I have rejoiced in the way of Your testimonies,*
> *As much as in all riches."*
>
> —Psalm 119:14

> *"I shall delight in Your commandments,*
> *Which I love.*
> *And I shall lift up my hands to Your commandments,*
> *Which I love;*
> *And I will meditate on Your statutes."*
>
> —Psalm 119:47-48

But there is another warning I must call your attention to:

> *"Now the serpent was more crafty than any beast of the field which the LORD God had made. And he said to the woman, "Indeed, has God said, 'You shall not eat from any tree of the garden'?"*
>
> —Genesis 3:1

> *"But I am afraid that, as the serpent deceived Eve by his craftiness, your minds will be led astray from the simplicity and purity of devotion to Christ."*
>
> —2 Corinthians 11:3

Variations of 'has God said' ring throughout the ages and in our lives today. Because the attacks are constant, we need constant reminders. Psalm 119 will remind you daily of the reality of what you have in front of you in the written word of God. They are certain and correct (Proverbs 22:21), and the only rock upon which to build a life (Matthew 7:24-27).

A Word About the (Human) Author of Psalm 119

It is not my purpose here to advocate for a specific human author of Psalm 119. Scholars have advocated for David, Daniel, and Ezra. Surely these men of faith were compelling examples of intimacy with God, lives transformed by God, and love for His word:

David: King of Israel, Man After God's Own Heart

> *"The law of the LORD is perfect, restoring the soul;*
> *The testimony of the LORD is sure, making wise the simple.*
> *The precepts of the LORD are right, rejoicing the heart;*
> *The commandment of the LORD is pure, enlightening the eyes.*
> *The fear of the LORD is clean, enduring forever;*
> *The judgments of the LORD are true; they are righteous altogether.*
> *They are more desirable than gold, yes, than much fine gold;*
> *Sweeter also than honey and the drippings of the honeycomb."*
>
> —Psalm 19:7-10

In language very similar to Psalm 119 (particularly Psalm 119:103-104) David lived a life of utter dependence and love for God in His word.

Daniel: Man of Conviction, Israeli Ambassador in the Babylonian Exile

> "To the Lord our God belong compassion and forgiveness, for we have rebelled against Him; nor have we obeyed the voice of the LORD our God, to walk in His teachings which He set before us through His servants the prophets."
>
> —Daniel 9:9-10

Daniel lived a life of resolved conviction and faithfulness, recognizing that the welfare of God's people was the result of their faithfulness to His word.

Ezra: Priest for the Returning Exiles in Israel

> "For Ezra had set his heart to study the law of the LORD and to practice it, and to teach His statutes and ordinances in Israel."
>
> —Ezra 7:10

Ezra presents to us a holistic approach to God's word: an engaged heart and a credible life as a foundation for teaching.

Words About the Word

Psalm 119 uses the following terms to describe various aspects of Scripture (which are identical to those in Psalm 19:7-10):

- *Law*: v.1, תורה, tôrāh, the Old Testament laws given to Moses. God's law provides the foundation for life and action.
- *Testimonies*: v.2, עֵדָה, ʿēḏāh, God's permanent witness, the basis of His covenant with His people.
- *Precepts*: v.4, דוּקְפ, piqqûḏ, collective mandates, how God wants things ordered.
- *Statutes*: v.5, חֹק, ḥōq, regulation, law, ordinance, decree, custom, of God's divine will.

- *Commandments*: v.6, מִצְוָה, miṣwāh, commandment. Our sovereign Lord's commands are not optional.
- *Judgments*: v.7, מִשְׁפָּט, mišpāṭ, a judgment, a legal decision, a legal case, a claim. His verdicts are both authoritative and liberating.
- *Word*: v.9, דָּבָר, dāḇār, word, speech; of anything God has spoken, commanded, or promised.

A Word About Commentaries

I have drawn from several classic commentaries in this volume, most notably Spurgeon's *Treasury of David* and *The Golden Alphabet*, Keil & Delitzsch, Matthew Henry, and William Swan Plumer's *Studies in the Psalms*. Quotes from Spurgeon presume King David as the human author of Psalm 119. For more technical commentary I recommend *Psalms (The Expositors Bible Commentary)* by William A. VanGemeren or *Psalms: An Introduction and Commentary* by Tremper Longman III.

The Format of this Devotional and a Personal Note

Psalm 119 is divided into 22 - 8 verse sections, 1 for each letter of the Hebrew alphabet. Other acrostic patterns in Scripture can be found in Psalms 9, 10, 24, 34, 37, 111, 112, 145, Proverbs 31:10-31, Lamentations 1-4, and Nahum 1:2-8. These are noted in the paper editions of the LSB (Legacy Standard Bible).

The ancient Hebrew language was designed with these patterns and for memorization, a legacy that is passed on to us through the generations into myriad languages.

I have provided a brief introduction to each section followed by a deeper dive into each verse.

I have long read a section of Psalm 119 as preparation for my daily devotions. It sharpens my mind and enflames my affections. I am reminded of the feast God has set before me in His word. I heartily recommend this discipline to you.

Psalm 119 is a prayer. As such, the notes you have before you are presented most often in the second person, addressed to God as prayers. I never want us to lose sight that God is near to us in His word (vv. 102, 151).

I urge you to meditate on Psalm 119 personally, slowly, and prayerfully. This devotional is meant to supplement and encourage your intimacy with God and time in His word, not to replace it. I have been generous with cross-references, encouraging you to enjoy the consistency of God's word and to explore it more deeply.

Psalm 119-Mem (vv. 97-104) to me represents the heart of this Psalm. My prayer for you is that vv. 103-104 be your experience more and more each day!

> *"I have not turned aside from Your ordinances,*
> *For You Yourself have taught me.*
> *How sweet are Your words to my taste! Yes, sweeter than honey to my mouth!*
> *From Your precepts I get understanding;*
> *Therefore I hate every false way."*

Mark D. Twombly
Belle Mead, NJ
2023

CHAPTER 1
Aleph: 'How Blessed!'

"Aleph. How blessed are those whose way is blameless,
Who walk in the law of the LORD.
How blessed are those who observe His testimonies,
Who seek Him with all their heart.
They also do no unrighteousness;
They walk in His ways.
You have ordained Your precepts,
That we should keep them diligently.
Oh that my ways may be established
To keep Your statutes!
Then I shall not be ashamed
When I look upon all Your commandments.
I shall give thanks to You with uprightness of heart,
When I learn Your righteous judgments.
I shall keep Your statutes;
Do not forsake me utterly!"

—Psalm 119:1-8

The Psalmist sets for us a tone of heart obedience which only grows. Notice 'the way of' in vv. 14, 27, 32-33. We are to rejoice in, understand, observe, and run in the way of Your word. This is the Great Commission (Matthew 28:18-20) in the Old Testament! This is no mere instruction, this is the full surrender of discipleship. Luke 9:23, Luke 14:33, Proverbs 2:1-5.

The Christian life is no mere hobby. See Mark 4:19-20; Psalm 119 is the best antidote I know of so that the effect of God's word is not hindered in its fruitfulness.

"These first eight verses are taken up with a contemplation of the blessedness which comes through keeping the statutes of the Lord. The subject is treated in a devout manner rather than in a didactic style. Heart-fellowship with God is enjoyed through a love of that word which is God's way of communing with the soul by his Holy Spirit . . . You are not only instructed, but influenced to holy emotion, and helped to express the same.

'The changes are rung upon the words "way" - "undefiled in the way," "walk in his ways," "O that my ways were directed"; "keep" - "keep his testimonies," "keep thy precepts diligently," "directed to keep," "I will keep"; and "walk" - "walk in the law," "walk in his ways." Yet there is no tautology, nor is the same thought repeated, though to the careless reader, it may seem so.

"The change from statements about others and about the Lord to more personal dealing with God begins in Psalm 119:3, and becomes more clear as we advance, till in the later verses the communion becomes most intense and soul moving. O that every reader may feel the glow."[1]

Psalm 119:1

> "Aleph. How blessed are those whose way is blameless,
> Who walk in the law of the LORD."

---

1. Spurgeon, Charles Haddon, *Treasury of David*, Psalm 119 introduction, e-Sword edition

'How blessed" 'hearkens back to Psalm 1:1-2, yet this verse moves us right to the parallels of Psalm 1:1-2 to what such a man does. 'Blessed' is the Hebrew אֶשֶׁר, 'ešer, a noun with the sense of a state of bliss. In America, we use the word 'happiness', which I find to be too shallow. Bliss is to be justly satisfied in the soul, not lustfully satiated in one's flesh. It has a depth and permanence about it, resilient in all circumstances. 'Blameless' is the Hebrew תָּמִים, tāmiym, which is an adjective with the sense of blameless, complete, and is often linked with truth, virtue, uprightness, and righteousness. It appears 12 times in Psalms, and one other in Psalm 119, Psalm 119:80 of a blameless heart 'Walk' is the Hebrew הָלַך, hālak which, with other related Hebrew words, describes the pathway or pattern of one's life behavior. Such a walk is also described in Psalm 119:3 ('in His ways') and Psalm 119:45 ('at liberty').

Father, may I experience an indescribable bliss, an inner wholeness as my pathways follow Your eternal paths (Proverbs 4:18)! Unspeakable bliss is found in greatly delighting in Your commandments (Psalm 112:1), of walking with Christ by faith (1 Peter 1:8-9)!

"Blessed are the undefiled!" meaning thereby, that we eagerly desire to become such ourselves, and wish for no greater happiness than to be perfectly holy.

"Purity in our way and walk is the truest blessedness.

"Settle it in your hearts as a first postulate and sure rule of practical science that holiness is happiness, and that it is our wisdom first to seek the Kingdom of God and his righteousness.

"Outward evil would little hurt us if we were entirely rid of the evil of sin, an attainment which with the best of us lies still in the region of desire, and is not yet fully reached, though we have so clear a view of it that we see it to be blessedness itself; and therefore we eagerly press towards it.

"He whose life is in a gospel sense undefiled, is blessed, because he could never have reached this point if a thousand blessings had not already been bestowed on him. By nature we are defiled and out of the way, and we must therefore have been washed in the atoning blood to remove defilement, and we must have been converted by the power of the Holy Ghost, or we should not have been turned into the way of peace, nor be undefiled in it.

"The blessedness which is thus set before us we must aim at, but we must not think to obtain it without earnest effort. David has a great deal to say about it; his discourse in this Psalm is long and solemn, and it is a hint to us that the way of perfect obedience is not learned in a day; there must be precept upon precept, line upon line, and after efforts long enough to be compared with the 176 verses of this Psalm we may still have to cry, 'I have gone astray like a lost sheep; seek thy servant; for I do not forget thy commandments.'"[2]

Psalm 119:2

"How blessed are those who observe His testimonies,
Who seek Him with all their heart."

Of inestimable value is Your word! To observe with all my heart has value beyond description. Enrapture my heart, let me soar the heights!

'Blessed' is the same as in v.1, a state of bliss. 'Observe' is the Hebrew נָצַר, nāṣar: A verb with the sense of guard, keep, observe, preserve, or hide. We see it used with respect to God's word in Psalm 119:100, 115. I am reminded of Psalm 119:165, the peace that ensues the loving of Your law. These seem elusive, but I trust in You to make it so.

" . . . they walk in the paths of that law, which they will not trifle in, but *press forward* in them *towards the mark*, taking every step by rule and never walking at all adventures."[3]

"God is not truly sought by the cold researches of the brain: we must seek him with the heart . . . It is in vain that we endeavour to comprehend him by reason; we must apprehend him by affection. But the heart must not be divided with many objects if the Lord is to be sought by us. God is one, and we shall not know him till our heart is one. A broken heart need not be distressed at this, for no heart is so whole in its seekings after

---

2. Spurgeon, Charles Haddon, *Treasury of David*, Psalm 119 - Aleph, e-Sword edition
3. Henry, Matthew, *Commentary on the Whole Bible*, on Psalm 119:2, e-Sword edition

God as a heart which is broken, whereof every fragment sighs and cries after the great Father's face. It is the divided heart which the doctrine of the text censures, and strange to say, in scriptural phraseology, a heart may be divided and not broken, and it may be broken but not divided; and yet again it may be broken and be whole, and it never can be whole until it is broken. When our whole heart seeks the holy God in Christ Jesus it has come to him of whom it is written, 'as many as touched him were made perfectly whole.'"[4]

Psalm 119:3

> "They also do no unrighteousness;
> They walk in His ways."

In this description of this man blessed beyond compare by 1) being blameless, walking in Your law (v.1) , and 2) seeking You with all their heart by observing Your testimonies (v.2), we see now he does no unrighteousness by means of walking in Your ways. I am reminded of Psalm 11:7 and Psalm 12:6, namely, the purity of those who follow the purity of Your Word. He is single minded in his understanding and actions. Psalm 119:9-11. There is no magic formula and there are 'no additives required.' In our pride, we want to add to Your word— yet that is a sure path to untruth and unrighteousness. "'Do not add to His words Or He will reprove you, and you will be proved a liar." (Proverbs 30:6)

"Life, to the outward observer, at any rate, lies much in doing, and he who in his doings never swerves from equity, both towards God and man, has hit upon the way of perfection, and we may be sure that his heart is right . . . they are honest, upright, and chaste, and touching justice and morality they are blameless. Therefore are they happy . . . It is not enough them to be blameless, they wish also to be actively righteous . . . a saint lives in society that he may serve his God by walking in his ways . . .

---

4. Spurgeon, Charles Haddon, *Treasury of David*, on Psalm 119:2, e-Sword edition

The surest way to abstain from evil is to be fully occupied in doing good. This verse describes believers as they exist among us: although they have their faults and infirmities, yet they hate evil, and will not permit themselves to do it; they love the ways of truth, right and true godliness, mid habitually they walk therein. They do not claim to be absolutely perfect except in their desires, and there they are pure indeed, for they pant to be kept from all sin, and to be led into all holiness."[5]

Psalm 119:4

"You have ordained Your precepts,
    That we should keep them diligently."

Your precepts are not simply for our knowledge or interest, though they are truth and inexhaustibly interesting (Proverbs 2:1-5). What is interesting (pun intended) is that they cannot be fully explored or enjoyed without walking in them, as vv. 1-3 bear out. The word is supremely powerful and effective! 'Ordain' is the Hebrew צָוָה, ṣāwāh: A verb with the sense of to order, direct, or command. So we see here that 'ordained' speaks not merely to its purpose, but to its authority and power. As an example of authority, see God's first command to man in Genesis 2:16. As to power, see Psalm 33:9 and Psalm 148:5 where God commanded creation into existence, as He also commands the new creation into existence (2 Corinthians 4:6, 1 Peter 2:9-10). Precepts is the Hebrew פִּקּוּד, piqqûd, דִּיסוּפְּק peqûdiym: A masculine noun with the sense of instruction how things should be ordered. How You want things ordered is how things should be done, for You are the King! I noticed the obvious but profound truth in Ecclesiastes 8:4: 'the word of the king is authoritative'. Your commands are not optional, merely the best advice available. You are the one and only Sovereign (1 Timothy 6:15)! 'Diligently' is the Hebrew מְאֹד, me'ōd, an adverb with the sense of greatly, abundance, might, power. How can I, a mere human, have the

---

5. Spurgeon, Charles Haddon, *Treasury of David*, on Psalm 119:3, e-Sword edition

power to obey? Here is the wonder of it all: the power is the word itself, Hebrews 4:12, 1 Thessalonians 2:13. Amazing.

"God's precepts require *careful* obedience: there is no keeping them by accident. Some give to God a careless service, a sort of hit or miss obedience, but the Lord has not commanded such service, nor will he accept it. His law demands the love of all our heart, soul, mind, and strength; and a careless religion has none of these . . . As a man diligent in business arouses himself to do as much trade as he can, so must we be eager to serve the Lord as much as possible. Nor must we spare pains to do so, for a diligent obedience will also be *laborious* and *self-denying* . . . So should we serve the Lord. Such a Master deserves diligent servants; such service he demands, and will be content with nothing less. How seldom do men render it, and hence many through their negligence miss the double blessing spoken of in this Psalm."[6]

Psalm 119:5

"Oh that my ways may be established
To keep Your statutes!"

Having seen the utter blessedness of walking from the heart in obedience to Your word (vv. 1-2) and Your righteous purposes in Your word (vv. 3-4), the Psalmist cries that His ways would be so established. 'Established' is the Hebrew כּוּן, kûn: A verb with the sense of *set up, make firm, establish, prepare*. It indicates to make upright, fixed, and steadfast. It sets the foundation and direction for one's life, setting a firm and confident course. It reminds me of Jesus' words in Matthew 7:24-27, echoes of Proverbs 10:9, of the confidence of walking in integrity.

" . . . not only that our eyes may be directed to behold God's statutes, but our hearts directed to keep them."[7]

---

6. Spurgeon, Charles Haddon, *Treasury of David*, on Psalm 119:4, e-Sword edition
7. Henry, Matthew, *Commentary on the Whole Bible*, on Psalm 119:5, e-Sword edition

"We cannot of ourselves keep God's statutes as he would have them kept, and yet we long to do so: what resort have we but prayer? We must ask the Lord to work our works in us, or we shall never work out his commandments . . . Our ways are by nature opposed to the way of God, and must be turned by the Lord's direction in another direction from that which they originally take or they will lead us down to destruction. God can direct the mind and will without violating our free agency, and he will do so in answer to prayer; in fact, he has begun the work already in those who are heartily praying after the fashion of this verse . . . The longing of the text is prompted by admiration of the blessedness of holiness, by a contemplation of the righteous man's beauty of character, and by a reverent awe of the command of God."[8]

Psalm 119:6

"Then I shall not be ashamed
When I look upon all Your commandments."

'Then' - when my ways are established to keep Your word (v5), then I shall not be ashamed when I look upon them! What a safeguard against the fear of man (Proverbs 29:25), men of the flesh who stand against You (Philippians 3:18-19). What confidence and boldness for the challenges of life (Proverbs 28:1) and for the anticipation of the return of Jesus (Matthew 24:45-46, 1 John 2:28). In our weakness we await You, our hope is in You and not in ourselves (Philippians 3:20). What joyous fellowship and freedom Adam and Eve had with You in the garden, and what tragic shame after they disobeyed. To 'look upon' is the Hebrew נבָט, naḇāṭ: a verb with the sense of look, watch, regard, to gaze upon with intense focus. It is used elsewhere in Psalm 119 in Psalm 119:15 as 'regard' and Psalm 119:18 as 'behold'. As expected, this word is used of the focus encouraged in Proverbs 4:25, 'let your gaze be fixed'. May I be captivated by Your word and undistracted from it.

---

8. Spurgeon, Charles Haddon, *Treasury of David*, on Psalm 119:5, e-Sword edition

"He has *respect to all the commandments*, one as well as another, because they are all backed with the same authority (Jas 2:10, Jas 2:11) and all levelled at the same end, the glorifying of God in our happiness."[9]

"He had known shame, and here he rejoices in the prospect of being freed from it. Sin brings shame, and when sin is gone, the reason for being ashamed is banished . . . Whenever we err we prepare ourselves for confusion of face and sinking of heart: if no one else is ashamed of me I shall be ashamed of myself if I do iniquity . . . An abiding sense of duty will make us bold, we shall be afraid to be afraid. No shame in the presence of man will hinder us when the fear of God has taken full possession of our minds . . . There is nothing to be ashamed of in a holy life; a man may be ashamed of his pride, ashamed of his wealth, ashamed of his own children, but he will never be ashamed of having in all things regarded the will of the Lord his God . . . A man may have a thousand virtues, and yet a single failing may cover him with shame."[10]

Psalm 119:7

"I shall give thanks to You with uprightness of heart,
When I learn Your righteous judgments."

The blessedness continues from vv. 1-6, of a blameless way, observing Your testimonies, walking in Your ways, keeping Your precepts diligently. If my ways are established to keep Your statutes, surely this is a cause of thankfulness and not shame when I learn more of them! This is not because of my perfection, but of Yours, not because of my sinlessness, but of Your grace and forgiveness. 'Uprightness' is the Hebrew יֹשֶׁר, yōšer: a noun with the sense of straightness, uprightness, or equity. The Old Testament often talks of two paths in life and warns people to stay on the straight path and not to stray onto the crooked path (Pro 2:13).' 'Learn' is the לָמַד, lāmaḏ: a verb with the sense of learn, study, teach, or to be taught, learned. It is elsewhere used with training

---

9. Henry, Matthew, *Commentary on the Whole Bible*, on Psalm 119:6, e-Sword edition
10. Spurgeon, Charles Haddon, *Treasury of David*, on Psalm 119:6, e-Sword edition

for battle. This is a full engagement of the heart and life, reflective of the latter part of Proverbs 21:29, namely, a sure way over a false façade.

"As long as we live we must be scholars in Christ's school, and sit at his feet; but we should aim to be head-scholars, and to get into the highest form. God's judgments are all righteous, and therefore it is desirable not only to learn them, but to be learned in them, *mighty in the scriptures.* [see Apollos in Acts 18:24] . . . he could not learn unless God taught him, and that divine instructions are special blessings, which we have reason to be thankful for . . . It is an easy thing to praise God in word and tongue; but those only are well learned in this mystery who have learned to *praise him with uprightness of heart,* that is, are inward with him in praising him, and sincerely aim at his glory in the course of their conversation as well as in the exercises of devotion. God accepts only the praises of the upright."[11]

"Be sure that he who prays for holiness will one day praise for happiness. Shame having vanished, silence is broken, and the formerly silent man declares, 'I will praise thee . . . ' He would himself be praiseworthy, but he counts God alone worthy of praise . . . there is no music like that which comes from a pure soul which standeth in its integrity. Heart praise is required, uprightness in that heart, and teaching to make the heart upright . . . If we are ever to learn, the Lord must teach us, and especially upon such a subject as his judgments, for they are a great deep. While these are passing before our eyes, and we are learning from them, we ought to praise God, for the original is not, 'when I have learned,' but, 'in my learning.'"[12]

Psalm 119:8

"I shall keep Your statutes;
Do not forsake me utterly!"

Why would the Psalmist cry not to be forsaken? I can think of three reasons. First, a sense of our sinfulness leads to a sense of unworthiness and Your just condemnation, Your abandonment of us for our

11. Henry, Matthew, *Commentary on the Whole Bible*, on Psalm 119:7, e-Sword edition
12. Spurgeon, Charles Haddon, *Treasury of David*, on Psalm 119:7, e-Sword edition

unfaithfulness. Second, and related, is our inability to keep Your law apart from You! Thirdly, faithfulness is a lonely road with few companions, often with only You. You draw near to us in Your word (Psalm 119:151). The fear of abandonment is real. First from You, then from others, see Psalm 27:9-10, Isaiah 41:10, Hebrews 13:5. Even Jesus was abandoned by all but a few earthly companions (John 6:67-69) who then abandoned Him when He needed them the most (Luke 22:1-62), and finally He was abandoned by You so we wouldn't be to accomplish our salvation (Matthew 27:46). Paul's life would also reflect this abandonment and salvation, see 2 Timothy 4:16-18. How precious then it is to have but a few companions in Your word (Psalm 119:74, Psalm 119:79, Philippians 2:1-4), but ultimately and utterly You Who will not utterly forsake me (Psalm 73:25-26).

"We cannot keep them unless we learn them; but we learn them in vain if we do not keep them. Those have well learned God's statutes who have come up to a full resolution, in the strength of his grace, to keep them . . . Good men see themselves undone if God forsakes them; for then the tempter will be too hard for them. "Though thou seem to forsake me, and threaten to forsake me, and dost, for a time, withdraw from me, yet let not the desertion be total and final; for that is hell."[13]

"A calm resolve . . . Feeling his own incapacity he trembles lest he should be left to himself, and this fear is increased by the horror which he has of falling into sin. The 'I will keep' sounds rightly enough now that the humble cry is heard with it. This is a happy amalgam: resolution and dependence . . . To be left, that we may discover our weakness, is a sufficient trial: to be altogether forsaken would be ruin and death . . . his grace will keep us keeping his law . . . The two 'I wills' needed to be seasoned with some such lowly petition, or it might have been thought that the good man's dependence was in some degree fixed upon his own determination. He presents his resolutions like a sacrifice, but he cries to heaven for the fire. [See 1 Kings 18:30-39]"[14]

---

13. Henry, Matthew, *Commentary on the Whole Bible*, on Psalm 119:8, e-Sword edition
14. Spurgeon, Charles Haddon, *Treasury of David*, Psalm 119:8, e-Sword edition

CHAPTER 2
Beth: 'Pure Delight'

"Beth. How can a young man keep his way pure?
By keeping it according to Your word.
With all my heart I have sought You;
Do not let me wander from Your commandments.
Your word I have treasured in my heart,
That I may not sin against You.
Blessed are You, O LORD; Teach me Your statutes.
With my lips I have told of
All the ordinances of Your mouth.
I have rejoiced in the way of Your testimonies,
As much as in all riches.
I will meditate on Your precepts
And regard Your ways.
I shall delight in Your statutes;
I shall not forget Your word."

—Psalm 119:9-16

In this octet the Psalmist goes deeper into the blessedness of the word by seeking its sanctifying impact to the core of his being. The blessedness described in vv.1-2 comes with wholehearted seeking (v.10) which is revealed in a consuming desire for holiness (vv. 9- 11). With such inner freedom from sin, he worships outwardly with his lips (vv. 12-13) and inwardly through rejoicing, meditation, and delight (vv. 14-16). In the New Testament, the Apostle Paul describes the unspeakable, eternal benefits of becoming 'obedient from the heart' (Romans 6:17-22).

'These verses start at the beginning of life. Though written by an old man, they were written for all young men. Only he who begins with God in the greenness of youth will be able to write like this from experience in the ripeness of age. No sooner did David introduce his subject with one octave of verses, then he felt compelled to look after young men in the next set of eight stanzas. How much he thought of youthful piety! In the Hebrew, each verse in this section begins with B. If thoughts on the Blessed Way make up his A, then thoughts on Blessed Young Men will fill up the next letter. Oh, to be with God early in life! To give Him the dew of the day of life is to make the most of life."[15] See also Ecclesiastes 12:1.

Psalm 119:9

> "Beth. How can a young man keep his way pure?
> By keeping it according to Your word."

How can Psalm 119:1-2 be possible, especially for a young man full of fleshly passion? According to Your word. 'Pure' is the Hebrew זָכָה, zākāh: a verb with the sense of clean, cleansed from sin. 'Keeping' is the Hebrew שָׁמַר, šāmar: a verb with the sense of watch, keep, preserve, guard, to be careful, be on one's guard. Purity is no accident, yet it cannot be done with one's own resources (Proverbs 20:9).

---

15. Spurgeon, Charles Haddon. *The Golden Alphabet* (Updated, Annotated): An Exposition of Psalm 119 (pp. 23-24). Aneko Press. Kindle Edition

" . . . the poet desires this, and supplicates God's gracious assistance in order to it. To purify or cleanse one's way or walk (זָכָה, cf. Psa 73:13; Pro 20:9) signifies to maintain it pure."[16]

"You must take heed to your daily life, as well as study your Bible, and you must study your Bible that you may take heed to your daily life . . . Wilful ignorance is in itself wilful sin, and the evil which comes of it is without excuse. Let each man, whether young or old, who desires to be holy have a holy watchfulness in his heart, and keep his Holy Bible before his open eye. There he will find every turn of the road marked down, every slough and miry place pointed out, with the way to go through unsoiled; and there, too, he will find light for his darkness, comfort for his weariness, and company for his loneliness, so that by its help he shall reach the benediction of Psa 119:1 of the Psalm, which suggested the Psalmist's enquiry, and awakened his desires."[17]

Psalm 119:10

"With all my heart I have sought You;
Do not let me wander from Your commandments."

'With all my heart'. Who can say this? We see it also in Psalm 119:34 ('keep it with all my heart), Psalm 119:58 ('I sought Your favor with all my heart'), Psalm 119:69 ('with all my heart I will observe Your precepts'), and Psalm 119:145 ('I cried with all my heart'). This f oft forgotten verse between vv. 9,11 about hiding the word in the heart. At the least it speaks of single-minded focus and a fighting of distractions. 'Sought' is the Hebrew שָׁרַדְ, dāraš: a verb with the sense of seek, inquire of, examine, require. When you require something, your focus is sharpened. So it is for my need of Your word. The meaning of 'wander' is straightforward, but the implications of wandering are stark in the Scriptures. Those who wander from Your word are rebuked by You as arrogant and cursed (Psalm 119:21), and rejected by You for their

---

16. Keil & Delitzsch, *Commentary on the Old Testament*, on Psalm 119:9, e-Sword edition
17. Spurgeon, Charles Haddon, *Treasury of David*, on Psalm 119:9, e-Sword edition

useless deceit (Psalm 119:118). Interestingly, it is used to describe the exhilaration of sex (Proverbs 5:19-20) and the intoxication of wine (Proverbs 20:1). If there is anything we surrender to, may it be Your word! So we see once again surrender to God is the key; I resolve to be single hearted towards You, with a cry for help not to wander. 'Unite my heart to fear Your name' (Psalm 86:11)

" . . . the more we have found of the pleasure there is in keeping God's commandments the more afraid we shall be of wandering from them and the more earnest we shall be in prayer to God for his grace to prevent our wanderings."[18]

"His heart had gone after God himself: he had not only desired to obey his laws, but to commune with his person. This is a right royal search and pursuit, and well may it be followed with the whole heart. The surest mode of cleansing the way of our life is to seek after God himself, and to endeavour to abide in fellowship with him. Up to the good hour in which he was speaking to his Lord, the Psalmist had been an eager seeker after the Lord, and if faint, he was still pursuing. Had he not sought the Lord he would never have been so anxious to cleanse his way . . . A true heart cannot long live without fellowship with God . . . We are to be such whole-hearted seekers that we have neither time nor will to be wanderers."[19]

Psalm 119:11

> "Your word I have treasured in my heart,
> That I may not sin against You."

Seeking a pure way in Your word (v.9) and desiring to be wholehearted and focused (v.10), the Psalmist treasures Your word in His heart to this end, even more so because it is personal, that He may not sin against You. Reflecting on Psalm 51:4, we recognize that all sin, as destructive as it is horizontally (relationship with others), it is because we are not aligned vertically (relationship with You), having broken our

---

18. Henry, Matthew, *Commentary on the Whole Bible*, on Psalm 119:10, e-Sword edition
19. Spurgeon, Charles Haddon, *Treasury of David*, on Psalm 119:10, e-Sword edition

relationship with the Source of all things. Because of this, the Psalmist stores up Your word in his heart as more valuable than all riches (v.14), and later expresses his desire to have his heart inclined to this invaluable inheritance (Psalm 119:111-112).

"One is said to hide (צָפַן) the word in one's heart when one has it continually present with him, not merely as an outward precept, but as an inward motive power in opposition to selfish action (Job 23:12)."[20]

"All that he had of the word written, and all that had been revealed to him by the voice of God, - all, without exception, he had stored away in his affections, as a treasure to be preserved in a casket, or as a choice seed to be buried in a fruitful soil: what soil more fruitful than a renewed heart, wholly seeking the Lord? The word was God's own, and therefore precious to God's servant. He did not wear a text on his heart as a charm, but he hid it in his heart as a rule. He laid it up in the place of love and life, and it filled the chamber with sweetness and light . . . Here is the best thing, - "thy word;" hidden in the best place, - "in my heart;" for the best of purposes, - "that I might not sin against thee." This was done by the Psalmist with personal care, as a man carefully hides away his money When he fears thieves, - in this case the thief dreaded was sin . . . No cure for sin in the life is equal to the word in the seat of life, which is the heart. There is no hiding from sin unless we hide the truth in our souls . . . When the word is hidden in the heart the life shall be hidden from sin. The parallelism between the second octave and the first is still continued. Psalm 119:3 speaks of doing no iniquity, while this verse treats of the method of not sinning."[21]

Psalm 119:12

> "Blessed are You, O LORD;
> Teach me Your statutes."

Having committed his heart to Your word, the Psalmist's heart is naturally raised in worship. It has been said that the depths of knowledge of

---

20. Keil & Delitzsch, *Commentary on the Old Testament*, on Psalm 119:11, e-Sword edition
21. Spurgeon, Charles Haddon, *Treasury of David*, on Psalm 119:11, e-Sword edition

Your word determine the heights of our worship. I am simply in awe of the power, perfection, and beauty of Your word! The Psalmist not only blesses You (Psalm 103:1-2), but desires more of You (Psalm 42:1, Psalm 63:1). 'Blessed' is the Hebrew בָּרַךְ bāraḵ: a verb with the sense of bless, kneel, salute, or greet. 'Teach' is the Hebrew לָמַד lāmaḏ: a verb with the sense of learn, study, teach, taught, or learned. It is a word signifying training. We see this sentiment expressed strongly in Psalm 119 from a man who wishes more than knowledge, but a changed heart (Psalm 119:2), intimate relationship (Psalm 119:10, Psalm 119:151), and a holy life (Psalm 119:5, Psalm 119:33).

"These are words of adoration arising out of an intense admiration of the divine character, which the writer is humbly aiming to imitate. He blesses God for all that he has revealed to him, and wrought in him; he praises him with warmth of reverent love, and depth of holy wonder . . . It is as if David had said—I see that in conformity to thyself my way to happiness must lie, for thou art supremely blessed; and if I am made in my measure like to thee in holiness, I shall also partake in thy blessedness . . . who would not wish to enter the school of such a Master to learn of him the art of holy living? To this Instructor we must submit ourselves if we would practically keep the statutes of righteousness. The King who ordained the statutes knows best their meaning, and as they are the outcome of his own nature he can best inspire us with their spirit . . . If we know the Lord's statutes we have the most essential education."[22]

Psalm 119:13

> "With my lips I have told of
> All the ordinances of Your mouth."

'Mouth' is the Hebrew פֶּה, peh: a noun meaning mouth, but often figuratively of speech. It is used, for example, in Psalm 33:6; the breath of Your mouth created the heavens! My lips can only sing of Your praise

---

22. Spurgeon, Charles Haddon, *Treasury of David*, on Psalm 119:12, e-Sword edition

(see Psalm 119:171) of what You have done. In this age of the 'little gods' heresy, may I speak not from my own imagination, but from what You have said and done. For who can tell of all Your mighty deeds and show forth all Your praise? (Psalm 106:2) It is a single, delightful pursuit of life. You perform; I can but proclaim! Amos 3:7-8, Jeremiah 23:28, 1 Peter 4:11.

"Thus he showed how full he was of the word of God, and what a holy delight he took in his acquaintance with it; for it is *out of the abundance of the heart that the mouth speaks* [Luke 6:45]. Thus he did good with his knowledge; he did not hide God's word from others, but hid it for them; and, out of that *good treasure in his heart*, brought forth good things, as the householder out of his store *things new and old* [Matthew 13:52]."[23]

"What the Lord has veiled, it would be presumption for us to uncover; but on the other hand, what the Lord has revealed, it would be shameful for us to conceal . . . By teaching, we learn. By training the tongue in holy speech, we master the whole body. By familiarity with the divine procedure, we are made to delight in righteousness. Even so, in a threefold manner, our way is cleansed by our proclaiming the way of the Lord. What a joy for anyone to be able to look back on a faithful testimony to divine truth! When weary with Sunday services, how sweet to feel that we have not spoken our own words, but the teachings of divine revelation."[24]

Psalm 119:14

> "I have rejoiced in the way of Your testimonies,
> As much as in all riches."

In one of the most stunning verses in the Bible, the Psalmist continues to rise up in praise as he seeks victory over sin, to be trained by You, and to proclaim Your truth. As he reflects on these, he recognizes what he has, incalculable riches! 'Oh that my ways may be established' (v.5)

---

23. Henry, Matthew, *Commentary on the Whole Bible*, on Psalm 119:13, e-Sword edition
24. Spurgeon, Charles Haddon . *The Golden Alphabet* (Updated, Annotated): An Exposition of Psalm 119 (pp. 32-34). Aneko Press. Kindle Edition.

is expressed in so many ways in this Psalm. As much as in all riches? How excited one is at the thought of acquiring great wealth, of somehow being 'set for life'. Father, we are not only set for this life, but for eternity! Why is my level of rejoicing so low? 'Rejoice' is the Hebrew שׂישׂ, śûś, śiyś: a verb with the sense of rejoice, exalt, jubilant celebration. 'Way of Your testimonies (also precept, commandment, and statutes) occurs in Psalm 119:14, Psalm 119:27, Psalm 119:32-33, and refers to the pathway or pattern of one's life which follows Your ways. See also Isaiah 26:8, which directs our desires towards You, our ultimate treasure (Psalm 73:25-26). In the New Testament, the Apostle prays that the eyes of our heart will be open to see the reality of these riches (see Ephesians 1:15-23, which prays towards seeing the infinite riches of Ephesians 1:1-14). Reflecting on Psalm 119:111-112, may my heart be inclined towards my inheritance! May I rejoice as one who has found great spoil (Psalm 119:72, Psalm 119:162)!

"*I have rejoiced in this as much as in all riches*, as much as ever any worldling rejoiced in the increase of his wealth. In the way of God's commandments I can truly say, Soul, take thy ease;" in true religion there is all riches, the unsearchable riches of Christ."[25]

"Delight in the Word of God is a sure proof that it has taken effect on the heart, and so is cleansing the life . . . The way was as dear to him as the Truth and the Life. There was no picking and choosing with David, or if he actually made a selection, he chose the most practical first. *Above all riches.* He compared his intense satisfaction with God's will with that of a man who possesses large and varied estates and the heart to enjoy them."[26]

Psalm 119:15

"I will meditate on Your precepts
And regard Your ways."

---

25. Henry, Matthew, *Commentary on the Whole Bible*, on Psalm 119:14, e-Sword edition
26. Spurgeon, Charles Haddon. *The Golden Alphabet* (Updated, Annotated): An Exposition of Psalm 119 (pp. 34-35). Aneko Press. Kindle Edition.

At first read, this seems understated. 'I will regard Your ways' comes across something like, 'I will also include You in my plans', which sounds almost dismissive of You. But a closer look at the text reveals something different. So far in this section, the Psalmist has expressed his need of Your word to make him pure (9, 11), the wholeheartedness he wants to bring to it (10), and his rejoicing in it 'as much as all riches' (14). It is with this understanding that he meditates on Your precepts. 'Regard' is the Hebrew נבט, nabāṭ: a verb with the sense of look or watch, with a focused gaze (Psalm 74:20, 119:6, 15, 18). So the 'regard' here might be better said, 'highest regard' in the sense that we see it in James 1:24-25, looking intently into Your perfect law. Because of its beauty and benefits - reflective of You, its Great Author - how could I look casually or look away?

"He who has an inward delight in anything will not long withdraw his mind from it . . . to some men meditation is a task; to the man of cleansed way it is a joy . . . No spiritual exercise is more profitable to the soul than that of devout meditation; why are many of us so exceeding slack in it?... I will think much about them so as to know what thy ways are; and next, I will think much of them so as to have thy ways in great reverence and high esteem. I will see what thy ways are towards me that I may be filled with reverence, gratitude, and love; and then, I will observe what are those ways which thou hast. prescribed for me, thy ways in which thou wouldest have me follow thee."[27]

Psalm 119:16

"I shall delight in Your statutes;
I shall not forget Your word."

'The Psalmist continues this section on rejoicing and meditating on Your word and culminates this with 'delight' and 'I shall not forget'. At this point, we are referring to a person's default thought patterns, a point

---

27. Spurgeon, Charles Haddon, *Treasury of David*, on Psalm 119:15, e-Sword edition

where he does not self-consciously point himself to Your word, but it is his starting point, where his mind goes when and before it goes anywhere else. 'Delight' is the Hebrew שׁעשׁע, šā`a`, verb which in this case has a sense of take delight in, fondle (see also Psalm 119:16, 40, 47). Father, You have created Your word to be treasured within and remembered (see vv. 9,11), and the Psalmist resolves not to forget it throughout the Psalm (Psalm 119:61, 84, 93, 109, 139, 141, 153, 176). The Psalmist does not forget despite all kinds of difficulty and opposition, and ends the Psalm with this resolution.

"When the law is written in the heart duty becomes a delight . . . Those that meditate in God's word, and delight in it, are in no great danger of forgetting it."[28]

"When we have no other solace, but are quite alone, it will be a glad thing for the heart to turn upon itself, and sweetly whisper, "I will delight myself." . . . here is no delighting ourselves with anything below that which God intended to be the soul's eternal satisfaction. The statute-book is intended to be the joy of every loyal subject. When the believer once peruses the sacred pages his soul burns within him as he turns first to one and then to another of the royal words of the great King, words full and firm, immutable and divine . . . Note how two "I wills" follow upon two "I haves." We may not promise for the future if we have altogether failed in the past; but where grace has enabled us to accomplish something, we may hopefully expect that it will enable us to do more."[29]

---

28. Henry, Matthew, *Commentary on the Whole Bible*, on Psalm 119:16, e-Sword edition
29. Spurgeon, Charles Haddon, *Treasury of David*, on Psalm 119:16, e-Sword edition

CHAPTER 3
Gimel: 'Bountiful Counselors'

"Gimel. Deal bountifully with Your servant,
That I may live and keep Your word.
Open my eyes, that I may behold
Wonderful things from Your law.
I am a stranger in the earth;
Do not hide Your commandments from me.
My soul is crushed with longing
After Your ordinances at all times.
You rebuke the arrogant, the cursed,
Who wander from Your commandments.
Take away reproach and contempt from me,
For I observe Your testimonies.
Even though princes sit and talk against me,
Your servant meditates on Your statutes.
Your testimonies also are my delight;
They are my counselors."

—Psalm 119:17-24

While the Psalmist finds life, fellowship, and illumination in You (vv. 17-18), he finds death, alienation, and despair on earth (vv.19-23, also Psalm 119:87). Seeking to be redeemed from the oppression of man (Psalm 119:134) by the arrogant and powerful who bring reproach and contempt, the Psalmist seeks continual illumination within through the counsel and comfort of Your word, which is ultimate truth (Psalm 119:43, Psalm 119:142, Psalm 119:151, Psalm 119:160).

"In this section the trials of the way appear to be manifest to the Psalmist's mind, and he prays accordingly for the help which will meet his case. As in the last eight verses he prayed as a youth newly come into the world, so here he pleads as a servant and a pilgrim, who growingly finds himself to be a stranger in an enemy's country. His appeal is to God alone, and his prayer is specially direct and personal. He speaks with the Lord as a man speaketh with his friend. [Exodus 33:11]"[30]

Psalm 119:17

> "Gimel. Deal bountifully with Your servant,
> That I may live and keep Your word."

I look to the Source of life to live. What is the purpose of life? To know You, which is life itself (Jeremiah 9:23-24, John 17:3). To keep Your word is the only way to truly live! I think of Your generosity, which is beyond belief (Romans 8:32). It would be enough that You do not destroy us in Your righteous anger (Psalm 78:38), but You do so much more than this, lavishing us with Your presence (Psalm 16:11, Psalm 36:7-9), Your grace (Ephesians 1:7), Your joy (1 Peter 1:8-9). 'Bountifully' is the Hebrew גָּמַל, gāmal: a verb with the sense of recompense another, bring to completion, do good, at times translates as 'deal bountifully' (Psalm 13:6, 116:7, 119:17, Proverbs 11:17, Isaiah 63:7). The sense here is completion or satisfaction. I see it as an elaboration on the bliss of 'blessed' in vv.1-3. May I ever be satisfied with Your likeness (Psalm 17:15)!

---

30. Spurgeon, Charles Haddon, *Treasury of David*, on Psalm 119 - Gimel, e-Sword edition

"He takes pleasure in acknowledging his duty to God, and he considers it the joy of his heart to be in the service of his God . . . The psalmist is asking God to let his wage be according to God's goodness and not according to his own merit. Reward me according to the largeness of your generosity, and not according to the meagerness of my service . . . Only the Lord can keep us alive, and it is mighty grace which preserves the life that we have forfeited by our sin . . . Spiritual life, without which this natural life is nothing more than existence, is also to be sought from the Lord's bounty, for it is the noblest work of divine grace, and through which the abundance of God is gloriously displayed . . . We may not want to live and sin, but we can pray to live and keep God's Word. Being is a poor thing if it is not well-being. Life is only worth keeping while we can keep God's Word . . . If we serve God, it is because He gives us grace. We work *for* Him because He works *in* us."[31]

Psalm 119:18

"Open my eyes, that I may behold
Wonderful things from Your law."

This is an often repeated prayer, asking You, whose word is living and active, always fresh, always delightful, to make it so by experience in my heart by Your Spirit. The unspeakably wonderful things are already there, if I could but see them! I am reminded of Ephesians 1:18, a prayer that the eyes of our hearts may be enlightened, and also Ephesians 3:18-19, that we might see what we can't see, and know by experience what we can't know, and to be filled with what we don't have, namely Your fullness by Your Spirit. 'Behold' reminds us of 2 Corinthians 3:18, that You would show us Your glory and that we would be transformed. How does that happen today? Moses beheld Your glory (Exodus 33:18-34:7, note both the sight and the word) and the Apostles beheld Your glory (John 1:14, Matthew 17:2, Mark 9:2, 2

---

31. Spurgeon, Charles Haddon . *The Golden Alphabet* (Updated, Annotated): An Exposition of Psalm 119 (pp. 40-41). Aneko Press. Kindle Edition

Peter 1:16-21), yet one of them said that Your word is 'more sure', 'as a lamp shining in a dark place, until the day dawns and the morning star arises in your hearts'. May my heart be enraptured by what You show me in Your word today. Even as I write this, it is, and I am in awe. 'Wonderful things' is relatively rare in the O.T., occurring just one other time as 'wonders' in Psalm 119:27.

> "The only thing worse than being blind is having sight but
> no vision."
>
> —Helen Keller

"The Tôra beneath the surface of its letter contains an abundance of such 'wondrous things,' into which only eyes from which God has removed the covering of natural short-sightedness penetrate."[32]

"It is far better to have the eyes opened than to be placed in the midst of the noblest prospects and remain blind to their beauty . . . He [the Psalmist] didn't have even half the Bible, but he treasured it more than some people cherish the whole thing. He felt that God had laid up great benefits and rewards in His Word, and he begs for power to perceive, appreciate, and enjoy them. We do not so much need God to give us more benefits, as we need the ability to see what He has already given.

The prayer implies a conscious darkness, a dimness of spiritual vision, a powerlessness to remove that defect, and a full assurance that God can remove it . . . The Bible is a land of wonder. It not only relates miracles, but is itself a world of wonders.

Yet what are these to closed eyes? And what person who is born blind can open his own eyes? God himself must reveal revelation to each heart. Scripture needs opening, but not half as much as our eyes do . . . it is a test of the true knowledge of God that it causes its possessor to thirst for deeper knowledge."[33]

---

32. Keil & Delitzsch, *Commentary on the Old Testament*, on Psalm 119:18, e-Sword edition
33. Spurgeon, Charles Haddon. *The Golden Alphabet* (Updated, Annotated): An Exposition of Psalm 119 (pp. 42-43). Aneko Press. Kindle Edition

Psalm 119:19

"I am a stranger in the earth;
Do not hide Your commandments from me."

"Think it not strange' - that I would feel out of place, that opposition would be normal, see 1 Peter 2:9-10, 1 Peter 4:12. I am no longer bound for destruction, Psalm 119:87, Philippians 3:18-19. Isn't it interesting that Your people, who are to see the futility of life under the sun (Ecclesiastes 1:14) provide the most benefit to it by seeking not it, but You! (Jeremiah 29:7, Philippians 2:14-15.)

"Upon earth we have no abiding resting-place, we sojourn here as in a strange land (Psa 119:19, Psa 39:13; 1Ch 29:15). Hence the poet prays in Psa 119:19 that God would keep His commandments, these rules of conduct for the journey of life, in living consciousness for him."[34]

"The Psalmist was a stranger for God's sake, else had he been as much at home as worldlings are; he was not a stranger to God, but a stranger to the world, a banished man so long as he was out of heaven . . . David implies that God's commands were his solace in his exile' they reminded him of home, and they showed him the way thither, and therefore he begged that they might never be hidden from him, by his being unable either to understand them or to obey them . . . What would be the use of opened eyes if the best object of sight were hidden from their view? While we wander here we can endure all the ills of this foreign land with patience if the word of God is applied to our hearts by the Spirit of God; but if the heavenly things which make for our peace were hid from our eyes we should be in an evil case, - in fact, we should be at sea without a compass, in a desert without a guide, in an enemy's country without a friend."[35]

---

34. Keil & Delitzsch, *Commentary on the Old Testament*, on Psalm 119:19, e-Sword edition
35. Spurgeon, Charles Haddon, *Treasury of David*, on Psalm 119:19, e-Sword edition

Psalm 119:20

> "My soul is crushed with longing
> After Your ordinances at all times."

Is 'crushed with longing' a sustainable state? Certainly, the goal is unsurpassed. 'Crushed' is the Hebrew גָּרַס, gāras: a verb with the sense of broken, crushed, wasting away. 'Longing' is the Hebrew תַּאֲבָה, ta'abāh: a noun with the sense of intense desire These words normally indicate a severe lack of health, yet is it not healthy to have no greater desire than this?

"Longing [see also Psalm 119:174] states the bias of mind in or at which the soul feels itself thus overpowered even to being crushed: it is crushing from longing after God's judgment, viz., after a more and more thorough knowledge of them."[36]

"'True godliness lies very much in desires. As we are not what we shall be, so also we are not what we would be. The desires of gracious men after holiness are intense, - they cause a wear of heart, a straining of the mind, till it feels ready to snap with the heavenly pull . . . Desires which can be put off and on like our garments are at best but mere wishes, and possibly they are hardly true enough to be called by that name, - they are temporary emotions born of excitement, and doomed to die when the heat which created them has cooled down. He who always longs to know and do the right is the truly right man. His judgment is sound, for he loves all God's judgments, and follows them with constancy. His times shall be good, since he longs to be good and to do good at all times."[37]

Psalm 119:21

> "You rebuke the arrogant, the cursed,
> Who wander from Your commandments."

---

36. Keil & Delitzsch, *Commentary on the Old Testament*, on Psalm 119:20, e-Sword edition
37. Spurgeon, Charles Haddon, *Treasury of David*, on Psalm 119:20, e-Sword edition

Wandering is far from innocuous—it is dangerous. It ignores the realities of this life and the next. It assumes that the default is good and man's heart is naturally good. Yet, so many seem so inoculated to the danger. In what way do You rebuke them? To wander is to be arrogant and cursed. Proverbs 1:32-33 and Psalm 73:18 open our eyes to the reality. 'Prone to wander, Lord I feel it' (from the hymn 'Come Thou Fount'). The Psalmist ends Psalm 119 with this concern: "'I have gone astray like a lost sheep; seek Your servant, For I do not forget Your commandments." (Psalms 119:176). You mercifully answer this prayer through the life giving reproof (Proverbs 15:31) of affliction (see vv. 67, 71).

"Here is, 1. The wretched character of wicked people. The temper of their minds is bad. They are proud; they magnify themselves above others. And yet that is not all: they magnify themselves against God, and set up their wills in competition with and opposition to the will of God, as if their hearts, and tongues, and all, were their own . . . 2. The wretched case of such. They are certainly cursed, for God resists the proud [1 Peter 5:5-6]; and those that throw off the commands of the law lay themselves under its curse (Gal 3:10), and he that now beholds them afar off will shortly say to them, Go, you cursed. The proud sinners bless themselves; God curses them."[38]

"God rebukes pride even when the multitudes pay homage to it, for he sees in it rebellion against his own majesty, and the seeds of yet further rebellions."[39]

Psalm 119:22

"Take away reproach and contempt from me,
For I observe Your testimonies."

The Psalmist asks for reproach (i.e. scorn) and contempt (i.e. disrespect) to be removed. Why? Because he observes (obeys continually) Your testimonies. As such, he invites neither man's disrespect nor Your

---

38. Henry, Matthew, *Commentary on the Whole Bible*, on Psalm 119:21, e-Sword edition
39. Spurgeon, Charles Haddon, *Treasury of David*, on Psalm 119:21, e-Sword edition

disapproval. If he has the former, the latter will sustain him, and if he has the approval of men, he knows it is but fleeting and Your approval will be his foundation. Still, the Psalmist dreads reproach and turns to Your word (Psalm 119:39). He knows that the contempt of men comes only from those who are contemptible to You (Psalm 123:3-4). He knows the security of his position and the doom that awaits those far from You (Psalm 141:8-10).

"No one likes to be traduced, or even to be despised. He who says, 'I care nothing for my reputation,' is not a wise man, for in Solomon's esteem 'a good name is better than precious ointment.' [Ecclesiastes 7:1] . . .

If through fear of reproach we forsake the divine testimony we shall deserve the coward's doom; our safety lies in sticking close to the true and to the right. God will keep those who keep his testimonies. A good conscience is the best security for a good name; reproach will not abide with those who abide with Christ, neither will contempt remain upon those who remain faithful to the ways of the Lord.

This verse stands as a parallel both in sense and position to Psa 119:6, and it has the catchword of 'testimonies,' by which it chimes with Psa 119:14."[40]

Psalm 119:23

"Even though princes sit and talk against me,
Your servant meditates on Your statutes."

It is good not to care what people think. When one knows You, one tends not to be intimidated. The fear of man truly is a snare (Proverbs 29:25), man apart from You should not be regarded (Isaiah 2:22) and are like the animals that perish (Psalm 49:20). All the powers of the earth are counted as less than nothing to You (Isaiah 40:17). It is good to realize this as I come into Your presence! Loving the approval of men

---

40. Spurgeon, Charles Haddon, *Treasury of David*, on Psalm 119:22, e-Sword edition

over Your approval is deadly, eternally so (John 12:42-43, Romans 1:32). It is surely right to obey You rather than men (Acts 4:19-20), and if I were to be a man pleaser, I could not be a servant of Christ (Galatians 1:10). Man at his best is foolish and weak (1 Corinthians 1:20-25). I want to be with those who are with You (Psalm 119:74, Psalm 119:79, Philippians 2:1-2). So, when 'princes' sit and talk against me, what do I do? I aim infinitely higher to hear Your word. Psalm 27:1-4 is perhaps the consummate example of this, a man experiencing intimacy with You internally while facing unspeakable opposition externally. The Psalmist would go deeper into this in v.24, delighting in Your constant counsel. Like Stephen, may I be like one with whom godless man cannot cope without turning to You (Acts 6:10). In fact, one might say, if there is not strong opposition in some quarters, we are not living the righteous life we should (Proverbs 29:27, 2 Timothy 3:12). You will give us the words to say when dragged before earthly authorities, giving opportunity to glorify You (Luke 21:12-19)! May I relish such opportunity. When we see all people and circumstances in light of Your presence, so much becomes clear. We can become afraid not of godless men, but for them (Psalm 62:9, Proverbs 21:29). Surely You are true, though every man be found a liar (Romans 3:4).

"He *meditated in God's statutes*, went on in his duty, and did not regard them; as a deaf man, he heard not. When they spoke against him, he found that in the word of God which spoke for him, and spoke comfort to him, and then none of these things moved him. Those that have pleasure in communion with God may easily despise the censures of men, even of princes."[41]

"Princes saw in him a greatness which they envied, and therefore they abused him. On their thrones they might have found something better to consider and speak about, but they turned the seat of judgment into the seat of the scorner. [Psalm 1:1] Most men covet a prince's good word, and to be spoken ill of by a great man is a great discouragement to them, but the Psalmist bore his trial with holy calmness . . . '*But thy*

---

41. Henry, Matthew, *Commentary on the Whole Bible*, on Psalm 119:23, e-Sword edition

servant did meditate in thy statutes.' This was brave indeed. He was God's servant, and therefore he attended to his Master's business; he was God's servant, and therefore felt sure that his Lord would defend him. He gave no heed to his princely slanderers, he did not even allow his thoughts to be disturbed by a knowledge of their plotting in conclave ... It is a praiseworthy thing when the resolve of our happy hours is duly carried out in our seasons of affliction."[42]

Psalm 119:24

"Your testimonies also are my delight;
They are my counselors."

Because the Psalmist was a stranger in the earth (v.19), crushed with longing after Your word (v.20), surrounded by arrogant men who reproached him (v.22), reviled by powerful men (v.23), he sought delight elsewhere. He sought it in Your word. Note the contrast in the Psalms with self-counsel (Psalm 13:2) leading to despair within (Psalm 42:5-6, Psalm 42:11, Psalm 43:5), which must be rejected along with the counsel of the wicked (Psalm 1:1). How wonderful it is to know that You are near in Your word (Psalm 119:151) and that You counsel me intimately and personally (Psalm 32:8), so of course Your word would be my constant delight (Psalm 1:2). Having Your word on my heart and lips (Deuteronomy 6:6-7), You guide me through them at all times and in all things (Proverbs 6:22). 'Delight' here is the Hebrew שַׁעֲשֻׁעִים , ša'ašu'iym: a noun which often describes the delight given to the one who follows Your word (Psalm 119:24, 77, 92, 143, 174). 'Counselors' here is a combination of שׁאִי, 'iyš: a noun meaning a man, individual and עֵצָה 'ēṣāh: a noun with the sense of advice or plan. An adequate rendering would be 'men of my counsel' (John Gill and Matthew Henry commentaries affirm this). While multiple wise words come from many human sources, they are ultimately 'given by one Shepherd' (Ecclesiastes

42. Spurgeon, Charles Haddon, *Treasury of David*, on Psalm 119:23, e-Sword edition

12:11). Oh Lord! Grant me grace to keep to the way of good men and walk in the paths of the righteous (Proverbs 2:20). When my anxious, sinful thoughts multiply within me, flood my mind with the delight of Your consolations (Psalm 94:19).

"While his enemies took counsel with each other the holy man took counsel with the testimonies of God . . . in our sorrows they are our delight, and in our difficulties they are our guide; we derive joy from them and discover wisdom in them. If we desire to find comfort in the Scriptures we must submit ourselves to their counsel, and when we follow their counsel it must not be with reluctance but with delight . . . The best answer to accusing princes is the word of the justifying King . . . In Psa 119:16 David said, 'I will delight in thy statutes,' and here he says 'they are my delight:' thus resolutions formed in God's strength come to fruit, and spiritual desires ripen into actual attainments. O that it might be so with all the readers of these lines."[43]

---

43. Spurgeon, Charles Haddon, *Treasury of David*, on Psalm 119:24, e-Sword edition

CHAPTER 4
Daleth: 'Revived to Run'

"Daleth. My soul cleaves to the dust;
Revive me according to Your word.
I have told of my ways, and You have answered me;
Teach me Your statutes.
Make me understand the way of Your precepts,
So I will meditate on Your wonders.
My soul weeps because of grief;
Strengthen me according to Your word.
Remove the false way from me,
And graciously grant me Your law.
I have chosen the faithful way;
I have placed Your ordinances before me.
I cling to Your testimonies;
O LORD, do not put me to shame!
I shall run the way of Your commandments,
For You will enlarge my heart."

—Psalm 119:25-32

Here in Daleth, You carry the Psalmist from cleaving to the dust to running the way of Your commandments. He sees himself as earthbound and in despair, so he pours out his heart to You (v.26, see Psalm 62:8), he cries for understanding (v.27), weeps in weakness for strength (v.28), repents from his own false way (vv. 29-30), clings to Your word as he had previously cleaved to the dust (v.31), and runs in Your ways with an expectation of enlarged capacity (v.32). In football terms, he took the ball and ran with it, he hastened and did not delay (Psalm 119:59-60) with his most prized possession of obedience to Your perfect law (Psalm 119:56).

"Here, it seems to me, we have the Psalmist in trouble bewailing the bondage to earthly things in which he finds his mind to be held. His soul cleaves to the dust, melts for heaviness, and cries for enlargement from its spiritual prison. In these verses we shall see the influence of the divine word upon a heart which laments its downward tendencies, and is filled with mourning because of its deadening surroundings. The word of the Lord evidently arouses prayer (Psalm 119:25-29), confirms choice (Psalm 119:30), and inspires renewed resolve (Psalm 119:32): it is in all tribulation whether of body or mind the surest source of help.

This portion has D for its alphabetical letter: it sings of Depression, in the spirit of Devotion, Determination, and Dependence."[44]

Psalm 119:25

"Daleth. My soul cleaves to the dust;
Revive me according to Your word."

While he 'cleaves' to the dust now, he would soon 'cling' to Your testimonies (v. 31). Both of these words are the Hebrew דָּבַק, dābaq: a verb with the sense of cling, join with, stay with. This same word is used of a man clinging or cleaving to his wife (Genesis 2:24). When one cleaves, it seems a permanent position. How would the Psalmist be freed from this

---

44. Spurgeon, Charles Haddon, *Treasury of David*, on Psalm 119 - Daleth, e-Sword edition

earth with its sin and despair? Only through Your resurrection power. 'Revive me according to Your word':

- When my soul cleaves to the dust (Psalm 119:25)
- When I am exceedingly afflicted (Psalm 119:107)
- When I need You to plead my cause and redeem me (Psalm 119:154)

". . . the Psalmist felt as if these ensigns of woe were glued to him, and his very soul was made to cleave to them because of his powerlessness to rise above his grief. Does he not also mean that he felt ready to die? Did he not feel his life absorbed and fast held by the grave's mould, half choked by the death-dust? It may not be straining the language if we conceive that he also felt and bemoaned his earthly-mindedness and spiritual deadness. There was a tendency in his soul to cling to earth which he greatly bewailed . . . Many are of the earth earthy, and never lament it; only the heaven-born and heaven-soaring spirit pines at the thought of being fastened to this world, and bird-limed by its sorrows or its pleasures . . . Many are of the earth earthy, and never lament it; only the heaven-born and heaven-soaring spirit pines at the thought of being fastened to this world, and bird-limed by its sorrows or its pleasures . . . David seeks quickening: one would have thought that he would have asked for comfort or upraising, but he knew that these would come out of increased life, and therefore he sought that blessing which is the root of the rest . . . the word of God shows us that he who first made us must keep us alive [Galatians 5:25] . . . it is a grand thing to see a believer in the dust and yet pleading the promise, a man at the grave's mouth crying, 'quicken me,' and hoping that it shall be done . . . Life is in both cases the object of pursuit that he may have life, and have it more abundantly [John 10:10]."[45]

Psalm 119:26

"I have told of my ways, and You have answered me;
Teach me Your statutes."

---

45. Spurgeon, Charles Haddon, *Treasury of David*, on Psalm 119:25, e-Sword edition

I see John 15:7 in this verse. Why? While the Psalmist cries out for help, that help comes in the form of Your word. I believe that, while it is a wondrous, unspeakable thing that we can come to You in prayer (Psalm 65:2, Psalm 62:8, Hebrews 4:16), it is infinitely more important that we hear from You than that You hear from us. For You to reprove and direct me away from my own heart to Yours (Proverbs 28:26) is necessary, for only You can show me the path of life (Psalm 16:11), for my ways apart from You can only end in darkness and death (Proverbs 4:19-20, Proverbs 14:12). Reflecting on the word 'way', which means path, journey, pattern of life:

- I have told of my ways, but I need an answer from You to speak into those ways (v.26)
- In order to understand the way of Your commands, I need to meditate on the wonderful things You do (v.27)
- I need false ways to be removed and replaced by Your living and active law (v. 29)
- I need to choose the faithful way of Your ordinances ever before me (v.30)
- Finally, I need to run in the way of Your commandments and in Your strength, unhesitatingly and boldly (I think of Psalm 119:59-60)

"Open confession is good for the soul. Nothing brings more ease and more life to a man than a frank acknowledgment of the evil which has caused the sorrow and the lethargy. Such a declaration proves that the man knows his own condition, and is no longer blinded by pride . . . It is God's way to forgive our sinful way when we from our hearts confess the wrong . . . He was not willing to sin through ignorance, he wished to know all the mind of God by being taught it by the best of teachers . . . This cry for teaching is frequent in the Psalm; in Psa 119:12 it followed a sight of God, here follows from a sight of self. Every experience should lead us thus to plead it with God."[46]

---

46. Spurgeon, Charles Haddon, *Treasury of David*, on Psalm 119:26, e-Sword edition

Psalm 119:27

"Make me understand the way of Your precepts,
So I will meditate on Your wonders."

I am intrigued by this verse. First, because it is intensely practical, asking You to show me 'how do I do this?' Second, because it anticipates wondrous works accomplished by Your word in me that I can look forward to meditating on. 'Way' is Hebrew דֶּרֶךְ, Derek: a noun with the sense of path, journey, way. I think immediately of Job 23:10: "But He knows the way I take; When He has tried me, I shall come forth as gold." May I understand my way, even while knowing that I can't fully understand it, Proverbs 20:24. These are the 3 verses in the Scripture with both 'understand' and 'way' (Psalm 119:27, Proverbs 14:8, Proverbs 20:24). 'Understand' is the Hebrew בִּין, biyn: a verb with the sense of discern, perceive, observe, pay attention to. Back to Job 23:10, it is only He who fully knows my way; mine is to have the discernment to trust Him.

". . . the surest way of keeping up our communion with God is by learning his statutes and walking intelligently in the way of his precepts. See 1Jn 1:6, 1Jn 1:7. 3. The good use he would make of this for the honour of God and the edification of others: 'Let me have a good understanding of the way of thy precepts; give me a clear, distinct, and methodical knowledge of divine things; so shall I talk with the more assurance, and the more to the purpose, of thy wondrous works.' We can **talk** with a better grace of God's wondrous works, the wonders of providence, and especially the wonders of redeeming love, when we understand the way of God's precepts and **walk** in that way."[47]

"Give me a deep insight into the practical meaning of thy word; let me get a clear idea of the tone and tenor of thy law. Blind obedience has but small beauty; God would have us follow him with our eyes open. Our understanding needs enlightenment and direction- he who made our understanding must also make us understand . . . he is not concerned

---

47. *The Pulpit Commentary*, on Psalm 119:27, e-Sword edition, with emphasis

about the subtleties of the law, but the commonplaces and everyday rules of it, which are described as 'the way of thy precepts.' . . . we take it to mean that in proportion as David understood the word of God he would meditate upon it more and more. It is usually so; the thoughtless care not to know the inner meaning of the Scriptures, while those who know them best are the very men who strive after a greater familiarity with them, and therefore give themselves up to musing upon them."[48]

Psalm 119:28

> "My soul weeps because of grief;
> Strengthen me according to Your word."

Grief over what? I believe it is the false way of v.29 and its consequences. It is a 'deep weeping' of the soul, and follows the cleaving of the soul to dust in v.25. I need strength to overcome the guilt and weakness, the natural consequence of sin, and that strength can only come from the food of Your word. 'Strengthen' is the Hebrew קוּם, qûm: a verb with the sense of arise, stand, establish or strengthen (see Psalm 119:28).

"There is one good point in this downcast state, for it is better to be melted with grief than to be hardened by impenitence. [See Proverbs 28:14] . . . In that prayer let us plead nothing but the word of God; for there is no plea like a promise, no argument like a word from our covenant God . . . Note how David records his inner soul-life. In Psa 119:20 he says, 'My soul breaketh;' in Psa 119:25, 'My soul cleaveth to the dust;' and here, 'My soul melteth.' Further on, in Psa 119:81, he cries, 'My soul fainteth;' in Psa 119:109, 'My soul is continually in my hand;' in Psa 119:167, 'My soul hath kept thy testimonies'; and lastly, in Psa 119:175, 'Let my soul live.' Some people do not even know that they have a soul, and here is David all soul. What a difference there is between the spiritually living and the spiritually dead."[49]

---

48. Spurgeon, Charles Haddon, *Treasury of David*, on Psalm 119:27, e-Sword edition
49. Spurgeon, Charles Haddon, *Treasury of David*, on Psalm 119:28, e-Sword edition

Psalm 119:29

> "Remove the false way from me,
> And graciously grant me Your law."

Something inferior must be removed and replaced with something superior. Father, You are about our maximum joy, and so You direct us away from that which will destroy and discourage to the invaluable riches of Your word (Proverbs 3:15, Proverbs 8:11). We see this expulsive power in Psalm 119:104, Psalm 119:128. Thomas Chalmers wrote of it in *The Expulsive Power of a New Affection*.[50] Having experienced the Lord (Psalm 34:8), nothing less will do. Yet, knowing this and even experiencing this, the sin in our hearts is often drawn elsewhere. So the Psalmist prays in desperation for God to take that away! He knows that transformation can be sought in God but not accomplished in self. The section began with the Psalmist cleaving to the dust and he needs help!

"He desired to be right and upright, true and in the truth; but he feared that a measure of falsehood would cling to him unless the Lord took it away, and therefore he earnestly cried for its removal. False motives may at times sway us, and we may fall into mistaken notions of our own spiritual condition before God, which erroneous conceits may be kept up by a natural prejudice in our own favour, and so we may be confirmed in a delusion, and abide under error unless grace comes to the rescue. No true heart can rest in a false view of itself; . . . if the law be not in our hearts the lie will enter . . . The only way to expel the lie is to accept the truth . . . a belief of the doctrines of grace is a grand preservative from deadly error . . . In Psa 119:21 David cries out against pride, and here against lying - these are much the same thing. Is not pride the greatest of all lies?"[51]

---

50. Piper, J. (2023, May 21). *"the expulsive power of a new affection": The life-changing insight of Thomas Chalmers*. Desiring God. https://www.desiringgod.org/articles/the-expulsive-power-of-a-new-affection
51. Spurgeon, Charles Haddon, *Treasury of David*, on Psalm 119:29, e-Sword edition

Psalm 119:30

> "I have chosen the faithful way;
> I have placed Your ordinances before me."

May my resolve be of You, my dependence upon You for the ability to follow through. You have made Your word so clear! So often my confusion arises from my compromise. The 'faithful way' indicates that the Psalmist commits himself not simply to faithful thinking (although it must start here), but to a faithful 'way', that is, doing. How much time is wasted in indecision and compromise! Make me true and united in heart towards you (Psalm 86:11).

". . . a man must choose one or the other, for there cannot be any neutrality in the case. Men do not drop into the right way by chance; they must choose it, and continue to choose it, or they will soon wander from it. Those whom God has chosen in due time choose his way. There is a doctrinal way of truth which we ought to choose, rejecting every dogma of man's devising; there is a ceremonial way of truth which we should follow, detesting all the forms which apostate churches have invented; and then there is a practical way of truth, the way of holiness, to which we must adhere whatever may be our temptation to forsake it . . . Men do not become holy by a careless wish: there must be study, consideration, deliberation, and earnest enquiry, or the way of truth will be missed. The commands of God must be set before us as the mark to aim at, the model to work by, the road to walk in. If we put God's judgments into the background we shall soon find ourselves departing from them."[52]

Psalm 119:31

> "I cling to Your testimonies;
> O LORD, do not put me to shame!"

---

52. Spurgeon, Charles Haddon, *Treasury of David*, on Psalm 119:30, e-Sword edition

'Cling' is the same Hebrew word as 'cleaves' in v.25. I awake in a battle as to what my soul would cling to. I feel as though I am holding on for dear life. Nothing else will do. All else is disorder, destruction, and death. I resonate with the words of Romans 6:21-23, 'what benefit'? Psalm 103:3, Psalm 116:12 - there is lasting benefit only in You. Surely my soul clings to You (Psalm 63:8), the Source of all good (Romans 12:9, Mark 10:18). I hold on for dear life as one being rescued, lost at sea, and find myself on the most glorious vessel imaginable. Why would I then throw myself into the sea of chaos and death?

"His choice was so heartily and deliberately made that he stuck to it for life, and could not be removed from it by the reproaches of those who despised the way of the Lord. What could he have gained by quitting the sacred testimony? Say rather, what would he not have lost if he had ceased to cleave to the divine word? It is pleasant to look back upon past perseverance and to expect grace to continue equally steadfast in the future. He who has enabled us to stick to him will surely stick to us . . . If we are not true to our profession we may be left to reap the fruit of our folly, and that will be the bitter thing called 'shame.' A brave heart is more wounded by shame than by any weapon which a soldier's hand can wield."[53]

Psalm 119:32

> "I shall run the way of Your commandments,
> For You will enlarge my heart."

The Psalmist has moved from being paralyzed and cleaving to the dust (v.25) to cleaving to Your word (v.31) and running in it. How did this happen? A confession of sin (v.26), a relinquishing of self (v.29), and a seeking of You and Your ways (v.30) revived him. Free from the weight and obstacles of sin (Proverbs 4:12, Hebrews 12:1-2), he was free to run! Because his life has the credibility of obedient action, his words have

---

53. Spurgeon, Charles Haddon, *Treasury of David*, on Psalm 119:31, e-Sword edition

weight and are not useless (Proverbs 12:14, Proverbs 12:26, Proverbs 15:7, Proverbs 26:7). 'Enlarge' is the Hebrew רָחַב, rāḥ̱b: a verb with the sense of enlarge, extend, open wide. We know that conditioned athletes often have larger physical hearts and greater capacity. Whether this is cause or effect is a matter of debate, but Lord, make it so! Increase my capacity from You and for You. May I receive and give much of You. May I hasten and not delay in it (Psalm 119:59-60)! Freed from sin, I flee to You in unspeakable joy and freedom. Surely the path of life has more joy and adventure than any other (Psalm 16:11, Proverbs 4:18).

"I will run the way of thy commandments . . . Not only walk but run in it; which is expressive of great affection to the commands of God, of great readiness and cheerfulness, of great haste and swiftness in the way of them, and of great delight and pleasure therein; when thou shall enlarge my heart; with the knowledge of God, his word, ways, worship, and ordinances; with his love more fully made known, and with an increase of love to him; with the fear of him, and a flow of spiritual joy and peace; and when delivered from straits and difficulties, from weights and pressures, and everything that may hinder walking or running;"[54]

"With energy, promptitude, and zeal he would perform the will of God, but he needed more life and liberty from the hand of God . . . the feet soon run when the heart is free and energetic. Let the affections be aroused and eagerly set on divine things, and our actions will be full of force, swiftness, and delight . . . He must change the heart, unite the heart, encourage the heart, strengthen the heart, and enlarge the heart, and then the course of the life will be gracious, sincere, happy, and earnest; so that from our lowest up to our highest state in grace we must attribute all to the free favour of our God. We must run; for grace is not an overwhelming force which compels unwilling minds to move contrary to their will our running is the spontaneous leaping forward of a mind which has been set free by the hand of God, and delights to show its freedom by its bounding speed.

---

54. John Gill, *Exposition on the Entire Bible*, on Psalm 119:32, e-Sword edition

What a change from Psa 119:25 to the present, from cleaving to the dust to running in the way. It is the excellence of holy sorrow that it works in us the quickening for which we seek, and then we show the sincerity of our grief and the reality of our revival by being zealous in the ways of the Lord . . . It is one of the great lacks of our age that heads count for more than hearts, and men are far more ready to learn than to love, though they are by no means eager in either direction."[55]

---

55. Spurgeon, Charles Haddon, *Treasury of David*, on Psalm 119:32, e-Sword edition

CHAPTER 5
He: 'Lord, Change Me!'

"He. Teach me, O LORD, the way of Your statutes,
And I shall observe it to the end.
Give me understanding, that I may observe Your law
And keep it with all my heart.
Make me walk in the path of Your commandments,
For I delight in it.
Incline my heart to Your testimonies
And not to dishonest gain.
Turn away my eyes from looking at vanity,
And revive me in Your ways.
Establish Your word to Your servant,
As that which produces reverence for You.
Turn away my reproach which I dread,
For Your ordinances are good.
Behold, I long for Your precepts;
Revive me through Your righteousness."

—Psalm 119:33-40

How do the prayers of the Psalmist, here, compare to mine? What am I asking God FOR? Notice the Psalmist does not pray things like, 'Lord enable me to . . .', or 'give the doctors or whoever wisdom to . . .', or anything like that. Those may not be bad things, but I am challenged to find prayers like those modeled for us in the Bible. No, here, the Psalmist essentially pleads, 'Lord, DO it!' I must go further to ask You to change me. Notice the pleas, which start with 'teach' me, then escalate from there:

- 'give me understanding' (v.34)
- 'make me walk' (v. 35)
- 'incline my heart' (v. 36)
- 'turn away my eyes' (v. 27)
- 'establish Your word' (v. 38)
- 'turn away my reproach' (v. 39)

All of which result in:

- observing Your ways with a whole heart (v. 33-34)
- delighting in Your commandments (v. 35)
- avoiding dishonest gain (v. 36)
- a revived and reverent life (vv. 37-40)

In other words, save me and change me, for I cannot save myself!

'A sense of dependence and a consciousness of extreme need pervade this section, which is all made up of prayer and plea. Psalm 119:25-32 trembled with a sense of sin, quivering with a childlike sense of weakness and folly, which caused the man of God to cry out for the help by which alone his soul could be preserved from falling back into sin.'[56]

Psalm 119:33

> "He. Teach me, O LORD, the way of Your statutes,
> And I shall observe it to the end."

---

56. Spurgeon, Charles Haddon, *Treasury of David*, on Psalm 119 - He, e-Sword edition

In this section, the Psalmist asks You to teach him the way (path) of Your commandments. Yet he realized that he needs even more. He needs understanding (v.34), resolve (v.35), motivation (v.36), focus (v.37), and assurance / fulfillment (v.38), all from You. The knowledge is just the beginning; to 'observe it to the end', to persevere with consistency, requires more than understanding or resolve, it requires Your intervention. This word for 'teach' is an interesting one, the Hebrew יָרָה, yārāh, a verb with the sense of shoot, throw, or pour. It is a word of action and accomplishment. It is used only one other place in Psalm 119, Psalm 119:102, in the past tense, 'You Yourself have taught me'. Only God can teach in this way, in an equipping, accomplishing way. This is distinct from the 'teach' of Psalm 119:12, the Hebrew לָמַד lāmaḏ which similarly is a word indicating 'training'. So the sense here is 'shoot me in the right direction'! It is a decision with no going back. It is reflected in Psalm 86:11 in an undivided heart. Like You, Father, may my children and those I disciple be trained and bear eternal fruit for Your kingdom. Psalm 127:5, 2 Timothy 2:2. Pour into me that I may pour into others.

"What he desires to be taught, not the notions or language of God's statutes, but the way of them - 'the way of applying them to myself and governing myself by them; teach me the way of my duty which thy statutes prescribe, and in every doubtful case let me know what thou wouldst have me to do, let me hear the word behind me, saying, This is the way, walk in it' Isa 30:21."[57]

"A sense of great slowness to learn drives us to seek a great teacher. What condescension it is on our great Jehovah's part that he deigns to teach those who seek him. The lesson which is desired is thoroughly practical; the holy man would not only learn the statutes, but the way of them, the daily use of them, their tenor, spirit, direction, habit, tendency . . . As Christ loves us to the end, so must we serve him to the end. The end of divine teaching is that we may persevere to the end."[58]

---

57. Henry, Matthew, *Commentary on the Whole Bible*, on Psalm 119:33, e-Sword edition
58. Spurgeon, Charles Haddon, *Treasury of David*, on Psalm 119:33, e-Sword edition

Psalm 119:34

> "Give me understanding, that I may observe Your law
> And keep it with all my heart."

I am convinced that if we just understood certain things, we would behave and respond differently. But the understanding must be more than mental; it must be volitional. And for that to happen, the affections must be stirred. Understanding must reach the affections. The Hebrew word indicates true understanding is evidenced by a response. Like the second son in the Parable of the Two Sons (Matthew 21:28-32), may our actions exceed our words. Like faithful disciples, may we hasten to observe (Psalm 119:59-60) and teach others to do so (Matthew 28:18-20) in word and example.

"We are in a state of complicated ruin, from which nothing but manifold grace can deliver us. Those who feel their folly are by the example of the Psalmist encouraged to pray for understanding: let each man by faith cry, 'Give me understanding.' Others have had it, why may it not come to me? It was a gift to them; will not the Lord also freely bestow it upon me?

We are not to seek this blessing that we may be famous for wisdom, but that we may be abundant in our love to the law of God."[59]

Psalm 119:35

> "Make me walk in the path of Your commandments,
> For I delight in it."

'Make me walk'. Despite the Psalmist's commitment to obey (v.33) and desire for understanding to do it (v.34), he realizes that this was not enough. A new heart and a new spirit are required; You must cause us to walk in Your statutes and observe Your ordinances (Ezekiel 36:26-27). Romans 7:22-8:4 expresses what happens through the Gospel

---

59. Spurgeon, Charles Haddon, *Treasury of David*, on Psalm 119:34, e-Sword edition

to move from realization to resolve to reality. 'Make me walk' is the Hebrew דָּרַךְ, dāraḵ: a verb with the sense of tread or bend. It has a sense of subduing or submission (see Habakkuk 3:19). It is the language of battle and conquest. Lord, You have vanquished sin and caused my soul to walk in triumphant victory over it! (Romans 8:37, Colossians 2:15, 2 Corinthians 2:14) The smell of victory follows us. This word is used of God leading us in His truth and in humility (Psalm 25:5, Psalm 25:9, see also Psalm 45:4), leading us in upright paths (Psalm 107:7, Proverbs 4:11, Isaiah 42:16, Isaiah 48:17, Habakkuk 3:19). The path of victory is the way of the believer. 'Delight' here is the Hebrew חָפֵץ, ḥāpēṣ, חָפַץ, ḥāpāṣ, a verb with the sense of delight, pleasure, favor. I may not gravitate towards Your commandments naturally, but by Your transforming power I do and I remain in delight.

"Since we are not sufficient of ourselves, our dependence must be upon the grace of God, for from him all our sufficiency is. God puts his Spirit within us, and so causes us to walk in his statutes (Eze 36:27), and this is that which David here begs. 2. That God would make him willing to do it, and would, by his grace, subdue the aversion he naturally had to it: 'Incline my heart to thy testimonies, to those things which thy testimonies prescribe; not only make me willing to do my duty, as that which I must do and therefore am concerned to make the best of, but make me desirous to do my duty as that which is agreeable to the new nature and really advantageous to me.' Duty is then done with delight when the heart is inclined to it: it is God's grace that inclines us, and the more backward we find ourselves to it the more earnest we must be for that grace."[60]

"This is the cry of a child that longs to walk, but is too feeble; of a pilgrim who is exhausted, yet pants to be on the march; of a lame man who pines to be able to run . . . O thou who didst once make me, I pray thee make me again: thou hast made me to know; now make me to go . . . Grace does not treat us as stocks and stones, to be dragged by horses or engines, but as creatures endowed with life, reason, will,

---

60. Henry, Matthew, *Commentary on the Whole Bible*, on Psalm 119:35, e-Sword edition

and active powers, who are willing and able to go of themselves if once made to do so. God worketh in us, but it is that we may both will and do according to his good pleasure [Philippians 2:13]. The holiness we seek after is not a forced compliance with command, but the indulgence of a whole-hearted passion for goodness, such as shall conform our life to the will of the Lord. . . Is practical godliness the very jewel of your soul, the coveted prize of your mind? If so, the outward path of life, however rough will be clean, and lead the soul upward to delight ineffable. He who delights in the law should not doubt but what he will be enabled to run in its ways, for where the heart already finds its joy the feet are sure to follow."[61]

Psalm 119:36

> "Incline my heart to Your testimonies
> And not to dishonest gain."

This hearkens back to v. 35, 'make me walk' and Ezekiel 36:26-27. There it is placed in order of effect (walk), and here the cause (heart) is exposed. It is almost as if the Psalmist catches himself; he senses both his inability and responsibility to walk in Your ways, the only solution to which is a changed heart. 'Incline' is the Hebrew נָטָה, nāṭāh: A verb with the sense of stretch out, extend, be attentive. It occurs some 29 times in Psalms 4, Psalm 119, Psalm 119:36, and Psalm 119:112 as an inclined heart toward Your word, and in Psalm 119:51 and Psalm 119:157 in the negative as turning aside from Your word. Coercion will not do, for delight is a duty. '. . . free affection is the foundation and beginning of duly obeying the Law, for what is drawn forth by constraint, or servile fear, cannot please God.'[62] This is why there cannot simply be a turning from vanity, but a revival in Your ways as the delight of the soul. The Psalmist had already found in v. 35 a delight in it, yet a heart that strayed. He knew that it was of such benefit and delight that he seems to cry to be coerced!

---

61. Spurgeon, Charles Haddon, *Treasury of David*, on Psalm 119:35, e-Sword edition
62. John Calvin, *Calvin's Commentaries*, on Deuteronomy 11:1

Father, may it be my first and not my last inclination to move towards You. The Psalmist implies here that there is no delight to be found in falsehood, so he asks You to incline his heart towards truth. In v. 37 he would further ask for eyes that turn likewise. Surely 'gain' as the world sees it is no gain apart from Christ (Philippians 3:7-8, 1 Timothy 6:5-6). Surely the heart determines the path, Proverbs 4:23.

"What would his goings be if his heart did not go? . . . The only way to cure a wrong leaning is to have the soul bent in the opposite direction. Holiness of heart is the cure for covetousness. What a blessing it is that we may ask the Lord even for an inclination. Our wills are free, and yet without violating their liberty, grace can incline us in the right direction. This can be done by enlightening the understanding as to the excellence of obedience, by strengthening our habits of virtue, by giving us an experience of the sweetness of piety, and by many other ways . . . Happy shall we be when we feel habitually inclined to all that is good. This is not the way in which a carnal heart ever leans; all its inclinations are in opposition to the divine testimonies . . . Our hearts must have some object of desire, and the only way to keep out worldly gain is to put in its place the testimonies of the Lord. If we are inclined or bent one way, we shall be turned from the other; the negative virtue is most surely attained by making sure of the positive grace which inevitably produces it."[63]

Psalm 119:37

> "Turn away my eyes from looking at vanity,
> And revive me in Your ways."

In Psalm 119:29 the Psalmist asked for the false way to be removed. Here the Psalmist seems to ask You to take away the attraction which remains towards that which dishonors You. It reminds me of Psalm 101:3, David's desire that worthless things not capture his heart. 'Turn away' is the

---

63. Spurgeon, Charles Haddon, *Treasury of David*, on Psalm 119:36, e-Sword edition

Hebrew עָבַר, ʿāḇar, verb wih the sense of pass through or over, go away. So we are not distracted, we move along and keep focused. 'Vanity' is the Hebrew שָׁוְא, šāw', a noun with the sense of emptiness, vanity, evil, ruin, fraud, or deceit. Distractions must be removed for truth to be seen and sought.

"The honours, pleasures, and profits of the world are the vanities, the aspect and prospect of which draw multitudes away from the paths of religion and godliness. The eye, when fastened on these, infects the heart with the love of them, and so it is alienated from God and divine things; and therefore, as we ought to make a covenant with our eyes, and lay a charge upon them, that they shall not wander after, much less fix upon, that which is dangerous (Job 31:1) . . . a traveller that stands gazing upon every object that presents itself to his view will not rid ground; but, if our eyes be kept from that which would divert us, our hearts will be kept to that which will excite us."[64]

"The prayer is not so much that the eyes may be shut as 'turned away;' for we need to have them open, but directed to right objects . . . It is a proof of the sense of weakness felt by the Psalmist and of his entire dependence upon God that he even asks to have his eyes turned for him; he meant not to make himself passive, but he intended to set forth his own utter helplessness apart from the grace of God . . . Vitality is the cure of vanity."[65]

Psalm 119:38

> "Establish Your word to Your servant,
> As that which produces reverence for You."

Long one of my memory verses, I trust Your word to produce godly character in my life. 'Establish' is the Hebrew קוּם, qûm, a verb with the sense of arise or stand. It can mean to establish or strengthen (Psalm 119:28). I think immediately of 'show Yourself strong' in Psalm 68:28. So

---

64. Henry, Matthew, *Commentary on the Whole Bible*, on Psalm 119:37, e-Sword edition
65. Spurgeon, Charles Haddon, *Treasury of David*, on Psalm 119:37, e-Sword edition

here, I read 'show Your word strong'. 'Produces reverence' is the Hebrew יִרְאָה, yir'āh, a noun meaning fear. The word usually refers to the fear of God and is viewed as a positive quality. Father, may the work of Your word in my life produce compelling fruit of Your character and wisdom.

"Make me sure of thy sure word: make it sure to me and make me sure of it . . . Practical holiness is a great help towards doctrinal certainty: if we are God's servants he will confirm his word in our experience. 'If any man will do his will, he shall know of the doctrine'; and so know it as to be fully assured of it . . . 'Establish thy word to thy fear,' namely, that men may be led to fear thee; since a sure faith in the divine promise is the fountain and foundation of godly fear . . . We cannot look for the fulfilment of promises in our experience unless we live under the influence of the fear of the Lord: establishment in grace is the result of holy watchfulness and prayerful energy. We shall never be rooted and grounded in our belief unless we daily practise what we profess to believe. Full assurance is the reward of obedience."[66]

Psalm 119:39

"Turn away my reproach which I dread,
For Your ordinances are good."

Disapproval can be devastating. To be unwelcome by men is difficult enough, but to be rejected by You cannot be endured, either in this life or the next. 'Turn away' is the Hebrew עָבַר, `ābar, a verb with the sense of pass through or over, go away. In this case, the word means to cause something to pass away. 'This too shall pass.' We can endure when we know there is an end (Romans 8:18-25, 2 Corinthians 4:17). 'Reproach' is the Hebrew חֶרְפָּה, ḥerpāh, a noun with the sense of reproach, scorn, taunt. We see this in Psalm 69:9, Jesus took the weight of the full reproach of men. 'Dread' is the Hebrew יָגֹר yāgōr which has the sense of a specific fear, and appears only 5 times in the O.T., notably of Job whose

---

66. Spurgeon, Charles Haddon, *Treasury of David*, on Psalm 119:38, e-Sword edition

worst fears were realized (Job 3:25). The Psalmist begs for this to be removed so that he can fully enjoy Your judgments. The reproach of man can surely obscure the goodness of God. So it is these days, where otherwise faithful men are caving to the reproaches of a world that hates You (Psalm 2). Why not stand firm in the presence of God (Psalm 27:1-4)? I fear that so many who appear godly on the outside have not been cultivating an inner life with You that will survive the storm (Psalm 1, Matthew 7:24-27), and often they are essentially unarmed, taking up their own clever ideas and not Your word (Ephesians 6:10-17).

"Persecution in the form of calumny may also be prayed against, for it is a sore trial, perhaps the sorest of trials to men of sensitive minds. Many would sooner bear burning at the stake than the trial of cruel mockings . . . If God turns away our eyes from falsehood, we may also expect that he will turn away falsehood from injuring our good name. We shall be kept from lies if we keep from lies . . . We mourn when we are slandered; because the shame is cast rather upon our religion than ourselves . . . When men rail at God's government of the world it is our duty and privilege to stand up for him, and openly to declare before him, 'thy judgments are good;' and we should do the same when they assail the Bible, the gospel, the law, or the name of our Lord Jesus Christ."[67]

Psalm 119:40

"Behold, I long for Your precepts;
Revive me through Your righteousness."

How does the Psalmist long for Your precepts? To the point of transformation, not simply information. 'Long' has the sense of 'inherent desire'. 'Revive' is the Hebrew הָיָה, ḥāyāh, a verb with the sense of alive, live, keep alive. Its use in Psalm 119 is of sustaining life (Psalm 119:25, 37, 40, 88). One would even say that it creates life, making

---

67. Spurgeon, Charles Haddon, *Treasury of David*, on Psalm 119:39, e-Sword edition

alive. In this sense, the prayer is being answered while it is being uttered (Isaiah 65:24, Matthew 6:8), for surely only Your revival can create longing for You. The answer is personal, not simply Your word, but Your righteousness. Surely You come with Your word (Psalm 119:151), and righteousness clothes those who are Yours (Psalm 24:5, Isaiah 59:17, Isaiah 61:10). Note the association of righteousness with salvation.

"He is deeply bowed down by a sense of his weakness and need of grace; but he does desire to be in all things conformed to the divine will. Where our longings are, there are we in the sight of God. We need quickening every hour of the day for we are so sadly apt to become slow and languid in the ways of God. It is the Holy Spirit who can pour new life into us; let us not cease crying to him. Let the life we already possess show itself by longing for more."[68]

---

68. Spurgeon, Charles Haddon, *Treasury of David*, on Psalm 119:40, e-Sword edition

CHAPTER 6
Vav: 'Free Worship'

"Vav. May Your lovingkindnesses also come to me, O LORD,
Your salvation according to Your word;
So I will have an answer for him who reproaches me,
For I trust in Your word.
And do not take the word of truth utterly out of my mouth,
For I wait for Your ordinances.
So I will keep Your law continually,
Forever and ever.
And I will walk at liberty,
For I seek Your precepts.
I will also speak of Your testimonies before kings
And shall not be ashamed.
I shall delight in Your commandments,
Which I love.
And I shall lift up my hands to Your commandments,
Which I love;
And I will meditate on Your statutes."

—Psalm 119:41-48

Whth hen Your lovingkindnesses come to me, I am free to drink from abundance (Psalm 36:8) that is infinite (Psalm 103:11). I will have a ready answer (v. 42), hope for new answers (v.43), resolve (v.44), utter freedom (v.45), confidence before all men (v.46), inner delight (v. 47), and unending worship (v. 48). This truly is 'salvation according to Your word' (v.41).

"In these verses holy fear is apparent and prominent. The man of God trembles lest in any way or degree the Lord should remove his favour from him. The eight verses are one continued pleading for the abiding of grace in his soul, and it is supported by such holy arguments as would only suggest themselves to a spirit burning with love to God."[69]

Psalm 119:41

"Vav. May Your lovingkindnesses also come to me, O LORD,
Your salvation according to Your word;"

'Lovingkindnesses' is plural I think of the 'fullness . . . grace upon grace' of John 1:16 and the 'lavished' of Ephesians 1:7-8. Is not Your 'lovingkindness' eternally enough? Yes, but I believe the Psalmist emphasizes its aboundance (I mistyped that, but I like it!) and its energy, i.e. it is always active. Chesed (Hebrew חֶסֶד) upon chesed! Grace upon grace, according to Your Word, according to Your Son.

"He needed much mercy and varied mercy, hence the request is in the plural. He needed mercy from God rather than from man, and so he asks for 'thy mercies.' The way sometimes seemed blocked, and therefore he begs that the mercies may have their way cleared by God, and may 'come' to him. He who said, 'Let there be light,' can also say, 'Let there be mercy.' It may be that under a sense of unworthiness the writer feared lest mercy should be given to others, and not to himself; he therefore cries, 'Bless me, even me also, O my Father.'"[70]

---

69. Spurgeon, Charles Haddon, *Treasury of David*, on Psalm 119 - Vav, e-Sword edition
70. Spurgeon, Charles Haddon, *Treasury of David*, on Psalm 119:41, e-Sword edition

Psalm 119:42

> "So I will have an answer for him who reproaches me,
> For I trust in Your word."

Continuing the thought from v.39, how shall we deal with those who reproach? I lean upon Your lovingkindness and not my efforts, the holiness of Christ and not my credentials. Any answer comes not from my own cleverness, but from Your word. The Psalmist had experienced, not simply concepts of truth, but an experience of it, filled personally with Your lovingkindness and truth. Surely 'By lovingkindness and truth iniquity is atoned for, And by the fear of the LORD one keeps away from evil.' (Proverbs 16:6). In wisdom we answer fools (Proverbs 26:4-5), and Father, may I be so filled with Your truth in the innermost being (Psalm 51:6) that evil men will not be able to withstand (Acts 6:10. 1 Corinthians 2:4), from a life that is not vacuous but credible (1 Corinthians 4:19-20, Proverbs 21:29). In these days extra-biblical and often non-biblical standards are being used by some professing Christians to judge Christians. May I discern from Your word, speak from Your word, and desire the fruitful impact of Your word in their lives. Proverbs 26:23-28 and James 3:13-18 are particularly apt; may I rightly discern root and fruit for Your glory. The response may not be positive, but I trust in You and Your word, You who will bring all things to light (1 Corinthians 4:5, Hebrews 4:12-13). Surely a right regard for Your word is the best antidote to fear. Psalm 56:4.

"This is an unanswerable answer. When God, by granting us salvation, gives to our prayers an answer of peace, we are ready at once to answer the objections of the infidel, the quibbles of the sceptical, and the sneers of the contemptuous. It is most desirable that revilers should be answered, and hence we may expect the Lord to save his people in order that a weapon may be put into their hands with which to rout his adversaries. When those who reproach us are also reproaching God, we may ask him to help us to silence them by sure proofs of his mercy and faithfulness . . . God hath more respect to a man's trust than to all else that is in him; for the Lord hath chosen faith to be the hand into which he will place his mercies and his salvation. If any reproach us for trusting in God, we reply to them with arguments the most conclusive when we show that God has kept his promises, heard our prayers, and supplied our needs. Even the most sceptical are forced to bow before the logic of facts."[71] See also Psalm 71:7.

Psalm 119:43

> "And do not take the word of truth utterly out of my mouth,
> For I wait for Your ordinances."

This is a curious prayer, perhaps borne out of the Psalmist's desire to have a ready answer (v. 42). Your word seems readily available, our issue being our desire and capacity for it! Why would you take Your word 'utterly' out of my mouth? First, this speaks of the Psalmist's treasuring Your word, perhaps aware that his very life depends on it (Deuteronomy 32:46-47, Deuteronomy 8:2-3, Job 23:12). Second, this speaks of the seriousness of the stewardship. In modern language, we would say, 'use it or lose it'. I think of the parable of the talents (Matthew 25:14-30), the uselessness of those who are talkers and not doers (Proverbs 26:7, James 1:22, Luke 6:46), the condemnation of those who have the word but reject it (Psalm 50:16-17, Proverbs 13:13), and the coming spiritual famine (Amos 8:11-12). May I gain more understanding through increasing faithfulness (Psalm 111:10 , John 14:21). 'For I wait for Your ordinances'. The Psalmist asks You to honor the desire that You give! Surely You will, surely You do. May my hope be that You would fill me and not empty me of Your word, Psalm 81:10.

"For how could I continue to proclaim thy word if I found it fail me? Such would seem to be the run of the meaning . . . This prayer may also refer to other modes by which we may be disabled from speaking in the name of the Lord' as, for instance, by our falling into open sin, by our becoming depressed and despairing, by our labouring under sickness or

---

71. Spurgeon, Charles Haddon, *Treasury of David*, on Psalm 119:42, e-Sword edition

mental aberration, by our finding no door of utterance, or meeting with no willing audience . . . God is the author of our hopes, and we may most fittingly entreat him to fulfil them. The judgments of his providence are the outcome of his word; what he says in the Scriptures he actually performs in his government; we may therefore look for him to show himself strong on the behalf of his own threatenings and promises, and we shall not look in vain."[72]

Psalm 119:44

"So I will keep Your law continually,
Forever and ever."

Who can make such an insane statement? A wish maybe, but a promise? Lord, how could I fulfill it? Knowing the truth of Psalm 119:1-2, I want to walk in Your ways always, to seek You with all my heart. How? The key may be in the word 'continually', which is the Hebrew תָּמִיד, tāmiyd: a noun with the sense of continuity, see Psalm 71:3. I see this as something of consistency, a pattern. My mind goes right to Proverbs 4:18-19, that our pattern would be in an upward and forward direction. Other references in the Psalms include Psalm 34:1, and in Psalm 119 we see it in Psalm 119:109 and Psalm 119:117.

"Not only does the Lord's faithfulness open our mouths against his adversaries, but it also knits our hearts to his fear, and makes our union with him more and more intense. Great mercies lead us to feel an inexpressible gratitude which, failing to utter itself in time, promises to engross eternity with praises . . . God's grace alone can enable us to keep his commandments without break and without end; eternal love must grant us eternal life, and out of this will come everlasting obedience . . . Undoubtedly the grace which enables us to bear witness with the mouth is a great help to ourselves as well as to others: we feel that the vows of the Lord are upon us, and that we cannot run back."[73]

---

72. Spurgeon, Charles Haddon, *Treasury of David*, on Psalm 119:43, e-Sword edition
73. Spurgeon, Charles Haddon, *Treasury of David*, on Psalm 119:44, e-Sword edition

Psalm 119:45

> "And I will walk at liberty,
> For I seek Your precepts."

How could it not be so? The way of freedom can only be pursued when the path is clear and the shackles of sin have been removed (Proverbs 4:11-12, Romans 6:20-23, 1 Corinthians 7:22-23). Surely the paths diverge, Proverbs 4:18-19. 'Liberty' is the Hebrew רָחָב, rāḥāḇ: an adjective with the sense of broad, wide, spacious, large. It is used one other time in Psalm 119, Psalm 119:96, 'Your commandment is exceedingly broad.' There is no end to the freedom of joyful discovery! I am reminded immediately of Psalm 18:19. Why would I retreat to the darkness of the forest when I can bask in the open freedom of the sun? Surely it is for freedom that Christ has set us free, Galatians 5:1. Surely 'eternal vigilance is the price of liberty' (attributed to Jefferson). 'Precepts' refers to instruction. It is counterintuitive to our flesh to think that following the instructions of another can bring us freedom. But so it is with You, my awesome and gracious God! 'He breaks the power of cancelled sin / He sets the prisoner free / His blood can make the foulest clean / His blood availed for me.' (from the hymn, 'All Hail the Power of Jesus' Name').

"Saints find no bondage in sanctity. The Spirit of holiness is a free spirit; he sets men at liberty and enables them to resist every effort to bring them under subjection. The way of holiness is not a track for slaves, but the King's highway for freemen, who are joyfully journeying from the Egypt of bondage to the Canaan of rest. God's mercies and his salvation, by teaching us to love the precepts of the word, set us at a happy rest; and the more we seek after the perfection of our obedience the more shall we enjoy complete emancipation from every form of spiritual slavery . . . He says, 'I shall walk,' indicating his daily progress through life; 'at liberty,' as one who is out of prison, unimpeded by adversaries, unencumbered by burdens, unshackled, allowed a wide range, and roaming without fear. Such liberty would be dangerous if a man were seeking himself or his own lusts; but when the one object sought after is the will of God, there can be no need to restrain the searcher . . . Is not this the way to the highest form of liberty, - to be always labouring to know the mind of God and to be conformed to it?"[74]

Psalm 119:46

> "I will also speak of Your testimonies before kings
> And shall not be ashamed."

Here the Psalmist has moved from fear of abandonment (v.43) to confidence to stand before kings without shame. So is the confidence of the word of God. May I boldly and rightly speak of Your testimonies before all people regardless of position in life, the confidence being in Your word and the motivation being the fear of You. Isaiah 2:22, Isaiah 40:17, Matthew 10:18-20. What an unspeakable joy it is to live without the fear of man but in the fear of You. "'If God spare my life, ere many years I will cause a boy who drives a plough to know more of the scriptures than you do." - William Tyndale to a credentialed priest. Surely shame should come to those who are in debt to Your word, regardless of station in life (Proverbs 13:13, Jeremiah 8:9, 1 Corinthians 1:27 context).

"He would speak of God's testimonies, and profess to build his hope upon them and make them his council, his guards, his crown, his all. We must never be afraid to own our religion, though it should expose us to the wrath of kings, but speak of it as that which we will live and die by, like the three children before Nebuchadnezzar, Dan 3:16; Act 4:20 . . . God's testimonies shall be the principal subject of his discourse with the kings, not only to show that he was not ashamed of his religion, but to instruct them in it and bring them over to it."[75]

"This is part of his liberty; he is free from fear of the greatest, proudest, and most tyrannical of men . . . He says, 'I will speak': prudence might have suggested that his life and conduct would be enough, and that it would be better not to touch upon religion in the presence of

---

74. Spurgeon, Charles Haddon, *Treasury of David*, on Psalm 119:45, e-Sword edition
75. Henry, Matthew, *Commentary on the Whole Bible*, on Psalm 119:46, e-Sword edition

royal personages who worshipped other gods, and claimed to be right in so doing. He had already most fittingly preceded this resolve by the declaration, 'I will walk,' but he does not make his personal conduct an excuse for sinful silence, for he adds, 'I will speak.'. . . The great hindrance to our speaking upon holy topics in all companies is shame, but the Psalmist will 'not be ashamed'; there is nothing to be ashamed of, and there is no excuse for being ashamed, and yet many are as quiet as the dead for fear some creature like themselves should be offended. When God gives grace, cowardice soon vanishes."[76]

Psalm 119:47

> "I shall delight in Your commandments,
> Which I love."

No one has ever accused me of having too much joy, too much delight. Yet, I have been known as someone who is serious about Your word. I am wired in such a way, that Your word revives me every day often just to survive, even if I am not overflowing with obvious delight. Would You move in my heart in such a way that this delight propels me to new heights and overflows to others? I want the reaction of others to my exhortations not to be so much of a 'have to' but rather, 'look at what he is experiencing through Your word!' I want that, and I don't want to miss out on the great wisdom, peace, and joy it so obviously brings. 'Delight' is the Hebrew שָׁעַע, šā`a`, a verb with the sense of to take delight in; to fondle. It refers to the default place one goes to for pleasure. May it be Your word, Lord!

"The more delight we take in the service of God the nearer we come to the perfection we aim at."[77]

"Next to liberty and courage comes delight. When we have done our duty, we find a great reward in it . . . Obey the command, and you will love it; carry the yoke, and it will be easy, and rest will come by it . . .

---

76. Spurgeon, Charles Haddon, *Treasury of David*, on Psalm 119:46, e-Sword edition
77. Henry, Matthew, *Commentary on the Whole Bible*, on Psalm 119:47, e-Sword edition

David did not delight in the courts of kings, for there he found places of temptation to shame, but in the Scriptures he found himself at home; his heart was in them, and they yielded him supreme pleasure . . . Lord, let thy mercies come to us that we may love thy word and way, and find our whole delight therein.

The verse is in the future, and hence it sets forth, not only what David had done, but what he would do; he would in time to come delight in his Lord's commands. He knew that they would neither alter, nor fail to yield him joy . . . All the Psalm is fragrant with love to the word, but here for the first time love is expressly spoken of. It is here coupled with delight, and in Psa 119:165 with 'great peace.'"[78]

Psalm 119:48

> "And I shall lift up my hands to Your commandments,
> Which I love;
> And I will meditate on Your statutes."

My mind goes immediately to Psalm 138:2, where Your word is spoken of in worshipful terms. This makes people uncomfortable, bringing accusations of 'bibliolatry'. I often reflect on two things in response. First, that Your word is personal and that You come with it (Psalm 119:151); You cannot be separated from Your word. As an example, both You and Your word - written and incarnate - are truth (John 14:6, John 17:17). Second, the accusation is an empty one; I have never met someone who has too high a view of Scripture, nor have I seen an outbreak of it. Yet, there is the warning of Jesus in John 5:39-40, which actually reinforces the truth of this verse, namely, that the word is a source of true worship; in fact, we cannot worship without it (John 4:24). So what is the Psalmist's response here? To lift up his hands in the heights of worship, and meditate on Your statutes to the depths of his soul. He exalts You in this way within and without in love.

---

78. Spurgeon, Charles Haddon, *Treasury of David*, on Psalm 119:47, e-Sword edition

Personally, I am just in awe at the perfection and power of Your word, and am grieved to my core when it is neglected.

"Prayer with lifted hands, and meditation with upward-glancing eyes will in happy union work out the best inward results. The prayer of Psa 119:41 is already fulfilled in the man who is thus struggling upward and studying deeply. The whole of this verse is in the future, and may be viewed not only as a determination of David's mind, but as a result which he knew would follow from the Lord's sending him his mercies and his salvation."[79]

---

79. Spurgeon, Charles Haddon, *Treasury of David*, on Psalm 119:48, e-Sword edition

CHAPTER 7
Zayin: 'Remembrance to Revival'

"Zayin. Remember the word to Your servant,
In which You have made me hope.
This is my comfort in my affliction,
That Your word has revived me.
The arrogant utterly deride me,
Yet I do not turn aside from Your law.
I have remembered Your ordinances from of old, O LORD,
And comfort myself.
Burning indignation has seized me because of the wicked,
Who forsake Your law.
Your statutes are my songs
In the house of my pilgrimage.
O LORD, I remember Your name in the night,
And keep Your law.
This has become mine,
That I observe Your precepts."

—Psalm 119:49-56

Lord, we challenge not the strength of Your memory, but recall the strength of Your promises as we set our hope on You. Through current affliction (v.50), derision (v. 51), wickedness (v. 53), wandering (v. 54), and darkness (v. 55) the Psalmist remembers Your faithfulness in the past (v. 52), Your name in the night (v. 53), to the point of revival to obedience as a most prized possession above all else (v. 56).

"This octrain deals with the comfort of the word. It begins by seeking the main consolation, namely, the Lord's fulfilment of his promise, and then it shows how the word sustains us under affliction, and makes us so impervious to ridicule that we are moved by the harsh conduct of the wicked rather to horror of their sin than to any submission to their temptations. We are then shown how the Scripture furnishes songs for pilgrims, and memories for night-watchers; and the Psalm concludes by the general statement that the whole of this happiness and comfort arises out of keeping the statutes of the Lord."[80]

Psalm 119:49

"Zayin. Remember the word to Your servant,
In which You have made me hope."

Feeling hopeless, and speaking with others in You who feel the same, what am I to do? Surely a dive into the deep end of the pool of Your word is in order. Surely You have not forgotten Your word, but it is likely that I have. So my asking You to remember is really my calling to mind and seeking You on the basis of Your promises. "This I recall to my mind, Therefore I have hope." (Lamentations 3:21). Surely I must be made to hope in You by experiencing hopelessness in all else. As a slave You have complete right over me, to make me do anything. Make me hope properly! 'Hope' is the Hebrew יָחַל, yāḥal: a verb with the sense of wait, hope. The word appears some 40 times in the N.T., 19 in the Psalms, 6 in Psalm 119, in all other references as 'wait' (Psalm 119:43, Psalm 119:74,

---

80. Spurgeon, Charles Haddon, *Treasury of David*, on Psalm 119 - Zayin, e-Sword edition

Psalm 119:81, Psalm 119:114, Psalm 119:147). In Psalm 130:5 the hope in the word is explicit. Surely I want to hope continually and praise You more (Psalm 71:14)! The hope in Psalms 43-45 is an exclusive hope; I cannot legitimately hope in You and in other things, for that is rank idolatry (Psalm 118:8-9, Jeremiah 17:5-8). "And now, Lord, for what do I wait? My hope is in You." (Psalms 39:7) In the New Testament, surely it is unseen hope that is the fuel of life and an anchor for the soul, Romans 8:24-25, Hebrews 6:19.

"God's word is his hope and his trust amidst all derision."[81]

"He asks for no new promise, but to have the old word fulfilled . . . there is no fear, for the Lord has never forgotten a single promise to a single believer . . . If we hope upon his word we have a sure basis: our gracious Lord would never mock us by exciting false hopes . . . Let but the Lord remember his promise, and the promised act is as good as done [see also Romans 4:20-21]."[82]

Psalm 119:50

"This is my comfort in my affliction,
That Your word has revived me."

This is not a hoping in future revival, but a remembrance of past revival. O Lord, You have done it! 'Revive' is the Hebrew חָיָה, chayah, to come to life and to be kept alive. Lord, You have saved and are sustaining me by Your very word (see also vv. 25, 107, 154, Matthew 4:4).

"The drunkard lifts his glass and sings, 'this is my comfort'; but the man whose hope comes from God feels the life-giving power of the word of the Lord, and he testifies, 'this is my comfort.' Paul said, 'I know whom I have believed.'[2 Timothy 1:12] Comfort is desirable at all times; but comfort in affliction is like a lamp in a dark place. Some are unable to find comfort at such times; but it is not so with believers, for their Saviour has said to them, 'I will not leave you comfortless.' Some

---

81. Keil & Delitzsch, *Commentary on the Old Testament*, on Psalm 119:49, e-Sword edition
82. Spurgeon, Charles Haddon, *Treasury of David*, on Psalm 119:49, e-Sword edition

have comfort and no affliction, others have affliction and no comfort; but the saints have comfort in their affliction."[83]

Psalm 119:51

"The arrogant utterly deride me,
Yet I do not turn aside from Your law."

This, in short, is why the fear of man is a snare (Proverbs 29:25). First, arrogance is not an example to follow, but an error to a avoid and something to hate as You hate (Proverbs 8:13). Such are not content to live unhindered (which would be bad enough), but to bring others down with them (Proverbs 1:10-11), hence the derision. The meaning of these words in Hebrew is straightforward. 'Yet I do not turn aside'. How does one remain undistracted (Proverbs 4:27)? I believe Psalm 27:1-4 is immensely helpful here. One can experience the most intense fellowship with You under the most external pressure. In fact, one could say this is the only path to the kind of intimacy and dependence that benefits us the most. First, it shows our need. Second, it shows the utter contrast between the perfection of God and the sinfulness of man. Third, it shows Your utter sufficiency and the sufficiency of Your word. Perhaps this derision will accomplish its opposite intent. Others mean evil, You mean good through it. Such is Your great Sovereignty! Certainly Psalm 1:1-2 comes into play here, for the wicked, sinners, and scoffers are everywhere (Psalm 12:8). Surely those who deride You will be put to derision by You (Psalm 2:4 KJV).

"He not only had not quite forsaken the law, but had not so much as declined from it. We must never shrink from any duty, nor let slip an opportunity of doing good, for fear of the reproach of men, or their revilings."[84]

"Proud men never love gracious men, and as they fear them they veil their fear under a pretended contempt. In this case their hatred revealed itself in ridicule, and that ridicule was loud and long . . . Men must have

---

83. Spurgeon, Charles Haddon, *Treasury of David*, on Psalm 119:50, e-Sword edition
84. Henry, Matthew, *Commentary on the Whole Bible*, on Psalm 119:51, e-Sword edition

strange eyes to be able to see farce in faith, and a comedy in holiness; yet it is sadly the case that men who are short of wit can generally provoke a broad grin by jesting at a saint. Conceited sinners make footballs of godly men . . . Thus the deriders missed their aim: they laughed, but they did not win. The godly man, so far from turning aside from the right way, did not even slacken his pace, or in any sense fall off from his holy habits . . . God's law is our highway of peace and safety, and those who would laugh us out of it wish us no good."[85]

Psalm 119:52

> "I have remembered Your ordinances from of old,
> O LORD, And comfort myself."

I remember the bedrock of my life, Your very word. Truly Your faithfulness is of old and extends to every generation, Psalm 90:1-2. How vital it is to come into Your presence, to hear from You for proper perspective and comfort, Psalm 73:17. We notice that this verse is sandwiched between the derision of the arrogant (v.51) and the disobedience of the wicked (v.53). What else can one do but look up!

"When we see no present display of the divine power it is wise to fall back upon the records of former ages, since they are just as available as if the transactions were of yesterday, seeing the Lord is always the same. Our true comfort must be found in what our God works on behalf of truth and right, and as the histories of the olden times are full of divine interpositions it is well to be thoroughly acquainted with them. Moreover, if we are advanced in years we have the providences of our early days to review, and these should by no means be forgotten or left out of our thoughts . . . While in our own hearts we humbly drink of the mercy of God in quietude, we are not without comfort in seasons of turmoil and derision; for then we resort to God's justice, and remember how he scoffs at the scoffers: 'He that sitteth in the heavens doth laugh, the Lord doth have them in derision.' [Psalm 2:4 KJV]

---

85. Spurgeon, Charles Haddon, *Treasury of David*, on Psalm 119:51, e-Sword edition

When he was greatly derided the Psalmist did not sit down in despair, but rallied his spirits. He knew that comfort is needful for strength in service, and for the endurance of persecution, and therefore he comforted himself . . . there is a Judge of all the earth who will avenge his own elect, and redress the ills of these disordered times."[86]

Psalm 119:53

> "Burning indignation has seized me because of the wicked,
> Who forsake Your law."

In Zayin (vv. 49-56), the Psalmist moves from affliction to derision to indignation to rejoicing in praise, all by the work of Your word. Here we must turn to Psalm 119:51; my focus must always be on You, both because my soul cannot sustain burning indignation nor the utter derision of people in my own strength. A wonderful example is found in Jeremiah 20:8-9. Here Jeremiah laments that the word of the Lord has resulted in reproach and derision constantly. Yet, it is far worse for him to hold it in than to proclaim it. 'Burning indignation' is the Hebrew זַלְעָפָה, zal'āpāh, a noun with the sense of burning heat. This word occurs only three times in the Old Testament (the others are Psalm 11:6, Lamentations 5:10) However, the English 'indignation' occurs 31 times in the NASB, and in all but 2 cases it is of the righteous anger of God. Notably we see it in Psalm 7:11 of You and 2 Corinthians 7:11 of Your people. As an expression of Your righteousness, it is a daily occurrence, because of the continual unrighteousness of man. As an outworking of Your righteousness, Your people are to be angry at their own sin and obviously repentant. This is the primary way in which Your anger comes out of and produces righteousness, while man's anger does not (James 1:20). It seized the Psalmist because of the wicked who forsake Your law. It is a God centered anger. We see this in the life of David at his own sin (2 Samuel 12:1-14) and in Jesus at the temple (Psalm 69:9, John 2:14-17).

---

86. Spurgeon, Charles Haddon, *Treasury of David*, on Psalm 119:52, e-Sword edition

"Every sin is a transgression of the law, but a course and way of wilful and avowed sin is downright forsaking it and throwing it off . . . He trembled to think of the dishonour thereby done to God, the gratification thereby given to Satan, and the mischiefs thereby done to the souls of men. He dreaded the consequences of it both to the sinners themselves (and cried out, *O gather not my soul with sinners! let my enemy be as the wicked*) and to the interests of God's kingdom among men, which he was afraid would be thereby sunk and ruined."[87]

"He was horrified at their action, at the pride which led them to it, and at the punishment which would be sure to fall upon them for it. When he thought upon the ancient judgments of God he was filled with terror at the fate of the godless; as well he might be. Their laughter had not distressed him, but he was distressed by a foresight of their overthrow . . . this forsaking of the law filled him with the most painful emotions: he was astonished at their wickedness, stunned by their presumption, alarmed by the expectation of their sudden overthrow, amazed by the terror of their certain doom . . . Those who are the firmest believers in the eternal punishment of the wicked are the most grieved at their doom. It is no proof of tenderness to shut one's eyes to the awful doom of the ungodly. Compassion is far better shown in trying to save sinners than in trying to make things pleasant all round. Oh that we were all more distressed as we think of the portion of the ungodly in the lake of fire!"[88]

Psalm 119:54

"Your statutes are my songs
In the house of my pilgrimage."

Something is wrong when Your word is not rejoiced in, and something wholly sweet and appropriate when it is. Statutes are decrees, and pilgrimage has to do with sojourning. I love this. My source of joy is

---

87. Henry, Matthew, *Commentary on the Whole Bible*, on Psalm 119:53, e-Sword edition
88. Spurgeon, Charles Haddon, *Treasury of David*, on Psalm 119:53, e-Sword edition

not the earthly place I dwell in (Philippians 3:20, Psalm 49:11-12, Luke 12:20-21, 2 Corinthians 5:1) but in the One Who dwells in me (Ezekiel 36:27, John 14:17, Romans 8:9-11, 1 Corinthians 3:16, 1 Corinthians 6:19)! We look for a better country, whose architect and builder is God (Hebrews 11:10-16). Falsehood is all around me and makes me bitter. Your decrees infuse me with truth and fill me with joy.

"God's statutes are here his 'songs,' which give him spiritual refreshing, sweeten the hardships of the pilgrimage, and measure and hasten his steps."[89]

"David knew that he was not at home in this world, but a pilgrim through it, seeking a better country. He did not, however, sigh over this fact, but he sang about it. He tells us nothing about his pilgrim sighs, but speaks of his pilgrim songs . . . Happy is the heart which finds its joy in the commands of God, and makes obedience its recreation . . . Saints find horror in sin, and harmony in holiness. The wicked shun the law, and the righteous sing of it. In past days we have sung the Lord's statutes, and in this fact we may find comfort in present affliction."[90]

Psalm 119:55

> "O LORD, I remember Your name in the night,
> And keep Your law."

This has become increasingly true of me as sin loses its luster and I can only be at peace if I am at peace with You (Isaiah 26:3). I am experiencing practically that which only righteousness satisfies (Matthew 5:6). Praise Your name! I remember Your goodness, Your character, Your promises. I see more clearly that there is no life outside of You. 'Remember' is the 'זָכַר, zākar, a verb with the sense of remember, mention, recall, think on. We see it in context in Psalm 119:49 ('remember the word to Your servant') and Psalm 119:52 ('I have remembered Your ordinances'). Your word is my source of both hope and comfort, a sure source I do

---

89. Keil & Delitzsch, *Commentary on the Old Testament*, on Psalm 119:54, e-Sword edition
90. Spurgeon, Charles Haddon, *Treasury of David*, on Psalm 119:54, e-Sword edition

well to keep in mind. I am reminded of Lamentations 3:21, how intentionally I need to bring to mind Your character as the source of my hope. By Your grace may my mind instruct me in the night (Psalm 16:7-8 ff), may it be a peaceful yet powerful school for life. Surely this is what it means to meditate and delight in Your word 'day and night' (Joshua 1:8, Psalm 1:2).

"When others slept I woke to think of thee, thy person, thy actions, thy covenant, thy name, under which last term he comprehends the divine character as far as it is revealed . . . We are to hallow the name of God, and we cannot do so if it slips from our memory . . . by the thoughts of the night he ruled the actions of the day. As the actions of the day often create the dreams of the night, so do the thoughts of the night produce the deeds of the day . . . Reader, are your thoughts in the dark full of light, because full of God? Is his name the natural subject of your evening reflections? Then it will give a tone to your morning and noonday hours. Or do you give your whole mind to the fleeting cares and pleasures of this world? If so, it is little wonder that you do not live as you ought to do. No man is holy by chance. If we have no memory for the name of Jehovah we are not likely to remember his commandments: if we do not think of him secretly we shall not obey him openly."[91]

Psalm 119:56

"This has become mine,
That I observe Your precepts."

My most prized possession: Your word and its work in my heart and life. Nothing desirable is compared to this (Proverbs 3:15) and diligence, particularly here, is a precious possession (Proverbs 12:27). Treasures of inestimable value await (Proverbs 2:1-6). The all-consuming pursuit of it, the price, pales in comparison to the eternal benefits. 'Then you will discern the fear of the LORD And discover the knowledge of God.'

---

91. Spurgeon, Charles Haddon, *Treasury of David*, on Psalm 119:55, e-Sword edition

"God's work is its own wages. A heart to obey the will of God is a most valuable reward of obedience;"[92]

"We are not rewarded for our works, but there is a reward in them . . . God first works in us good works, and then rewards us for them."[93]

"Do not fear, Abram, I am a shield to you; Your reward shall be very great." – from Genesis 15:1

"In keeping them there is great reward." – from Psalm 19:11

92. Henry, Matthew, *Commentary on the Whole Bible*, on Psalm 119:55, e-Sword edition
93. Spurgeon, Charles Haddon, *Treasury of David*, on Psalm 119:55, e-Sword edition

CHAPTER 8
Heth: 'Ask, Seek, Knock, and Go'

"Heth. The LORD is my portion;
I have promised to keep Your words.
I sought Your favor with all my heart;
Be gracious to me according to Your word.
I considered my ways
And turned my feet to Your testimonies.
I hastened and did not delay
To keep Your commandments.
The cords of the wicked have encircled me,
But I have not forgotten Your law.
At midnight I shall rise to give thanks to You
Because of Your righteous ordinances.
I am a companion of all those who fear You,
And of those who keep Your precepts.
The earth is full of Your lovingkindness, O LORD;
Teach me Your statutes."

—Psalm 119:57-64

Because You are my portion (v. 57) and Your favor overrules the favor of men (v. 58) , I have promised to keep Your words, live a life that is dependent upon Your grace, examining my ways before You, running in Your commands. Neither the wicked nor the dark of night can keep me from You. I seek Your presence in those who fear You (v. 63) and see Your lovingkindness all about in a world that doesn't.

"In this section the Psalmist seems to take firm hold upon God himself; appropriating him (Psa 119:57), crying out for him (Psa 119:58), returning to him (Psa 119:59), solacing himself in him (Psa 119:61, Psa 119:62), associating with his people (Psa 119:63), and sighing for personal experience of his goodness (Psa 119:64). Note how Psa 119:57 is linked to the last of the former one, of which indeed it is an expanded repetition. 'This I had because I kept thy precepts. Thou art my portion, O Lord: I have said that I would keep thy words.'"[94]

Psalm 119:57

"The LORD is my portion;
I have promised to keep Your words."

Jesus was the ultimate example of this, John 4:34. 'Portion' is the Hebrew חֵלֶק, ḥēleq, a noun with the sense of portion, territory. Normally a portion is limited in some way. But You, O Lord, are infinite! This is used as 'inheritance' in Psalm 16:5, a forever portion in Psalm 73:26, and my portion in the land of the living, Psalm 142:5. With You as my portion, I should be forever satisfied, freed from the desire for lesser things. Because You are my portion, I take my fill in the means which You have provided, Your living word. Unlike earthly food, which in one sense is less necessary (Job 23:12), Your word is a delicious delight (Psalm 19:10, Psalm 119:103-104) which we need not fear gorging ourselves on (Psalm 81:10)! Filled, may I be free from lesser, destructive desires (Proverbs 17:14-15). The satisfaction is not merely in the eating, but in the experience of doing (James 1:25).

---

94. Spurgeon, Charles Haddon, *Treasury of David*, on Psalm 119 - Heth, e-Sword edition

"The poet is lost in wonder while he sees that the great and glorious God is all his own! Well might he be so, for there is no possession like Jehovah himself . . . Who that is truly wise could hesitate for a moment when the infinitely blessed God is set before him to be the object of his choice? . . . With much else to choose from, for he was a king, and a man of great resources, he deliberately turns from all the treasures of the world, and declares that the Lord, even Jehovah, is his portion . . . he preferred the word of God to the wealth of worldlings. It was his firm resolve to keep - that is, treasure up and observe - the words of his God, and as he had aforetime solemnly expressed it in the presence of the Lord himself, so here he confesses the binding obligation of his former vow. Jesus said, 'If a man love me, he will keep my words,' . . . Full assurance is a powerful source of holiness. The very words of God are to be stored up; for whether they relate to doctrine, promise, or precept, they are most precious. When the heart is determined to keep these words, and has registered its purpose in the court of heaven, it is prepared for all the temptations and trials that may befall it; for, with God as its heritage, it is always in good case."[95]

Psalm 119:58

"I sought Your favor with all my heart;
Be gracious to me according to Your word."

A frequent heart cry, Your favor is my very life. Your agenda for me is the ultimate grace. May I seek nothing less. Favor here is the Hebrew פָּנֶה, pāneh, a noun with the sense of face. The LSB translates it as 'I have sought to please Your face'. It occurs 121 times in Psalms, first in Psalm 4:6 as 'countenance', often as 'before' (see Psalm 62:8), 'presence' (see Psalm 44:3) or 'face', the latter most notably in Psalm 27:8-9. This is 1 of 4 times in Psalm 119, the others being Psalm 119:135 as 'face', Psalm 119:169-170 as 'before'. To seek Your favor is to seek Your face. To receive

---

95. Spurgeon, Charles Haddon, *Treasury of David*, on Psalm 119:57, e-Sword edition

Your promises according to Your word is the ultimate grace. We notice Daniel 9:13, how we are to seek Your favor, namely, in turning from our iniquity and giving attention to Your truth.

"Having taken God for his portion, he entreated his favour, as one that knew he had forfeited it, was unworthy of it, and yet undone without it, but for ever happy if he could obtain it . . . . The gracious soul is entirely set upon the favour of God, and is therefore importunate for it."[96]

"A fully assured possession be his God will seek his face, longing for his presence. Seeking God's presence is the idea conveyed by the marginal reading, 'thy face,' and this is true to the Hebrew . . . the light of his countenance gives us an antepast of heaven . . . The whole of God's favours are ready for those who seek them with their whole hearts . . . God has revealed such an infinity of mercy in his word that it would be impossible to conceive of more. See how the Psalmist dwells upon favour and mercy, he never dreams of merit. He does not demand, but entreat; for he feels his own unworthiness . . . God is his portion, and yet he begs for a look at his face . . . The confidence of faith makes us bold in prayer, but it never teaches us to live without prayer, or justifies us in being other than humble beggars at mercy's gate."[97]

Psalm 119:59

> "I considered my ways
> And turned my feet to Your testimonies."

What godly man ever said, 'I thought upon my ways, and justified myself.' (see also Proverbs 20:9)? While I explore the wonders of Your righteousness, I cannot help but see the depth of my sin and cry out, 'Oh that my ways may be established to keep Your statues!' (Psalm 119:5). I tell of my ways, but You answer decisively (Psalm 119:26), my ways may seem right to me

---

96. Henry, Matthew, *Commentary on the Whole Bible*, on Psalm 119:58, e-Sword edition
97. Spurgeon, Charles Haddon, *Treasury of David*, on Psalm 119:58, e-Sword edition

even when they could not be more wrong (Proverbs 14:12, Proverbs 16:25, Proverbs 28:26, Jeremiah 17:7). Save me from such delusion, even if it appears righteous (Jeremiah 10:8)! 'Turned' is the language of repentance, a change of mind which results in a change of behavior.

In my pride my default is to consider my ways and explore them (see Psalm 36:1-2). Even if not in sinful pride, it can often be in despair (Psalm 42:5), taking my own counsel (Psalm 13:2). The godly man considers this and turns away and towards You. Father, I praise You for and pray for grace to turn more frequently and more deeply. 'Considered' is the same as 'reckoned' in Genesis 15:6, and 'turn' is often a returning or turning back, most notably in 2 Kings 23:25, of Josiah, who 'turned to the LORD with all his heart and with all his soul and with all his might, according to all the law of Moses'. May I be like him! In the next verse, Psalm 119:60, we see the speed with which this turning occurs, with haste and without delay.

"While studying the word he was led to study his own life, and this caused a mighty revolution. He came to the word, and then he came to himself, and this made him arise and go to his father. Consideration is the commencement of conversion: first we think and then we turn. When the mind repents of ill ways the feet are soon led into good ways; but there will be no repenting until there is deep, earnest thought. Many men are averse to thought of any kind, and as to thought upon their ways, they cannot endure it, for their ways will not bear thinking of . . . Action without thought is folly, and thought without action is sloth: to think carefully and then to act promptly is a happy combination . . . If we are in the dark, and mourn an absent God, our wisest method will be not so much to think upon our sorrows as upon our ways: though we cannot turn the course of providence, we can turn the way of our walking, and this will soon mend matters. If we can get our feet right as to holy walking, we shall soon get our hearts right as to happy living."[98]

---

98. Spurgeon, Charles Haddon, *Treasury of David*, on Psalm 119:59, e-Sword edition

Psalm 119:60

"I hastened and did not delay
To keep Your commandments."

Having sought Your favor (Psalm 119:58), considered his ways, and turned toward Your testimonies (Psalm 119:59), the Psalmist now takes action to obey swiftly. We understand that the blessing is in the doing (Psalm 1:1-2, Matthew 7:24-27, James 1:25, John 13:17, 14:21, Psalm 111:10). As is often said by parents, 'delayed obedience is not obedience'. We don't have other things to do before or in preparation for obedience, as important as we think those things may be (Luke 8:21, 10:42). You are my King, and obedience is not only not optional, but it is the best possible option! How favorable You are to me! Continuing in the context of the Psalm, this resolution is necessary to avoid the cords of the wicked.

"Speed in repentance and speed in obedience are two excellent things. We are too often in haste to sin; O that we may be in a greater hurry to obey. Delay in sin is increase of sin . . . we are eager to make up for lost time by dashing forward to fulfil the precept . . . Many are zealous to obey custom and society, and yet they are slack in serving God. It is a crying shame that men should be served post-haste, and that God's work should have the go-by, or be performed with dreamy negligence."[99]

Psalm 119:61

"The cords of the wicked have encircled me,
But I have not forgotten Your law."

'The cords of the wicked have encircled me'. Emotion, or reality? For the Christian, it is hard to tell, for our citizenship is in heaven (Philippians 3:20), the world system has a different ruler (1 John 2:15-16, 1 John 3:13, 1 John 5:19), and we are hated in big and small ways because of Jesus (John 15:18-19). One could say there are 'micro-aggressions' which are debatable and macro-aggressions which are historical and very real

---

99. Spurgeon, Charles Haddon, *Treasury of David*, on Psalm 119:60, e-Sword edition

today. We are surrounded by this, and it challenges our perception of reality. Should I just go along? There is a sense in which I must be content and at peace with You, but I can never be at peace with sin. Lord, how do I endure? 'But I have not forgotten Your law.' Surely You are true though every man be found a liar (Romans 3:4). Surely indignation is the right response to this immersive injustice (Psalm 119:53), yet there is comfort in You (Psalm 119:52) - yes, only in You in Your word! Notice the comfort comes before the indignation because it is needed! May I go back to where I started, never forgetting Your law and comforting myself in You, God of truth (Psalm 31:5, Isaiah 65:16). When surrounded, I find perhaps the sweetest refuge (Psalm 27:3-4).

"Ungodly men grow worse, and become more and more daring, so that they go from ridicule to robbery. Much of this bold opposition arose from their being banded together: men will dare to do in company what they durst not have thought of alone . . . How much the ungodly have plundered the saints in all ages, and how often have the righteous borne gladly the spoiling of their goods! [Hebrews 10:34] . . . Neither his sense of injustice, nor his sorrow at his losses, nor his attempts at defence diverted him from the ways of God . . . He might have forgotten himself if he had forgotten the law; as it was, he was ready to forgive and forget the injuries done him, for his heart was taken up with the word of God. The bands of the wicked had not robbed him of his choicest treasure, since they had left him his holiness and his happiness . . . He could not be either bribed or bullied into sin. The cordon of the ungodly could not keep God from him, nor him from God- this was because God was his portion, and none could deprive him of it either by force or fraud. That is true grace which can endure the test: some are barely gracious among the circle of their friends, but this man was holy amid a ring of foes."[100]

Psalm 119:62

"At midnight I shall rise to give thanks to You
Because of Your righteous ordinances."

---

100. Spurgeon, Charles Haddon, *Treasury of David*, on Psalm 119:61, e-Sword edition

Meditation and prayer are to be day and night (Joshua 1:8, Psalm 1:2). I have risen in the middle of the night and prayed often, but it wasn't planned. Although many times I have resented it, I realize that it is of You, Lord. Ordinances here are judgments. I find that, even though increasingly my default thoughts are toward You, the sinful flesh refuses to die. This is Your means of strengthening me even as I sleep. Yet, I need to make nightly delight in You a priority. How do I get to the point of retiring and waking delighting in You? Psalm 17:15, Psalm 132:4.

"Great and good thoughts kept him awake, and refreshed him, instead of sleep; and so zealous was he for the honour of God that when others were in their beds he was upon his knees at his devotions."[101]

"He thought not of thieves, but of thanks; not of What *they* would steal, but of what *he* would give to his God. A thankful heart is such a blessing that it drives out fear and makes room for praise. Thanksgiving turns night into day, and consecrates all hours to the worship of God. Every hour is canonical to a saint . . . . David was charmed with these judgments. Like Paul, he could say, 'I delight in the law of God after the inward man.' [Romans 7:22] He could not find time enough by day to study the words of divine wisdom, or to bless God for them, and so he gave up his sleep that he might tell out his gratitude for such a law and such a Law-giver."[102]

Psalm 119:63

"I am a companion of all those who fear You,
And of those who keep Your precepts."

How good - yes, even how necessary - it is for us to have godly companions. I want to fear You; bring me those who fear You. I want to keep Your precepts; bring me those who keep Your precepts. I am reminded of Psalm 119:74 and Psalm 119:79, how good it is to be appreciated and sought after. 'Companion' is the Hebrew חָבֵר, ḥāḇēr, a

---

101. Henry, Matthew, *Commentary on the Whole Bible*, on Psalm 119:62, e-Sword edition
102. Spurgeon, Charles Haddon, *Treasury of David*, on Psalm 119:62, e-Sword edition

noun with the sense of friendship, association, companionship, as in Ecclesiastes 4:10. It occurs just 11 times in the Old Testament, just one other time in the Psalms, Psalm 45:7. We need each other! How good it is for us to dwell in unity (Psalm 133:1). It is sweet because it is rare. Loyalty is the exception (Proverbs 20:6) and betrayal is common. Only You are the Rock I can come to continually (Psalm 71:3-4) and never be disappointed (Deuteronomy 32:3-4, 2 Samuel 22:32, Isaiah 28:16). In all of this, may I walk closest with You, seeking to be a good man who seeks good men (Proverbs 2:20) but seeks You above all (Psalm 27:4).

" . . . so did him honour and helped to support his kingdom among men. Our love to the saints is then sincere when we love them for the sake of what we see of God in them and the service they do to him . . . He had not only a spiritual communion with them in the same faith and hope, but he joined with them in holy ordinances in the courts of the Lord, where rich and poor, prince and peasant, meet together . . . Though he was a king, he would associate with the poorest of his subjects that feared God, Psa 15:4: Jas 2:1."[103]

"The holy man spent his nights with God and his days with God's people. Those who fear God love those who fear him, and they make small choice in their company so long as the men are truly God-fearing. David was a king, and yet he consorted with 'all' who feared the Lord, whether they were obscure or famous, poor or rich. He was a fellow-commoner of the College of All-saints . . . He looked for inward godly fear, but he also expected to see outward piety in those whom he admitted to his society; . . . David was known to be on the godly side . . . the men of Belial hated him for this, and no doubt despised him for keeping such unfashionable company as that of humble men and women who were strait-laced and religious; but the man of God is by no means ashamed of his associates; so far from this, he even glories to avow his union with them, let his enemies make what they can of it. He found both pleasure and profit in saintly society; he grew better by consorting with the good, and derived honour from keeping right honourable company . . . A man

---

103. Henry, Matthew, *Commentary on the Whole Bible*, on Psalm 119:62, e-Sword edition

is known by his company . . . those who loved the saints on earth shall be numbered with them in heaven."[104]

Psalm 119:64

> "The earth is full of Your lovingkindness, O LORD;
> Teach me Your statutes."

I am reminded immediately of Psalm 33:5. Father, give me eyes to see it! Your lovingkindness abounds on the earth (Psalm 98:3, Psalm 103:11, Jeremiah 9:24) and how awesome are Your deeds and lovingkindness towards the sons of men (Psalm 66:5, Psalm 107:8, Psalm 107:15, Psalm 107:21, Psalm 107:31). Teach me to see, teach me to act in the reality of Your power. 'Lovingkindness' is the Hebrew חֶסֶד, ḥesed, a noun with the sense of kindness, lovingkindness, mercy, goodness, faithfulness, love, see it repeated in Psalm 136 and in the plural in Lamentations 3:22. Why do I act as if it does not exist? May I joyfully run in the way today (Psalm 119:32), knowing that You have brought me into a broad place of freedom (Psalm 18:19).

"He implores for himself the inward teaching concerning His word as the highest and most cherished of mercies."[105]

"He had learned that far beyond the bounds of the land of promise and the race of Israel the love of Jehovah extended, and in this verse he expressed that large-hearted idea of God which is so seldom seen. Surely he who fills the universe with his grace will grant such a request as this to his own child . . . those who have resolved to obey are the most eager to be taught . . . Those who wish to keep a law are anxious to know all its clauses and provisions lest they should offend through inadvertence. He who dares not care to be instructed of the Lord has never honestly resolved to be holy."[106]

---

104. Spurgeon, Charles Haddon, *Treasury of David*, on Psalm 119:63, e-Sword edition
105. Keil & Delitzsch, *Commentary on the Old Testament*, on Psalm 119:64
106. Spurgeon, Charles Haddon, *Treasury of David*, on Psalm 119:64, e-Sword edition

CHAPTER 9

Teth: 'Treasure in Affliction'

"Teth. You have dealt well with Your servant,
O LORD, according to Your word.
Teach me good discernment and knowledge,
For I believe in Your commandments.
Before I was afflicted I went astray,
But now I keep Your word.
You are good and do good;
Teach me Your statutes.
The arrogant have forged a lie against me;
With all my heart I will observe Your precepts.
Their heart is covered with fat,
But I delight in Your law.
It is good for me that I was afflicted,
That I may learn Your statutes.
The law of Your mouth is better to me
Than thousands of gold and silver pieces."

—Psalm 119:65-72

H aving been dealt well with (v. 65) through affliction that brought learning to the point of obedience (vv. 67, 71), perhaps the greatest benefit to the Psalmist was a teachable spirit (vv. 66, 68), a desire to obey (vv. 69), and a treasuring of true treasure (vv. 70, 72). 'Dealt' has the sense of 'accomplish'. Surely 'the lines have fallen to me in pleasant places' (Psalm 16:6) not because of my portion in this life, but because You are my portion (Psalm 16:5).

"In this ninth section the verses all begin with the letter Teth. They are the witness of experience, testifying to the goodness of God, the graciousness of his dealings, and the preciousness of his word. Especially the Psalmist proclaims the excellent uses of adversity, and the goodness of God in afflicting him. Psa 119:65 is the text of the entire octave."[107]

Psalm 119:65

"You have dealt well with Your servant,
O LORD, according to Your word."

The only way You can deal well with me is according to Your word, and praise You, not according to my self-centered desires. I am reminded of Psalm 119:26, You answer me with Your statutes! 'Dealt' has the sense of 'accomplish', and 'well' has the sense of for my benefit, my welfare.

"It is a wonder that he has not long ago discharged us, or at least reduced our allowances, or handled us roughly; yet we have had no hard dealings, all has been ordered with as much consideration as if we had rendered perfect obedience. We have had bread enough and to spare, our livery has been duly supplied, and his service has ennobled us and made us happy as kings. Complaints we have none. We lose ourselves in adoring thanksgiving, and find ourselves again in careful thanks-living."[108]

---

107. Spurgeon, Charles Haddon, *Treasury of David*, on Psalm 119 - Teth, e-Sword edition
108. Spurgeon, Charles Haddon, *Treasury of David*, on Psalm 119:65, e-Sword edition

Psalm 119:66

"Teach me good discernment and knowledge,
For I believe in Your commandments."

'Teach' has the sense of training for war. Good discernment and knowledge come in no small part from the affliction the Lord uses in our lives (Psalm 119:67, Psalm 119:71). Discernment and knowledge are by nature ultimately good (Proverbs 16:20, Proverbs 19:8). 'Good' is the Hebrew בוּט, ṭûḇ, a noun with the sense of property, goods, goodness, fairness, beauty; it is for useful enjoyment. 'Discernment' is the Hebrew ם טַע, ṭa'am, a noun with the sense of taste, judgment, discernment, discretion. This is the only use of this word in Psalms. 'Knowledge' is the Hebrew תעַדַּ, da'aṭ, a noun with the sense of knowledge, knowing, learning, discernment, insight, and notion. It is often associate with wisdom in Proverbs. Surely Your word shapes my affections and directs my paths (Psalm 119:103-104).

"A sight of our errors and a sense of our ignorance should make us teachable. We are not able to judge, for our knowledge is so sadly inaccurate and imperfect; if the Lord teaches us knowledge we shall attain to good judgment, but not otherwise. The Holy Ghost alone can fill us with light, and set the understanding upon a proper balance: let us ardently long for his teachings, since it is most desirable that we should be no longer mere children in knowledge and understanding."[109]

Psalm 119:67

"Before I was afflicted I went astray,
But now I keep Your word."

See also Psalm 119:71. This resonates with me more the more I meditate on it. As much as my love for Your word grows, so does my realization of the depravity of the sin nature. This leads to both discouragement

---

109. Spurgeon, Charles Haddon, *Treasury of David*, on Psalm 119:66, e-Sword edition

and a resolve to fight, seeing the reality of Romans 6:21, that there was only detriment to experienced sin, and of the warnings of Ecclesiastes and Proverbs, that unexperienced (although sometimes desired) sin will only lead to death (e.g. Proverbs 12:28, Proverbs 6:32, 1 Peter 2:11), even if just in my thoughts (Matthew 5:27-28, Galatians 6:7-8, James 1:14-16)! 'Afflicted' is the Hebrew עָנָה, `ānāh, a verb with the sense of afflicted, oppressed, humbled. Better to experience even relatively painful and extreme loss in this life then to lose one's life eternally (Matthew 18:8). Even if that is not my destiny, to be encumbered this life is to miss the eternal joy and benefit to others. Father, how gracious of You to enable me to share Your holiness (Hebrews 12:10)! Of this, Luther said, 'I want you to know how to study theology in the right way. I have practiced this method myself. . . . Here you will find three rules. They are frequently proposed throughout Psalm [119] and run thus: oration, meditatio, tentatio [prayer, meditation, trial]. (Plass, 1359)[110] As much as the Psalmist sought good discernment and knowledge (Psalm 119:66), he would soon realize that the answer to this plea requires affliction.

"How beneficial has the school of affliction through which he has attained to this, been to him! The word proceeding from the mouth of God is now more precious to him than the greatest earthly riches [see v. 72]."[111]

"Often our trials act as a thorn hedge to keep us in the good pasture, but our prosperity is a gap through which we go astray . . . the spiritual man who prizes growth in grace will bless God that those dangerous days are over, and that if the weather be more stormy it is also more healthy . . . Why is it that a little ease works in us so much disease? Can we never rest without rusting? What weak creatures we are to be unable to bear a little pleasure! What base hearts are those which turn the abundance of God's goodness into an occasion for sin . . . Grace is in that heart which profits by its chastening. It is of no use

110. *Martin Luther: Lessons from his life and Labor*. Desiring God. (2023, May 22). https://www.desiringgod.org/messages/martin-luther-lessons-from-his-life-and-labor
111. Keil & Delitzsch, *Commentary on the Old Testament*, on Psalm 119:67, e-Sword edition

to plough barren soil. When there is no spiritual life affliction works no spiritual benefit; but where the heart is sound trouble awakens conscience, wandering is confessed, the soul becomes again obedient to the command, and continues to be so . . . Before his trouble he wandered, but after it he kept within the hedge of the word, and found good pasture for his soul: the trial tethered him to his proper place; it kept him, and then he kept God's word. Sweet are the uses of adversity, and this is one of them, it puts a bridle upon transgression and furnishes a spur for holiness."[112]

Psalm 119:68

"You are good and do good;
Teach me Your statutes."

"Why do you call Me good? No one is good except God alone." – Jesus (see Mark 10:18, Luke 18:19). 'Good' is the Hebrew טוֹב, ṭôḇ, an adjective with the sense of good, well-pleasing, fruitful, morally correct, proper, convenient. 'Do good' is the Hebrew יָטַב, yāṭaḇ, a verb with the sense of be good, well, pleasing. It is the same as 'well' in v.65. Lord, You can only be good and Your actions perform good; You are its very Source and Definition. From the very beginning Your creation was good (e.g. Genesis 1:4). Your actions are good simply because You do them. Certainly I have no good besides You (Psalm 16:2), and no earthly thing can compare with You (Psalm 73:28)! As a result, where else do I go for teaching? You alone have the words of eternal life (John 6:68). Surely I am in constant need of Your instruction (Psalm 32:8, Job 42:4). Because You are good, You instruct sinners like me (Psalm 25:8). Help me to be a good man who is instructed by good men and qualified to instruct others (Proverbs 2:20, 2 Timothy 2:2).

"The streams of God's goodness are so numerous, and run so full, so strong, to all the creatures, that we must conclude the fountain that is in

---

112. Spurgeon, Charles Haddon, *Treasury of David*, on Psalm 119:67, e-Sword edition

himself to be inexhaustible. Instruct me in my duty, incline me to it, and enable me to do it."[113]

"God is essential goodness in himself, and in every attribute of his nature he is good in the fullest sense of the term; indeed, he has a monopoly of goodness, for there is none good but one, that is God . . . God is not latent and inactive goodness; he displays himself by his doings, he is actively beneficent, he does good . . . Facts about God are the best praise of God. All the glory we can give to God is to reflect his own glory upon himself . . . He who mourns that he has not kept the word longs to be taught it, and he who rejoices that by grace he has been taught to keep it is not less anxious for the like instruction to be continued to him."[114]

Psalm 119:69

> "The arrogant have forged a lie against me;
> With all my heart I will observe Your precepts."

Psalm 119:69 may give a clue as to where the affliction of v.67 and v.71 come from. Arrogant men forge lies against humble men. I am marveling less, but I still marvel, at the apparent ease and impunity with which this happens. Is there no shame? May I not be naïve, let me also not be intimidated. These poor people, whose heart is so encased in fat (v.70) - surely You have placed them in slippery places (Psalm 73:18). The Psalmist directs his attention away from the arrogant and doubles down on his focus on You and the promises of obedience to Your word. Is not the nearness of God ultimate good (Psalm 73:28) and incalculable treasure (Philippians 3:7-14)? May I measure all things by this, seeking the things which draw me closer to You and make me more like You above all else.

"He did not fear their malice, nor was he by it deterred from his duty: They have forged a lie against me. Thus they aimed to take away his good name. Nay, all we have in the world, even life itself, may be brought into

113. Henry, Matthew, *Commentary on the Whole Bible*, on Psalm 119:68, e-Sword edition
114. Spurgeon, Charles Haddon, *Treasury of David*, on Psalm 119:68, e-Sword edition

danger by those who make no conscience of forging a lie . . . He will bear it patiently; he will keep that precept which forbids him to render railing for railing, and will with all his heart sit down silently. He will go on in his duty with constancy and resolution: 'Let them say what they will, I will keep thy precepts, and not dread their reproach.' . . . Senseless, secure, and stupid; they are past feeling: thus the phrase is used, Isa 6:10 . . . I would not change conditions with them."[115]

"My one anxiety shall be to mind my own business and stick to the commandments of the Lord. If the mud which is thrown at us does not blind our eyes or bruise our integrity it will do us little harm. If we keep the precepts, the precepts will keep us . . . When slanderers drive us to more resolute and careful obedience they work our lasting good; falsehood hurled against us may be made to promote our fidelity to the truth, and the malice of men may increase our love to God. If we try to answer lies by our words we may be beaten in the battle; but a holy life is an unanswerable refutation of all calumnies."[116]

Psalm 119:70

> "Their heart is covered with fat,
> But I delight in Your law."

Of the arrogant who forge lies against the righteous, 'their heart is covered with fat', similarly the Psalmist in contrast observes Your precepts and delights in Your law. Thinking of the testimony of Scripture, the dead go further into the deadness of their hearts, while the spiritually living go from life to delight. The idea behind 'covered' is 'insensitive' or 'unfeeling'. I am reminded of Isaiah 6:10, Proverbs 28:14, the contrast between hardness and softness. We see this also in Hebrews 3:13. We need Your word and Your people to maintain hearts that are humbly soft towards You. I am reminded also of Proverbs 1:19, and 2 Peter 2:18-19 - the promise of freedom apart from You brings utter enslavement.

---

115. Henry, Matthew, *Commentary on the Whole Bible*, on Psalm 119:69, e-Sword edition
116. Spurgeon, Charles Haddon, *Treasury of David*, on Psalm 119:69, e-Sword edition

"Proud men grow fat through carnal luxuries, and this makes them prouder still. They riot in their prosperity, and fill their hearts therewith till they become insensible, effeminate, and self-indulgent. A greasy heart is something horrible; it is a fatness which makes a man fatuous, a fatty degeneration of the heart which leads to feebleness and death. The fat in such men is killing the life in them . . . How much better is it to joy in the law of the Lord than to joy in sensual indulgences. This makes the heart healthy, and keeps the mind lowly. No one who loves holiness has the slightest cause to envy the prosperity of the worldling. Delight in the law elevates and ennobles, while carnal pleasure clogs the intellect and degrades the affections. There is and always ought to be a vivid contrast between the believer and the sensualist, and that contrast is as much seen in the affections of the heart as in the actions of the life: their heart is as fat as grease, and our heart is delighted with the law of the Lord. Our delights are a better test of our character than anything else: as a man's heart is, so is the man . . . When law becomes delight, obedience is bliss. Holiness in the heart causes the soul to eat the fat of the land. To have the law for our delight will breed in our hearts the very opposite of the effects of pride; deadness, sensuality, and obstinacy will be cured, and we shall become teachable, sensitive, and spiritual."[117]

Psalm 119:71

> "It is good for me that I was afflicted,
> That I may learn Your statutes."

In the scope of Teth, we see a radical redefinition of what is good compared with our inclinations. 'You have dealt well' (v.65). How so? According to Your word, but magnified and focused in affliction, whether that be through Your sovereignty in difficult circumstances, or with difficult people - in this case, crafty, arrogant liars (v. 69). The pressure within and without grows us (see Romans 5:1-5, Romans

---

117. Spurgeon, Charles Haddon, *Treasury of David*, on Psalm 119:70, e-Sword edition, with emphasis

8:28-30, James 1:2-4 among many others!). Hope in a perfect result! See the notes on v. 67. 'It is good' because 'You are good and do good' (v.68). 'Good' here is a variation of what we see in vv. 65 ('well') and v.68. The sinfulness of our hearts reveals that this must be a primary means of seeing and seeking Your goodness. 'Learn' is the same as 'teach' in v.68, is common in Psalm 119, and has a sense of training. I think of the regular angst of this life. Am I as eager to rid myself of sin as I am to rid myself of pain? Father, how sweet this is in that it drives me to see and to seek You. "Yield now and be at peace with Him; Thereby good will come to you." (Job 22:21) How would I yield without affliction? And how would I receive Your goodness without yielding to it?

"*Waters of a full cup are wrung out to* God's people, Psa 73:10. 2. That it has been the advantage of God's people to be afflicted . . . *Therefore* God visited him with affliction, that he might learn God's statutes; and the intention was answered: the afflictions had contributed to the improvement of his knowledge and grace. He that chastened him taught him. *The rod and reproof give wisdom.* [Proverbs 29:15]"[118]

"Even though the affliction came from bad men, it was overruled for good ends . . . It was not good to the proud to be prosperous, for their hearts grew sensual and insensible; but affliction was good for the Psalmist. Our worst is better for us than the sinner's best. It is bad for sinners to rejoice, and good for saints to sorrow . . . We prayed the Lord to teach us (Psa 119:66), and now we see how he has already been doing it. Truly he has dealt well with us, for he has dealt wisely with us . . . To be larded by prosperity is not good for the proud; but for the truth to be learned by adversity is good for the humble. Very little is to be learned without affliction. If we would be scholars we must be sufferers."[119]

---

118. Henry, Matthew, *Commentary on the Whole Bible*, on Psalm 119:71, e-Sword edition
119. Spurgeon, Charles Haddon, *Treasury of David*, on Psalm 119:71, e-Sword edition

Psalm 119:72

"The law of Your mouth is better to me
Than thousands of gold and silver pieces."

If this is to be believed, I am set not only for life, but for eternity. See also Psalm 119:14, Psalm 119:162. I think of the worldly exhilaration of having a 'pile of gold'. To many, the thought is winning the lottery (notwithstanding the warnings against gaining wealth too quickly (e.g. Proverbs 20:21). Imagine having access to a supreme king and all his resources. I believe that is the sense here. Note 'law of Your mouth'. This is personal speech from You, Lord. Incredible. How can I not be attentive and receive all that I can as You speak personally to me? With riches, the human inclination is to take it and do whatever I want in this world. With Your word, I receive it deeply into my soul and do what You desire, ultimate wisdom and prosperity. We see the words of Your mouth also in Psalm 119:13, Psalm 119:88. In Psalm 33:6 we see Your word created all things! (see also Hebrews 1:1-3) In Psalm 138:4, all kings will give thanks to You, having heard the words of Your mouth.

" . . . by his afflictions he learned God's statutes, and the profit did so much counterbalance the loss, he was really a gainer by them; for God's law, which he got acquaintance with by his affliction, was *better* to him than all the *gold* and *silver* which he lost by his affliction. 1. David had but a little of the word of God in comparison with what we have, yet see how highly he valued it; . . . He had a great deal of gold and silver in comparison with what we have, yet see how little he valued it. His riches increased, and yet he did not set his heart upon them, but upon the word of God. That was better to him, yielded him better pleasures, and better maintenance, and a better inheritance, than all the treasures he was master of."[120]

"Things written are as dried herbs; but speech has a liveliness and dew about it. We do well to look upon the word of the Lord as though

---

120. Henry, Matthew, *Commentary on the Whole Bible*, on Psalm 119:72, e-Sword edition

it were newly spoken into our ear; for in very truth it is not decayed by years, but is as forcible and sure as though newly uttered. Precepts are prized when it is seen that they come forth from the lips of our Father who is in heaven. The same lips which spoke us into existence have spoken the law by which we are to govern that existence . . . Wealth is good in some respects, but obedience is better in all respects . . . It is a sure sign of a heart which has learned God's statutes when it prizes them above all earthly possessions; and it is an equally certain mark of grace when the precepts of Scripture are as precious as its promises. The Lord cause us thus to prize the law of his mouth.

See how this portion of the Psalm is flavoured with goodness. God's dealings are good (Psa 119:65), holy judgment is good (Psa 119:66), affliction is good (Psa 119:67), God is good (Psa 119:68), and here the law is not only good, but better than the best of treasure. Lord, make us good through thy good word. Amen."[121]

---

121. Spurgeon, Charles Haddon, *Treasury of David*, on Psalm 119:72, e-Sword edition

CHAPTER 10
Yodh: 'Godly Comfort and Companionship'

"Yodh. Your hands made me and fashioned me;
Give me understanding, that I may learn Your
commandments.
[74] May those who fear You see me and be glad,
Because I wait for Your word.
[75] I know, O LORD, that Your judgments are righteous,
And that in faithfulness You have afflicted me.
[76] O may Your lovingkindness comfort me,
According to Your word to Your servant.
[77] May Your compassion come to me that I may live,
For Your law is my delight.
[78] May the arrogant be ashamed, for they subvert me with
a lie;
But I shall meditate on Your precepts.
[79] May those who fear You turn to me,
Even those who know Your testimonies.
[80] May my heart be blameless in Your statutes,
So that I will not be ashamed."

—Psalm 119:73-80

What precious words of comfort and companionship! We see Your nearness in fashioning me (v. 73) and my circumstances (v. 75). You comfort me with Your word (vv. 76-77) and protect me from the influence of the arrogant (v. 78). You provide priceless companions through the work of Your word (vv. 74, 79). In all of this, may I continue to be blameless in Your statutes that I might receive its benefits (v. 80).

"We have now come to the tenth portion, which in each stanza begins with Jod, but it certainly does not treat of jots and titles and other trifles. Its subject would seem to be personal experience and its attractive influence upon others. The prophet is in deep sorrow, but looks to be delivered and made a blessing. Endeavouring to teach, the Psalmist first seeks to be taught (Psa 119:73), persuades himself that he will be well received (Psa 119:74), and rehearses the testimony which he intends to bear (Psa 119:75). He prays for more experience (Psa 119:76, Psa 119:77), for the baffling of the proud (Psa 119:78), for the gathering together of the godly to him (Psa 119:79), and for himself again that he may be fully equipped for his witness-bearing and may be sustained in it (Psa 119:80). This is the anxious yet hopeful cry of one who is heavily afflicted by cruel adversaries, and therefore makes his appeal to God as his only friend."[122]

Psalm 119:73

"Your hands made me and fashioned me;
Give me understanding, that I may learn Your commandments."

You who crafted me are eminently qualified to rule my life. In fact, for me to have understanding, You must. I think of Psalm 139:13, Psalm 139:24, how You, O Lord, are Master and Creator of things seen and unseen, from the `āśāh, and has the sense of accomplished or completed. 'Fashioned' is כּוּן, kûn and has the sense of having established or

---

122. Spurgeon, Charles Haddon, *Treasury of David*, on Psalm 119 - Yodh, e-Sword edition

prepared. This leads me to Ephesians 2:10 and to pray, 'Lord, You have created me for a purpose, help me to know what it is and how Your commandments enable me to live out that purpose!' Creation and new creation, established, sustained, and growing by Your hand! How can we truly live without the Source of life at the center?

"If God had roughly made us, and had not also elaborately fashioned us, this argument would lose much of its force; but surely from the delicate art and marvellous skill which the Lord has shown in the formation of the human body, we may infer that he is prepared to take equal pains with the soul till it shall perfectly bear his image."[123]

Psalm 119:74

> "May those who fear You see me and be glad,
> Because I wait for Your word."

Because I am so wonderful? Surely not. I have no good besides You (Psalm 16:2). Those who fear You want more of You, and recognize that comes primarily from Your word, and secondarily the work of the word in others for our mutual benefit (e.g. see Colossians 3:16). We see a parallel with Psalm 119:79, where those who fear You turn to me. Why gladness? 'Glad' is the Hebrew שָׂמַח, śāmaḥ, a verb with the sense of rejoice; to be joyful, to be glad; to gloat. It describes a state and agitation of rejoicing, of being happy. This is the only occurrence of the word in Psalm 119. See also the example of David in 2 Chronicles 15:9. Those who fear You are glad because I wait for Your word. May I always have an apt word from Your word for others that they look forward to and even depend upon. What a joy to be used in this way, to draw deeper for Your word both for my benefit and overflowing to the benefit of others. See Ezra 7:10, Proverbs 10:21, Proverbs 12:26, Isaiah 50:4. The beauty is that I lead by example; an excellent teacher must be a devoted learner. Praise You, Father! I have beloved friends that I can depend on, and, by Your grace, can depend on me.

---

123. Spurgeon, Charles Haddon, *Treasury of David*, on Psalm 119:73, e-Sword edition

"When a man of God obtains grace for himself he becomes a blessing to others, especially if that grace has made him a man of sound understanding and holy knowledge. God-fearing men are encouraged when they meet with experienced believers . . . It is good for the eyes to see a man whose witness is that the Lord is true; it is one of the joys of saints to hold converse with their more advanced brethren . . . We do not only meet to share each others' burdens, but to partake in each others' joys, and some men contribute largely to the stock of mutual gladness. Hopeful men bring gladness with them. Despondent spirits spread the infection of depression, and hence few are glad to see them, while those whose hopes are grounded upon God's word carry sunshine in their faces, and are welcomed by their fellows."[124]

Psalm 119:75

> "I know, O LORD, that Your judgments are righteous,
> And that in faithfulness You have afflicted me."

In this section, Yodh, the Psalmist seeks comfort (v. 76) and compassion (v. 77) because of Your affliction (v.75) and the subversion of the arrogant (v. 78). We had just seen in v. 67 and v.71 the good that comes from affliction, and now we see here that this affliction is from You and an expression of Your faithfulness. Of course this is true, since all good comes from You. This is part of the 'exceeding faithfulness' of Your word (v. 138). Through affliction we truly seek You (Psalm 78:34, Hosea 5:15). Through affliction comes praise and satisfaction (Psalm 74:21, Psalm 22:26).

The idea behind 'afflicted' is to be bowed down. Oh what a need we have to be humbled! With the slightest relief we stray and seek our own. What a wonderful teacher affliction from You is. Through it we see you, in particular we see here the incredible combination of righteousness and faithfulness. We see this combination elsewhere in these Scriptures:

---

124. Spurgeon, Charles Haddon, *Treasury of David*, on Psalm 119:74, e-Sword edition

Deuteronomy 32:4, 1 Samuel 26:23, Psalm 40:10, Psalm 96:13, Psalm 119:75, Psalm 119:138, Psalm 143:1, Isaiah 11:5, Isaiah 16:5

"Saints are sure about the rightness of their troubles, even when they cannot see the intent of them . . . It was not because God was unfaithful that the believer found himself in a sore strait, but for just the opposite reason: it was the faithfulness of God to his covenant which brought the chosen one under the rod . . . Our heavenly Father is no Eli [see 1 Samuel 2:29]: he will not suffer his children to sin without rebuke, his love is too intense for that."[125]

Psalm 119:76

"O may Your lovingkindness comfort me,
According to Your word to Your servant."

'O may Your lovingkindness comfort me', yet how often I have refused to be comforted (Psalm 77:2). Why is that? 'According to Your word' is, in my pride, the last thing I want. I want to be comforted on my terms, not on Yours Lord! That is not true comfort, yet my flesh deceives me. As I learned in my early counseling sessions, I had to come to grips with the reality that I just wanted relief, I didn't want You. I wanted temporary relief, then go on to running my own life. Your lovingkindness is such that You won't allow that. You know that only in surrender to You there is true and lasting peace. "Yield now and be at peace with Him; Thereby good will come to you." (Job 22:21)

"Having confessed the righteousness of the Lord, he now appeals to his mercy, and while he does not ask that the rod may be removed, he earnestly begs for comfort under it. Righteousness and faithfulness afford us no consolation if we cannot also taste of mercy, and, blessed be God, this is promised us in the word, and therefore we may expect it . . . Blessed be his name, notwithstanding our faults we are still his servants, and we serve a compassionate Master . . . That phrase, 'according to thy

---

125. Spurgeon, Charles Haddon, *Treasury of David*, on Psalm 119:75, e-Sword edition

word,' is a very favourite one; it shows the motive for mercy and the manner of mercy. Our prayers are according to the mind of God when they are according to the word of God."[126]

Psalm 119:77

"May Your compassion come to me that I may live,
For Your law is my delight."

My very life depends on this. I am reminded of v.58 and my great need for Your favor, for Your grace. 'For Your law is my delight.' The Psalmist understood the connection between delight and life. Life to the full comes in the delight of Your law, and with that delight comes an understanding of dependence upon You. 'Compassion' is the Hebrew רחם, raham, a noun with the sense of womb, compassion, mercy, affection. With this compassion certainly there is safety and security. In v.92, the Psalmist indicates that this delight is what sustained His life. Surely we live not on bread alone, but on Your word (Deuteronomy 8:3, Job 23:12, Matthew 4:4). Like a child in the womb, certainly we are at our most safest and secure in You. May I always live with this sense of dependent delight!

"He was so hard pressed that he was at death's door if God did not succour [satisfy] him . . . Yet no true child of God can live without the tender mercy of the Lord; it is death to him to be under God's displeasure . . . Then we do not merely exist, but live; we are lively, full of life, vivacious, and vigorous. We know not what life is till we know God . . . .To delight in the word when it rebukes us, is proof that we are profiting under it."[127]

Psalm 119:78

"May the arrogant be ashamed, for they subvert me with a lie;
But I shall meditate on Your precepts."

---

126. Spurgeon, Charles Haddon, *Treasury of David*, on Psalm 119:76, e-Sword edition
127. Spurgeon, Charles Haddon, *Treasury of David*, on Psalm 119:77, e-Sword edition

Similar to Psalm 119:69, the Psalmist replaces a lie with Your law. Lying is apparently one of the results of arrogance; it is the arrogant who forge lies and subvert the righteous (see also Proverbs 17:15). In these days, as in all times, it seems to be done with impunity and with no shame. And so we pray - for our sake and for theirs - that shame would come upon them, and upon us if we follow the same path. Psalm 101:6-7 is a wonderful meditation here; they may attack from the outside, but we don't allow them inside our hearts. It is God's thoughts, not ours, which dominate our thinking and our hearts, Isaiah 55:8-11. What hope it is that, 'the mouths of those who speak lies will be stopped' (Psalm 63:11) and, 'Truthful lips will be established forever, But a lying tongue is only for a moment.' (Proverbs 12:19).

"How little he valued the will - will of sinners . . . Even those that deal most fairly may meet with those that deal perversely . . . it does not hurt us, and therefore should not move us . . . God's dealing favourably with him might make them ashamed to think that they had dealt perversely with him."[128]

"He would leave the proud in God's hands, and give himself up to holy studies and contemplations . . . The proud are not worth a thought. The worst injury they can do us is to take us away from our devotions; let us baffle them by keeping all the closer to our God when they are most malicious in their onslaughts."[129]

Psalm 119:79

"May those who fear You turn to me,
Even those who know Your testimonies."

Because of his orientation towards Your word, the Psalmist had those who fear You see him and be glad (v. 74), and now asks that they turn to him, perhaps again. The truth of Psalm 119:63 is surely reflected here. Lord, what a unifier Your word is and who You are! There is no greater

---

128. Henry, Matthew, *Commentary on the Whole Bible*, on Psalm 119:78, e-Sword edition
129. Spurgeon, Charles Haddon, *Treasury of David*, on Psalm 119:78, e-Sword edition

companionship. Note both the affirmation and the equality here. While the Psalmist may have been more advanced in the word (the fact that he wrote this Psalm makes this likely), yet here we see 'even those who know Your testimonies'. The picture here isn't necessarily that they come to him to know Your word, but that they already have a knowledge of it that draws them to him. The Psalmist needs them as much as they need him, particularly in light of the oppression described in v.78. Certainly David experienced this in 2 Chronicles 15:9. I am reminded of Colossians 3:16 and context, namely, that as Your word dwells in us individually, it draws us together indelibly. How could it not be so given the reality of Your word? Being in Your word and sharing it with one another, we recognize the Source, the one Shepherd who is leading, feeding, and caring for us all (Ecclesiastes 12:11).

"Those who are right with God are also anxious to be right with his children . . . We cannot afford to lose the love of the least of the saints, and if we have lost their esteem we may most properly pray to have it restored. David was the leader of the godly party in the nation, and it wounded him to the heart when he perceived that those who feared God were not as glad to see him as aforetime they had been . . . those who are dear to God, and are instructed in his word, should be very precious in our eyes, and we should do our utmost to be upon good terms with them.

David has two descriptions for the saints, they are God-fearing and God-knowing. They possess both devotion and instruction; they have both the spirit and the science of true religion. We know some believers who are gracious, but not intelligent; and, on the other hand, we also know certain professors who have all head and no heart - he is the man who combines devotion with intelligence. We neither care for devout dunces nor for intellectual icebergs. When fearing and knowing walk hand in hand they cause men to be thoroughly furnished unto every good work. [2 Timothy 3:17]"[130]

---

130. Spurgeon, Charles Haddon, *Treasury of David*, on Psalm 119:79, e-Sword edition

Psalm 119:80

"May my heart be blameless in Your statutes,
So that I will not be ashamed."

There is no higher goal than Your righteousness, which is to be blameless in Your statutes. Surely this is ultimate spiritual strength, for "The wicked flee when no one is pursuing, But the righteous are bold as a lion." (Proverbs 28:1). Walking in Your ways is ultimate strength and confidence. It is also ultimate blessing, seen in Psalm 119:1-2, which hearkens back to Psalm 1:1-2. It is a compelling picture of what I want to be, the opposite of ashamed. When ashamed, I shrink back, but when blameless before You, I seek further righteousness. 'Blameless' is the Hebrew תָּמִים, tāmiym, an adjective with the sense of blameless, complete, true, virtuous, upright, righteous. Yet, who can claim blamelessness (Proverbs 20:9)? "But there is forgiveness with You, That You may be feared." (Psalms 130:4). Notice also the Psalmist seeks not just blameless actions, but a blameless heart from which actions flow (Proverbs 4:23). Like the Psalmist, Lord, may I seek truth in the innermost being (Psalm 51:6)! This can only happen through the finished work of Christ, the rule of the Father, and the presence of the Holy Spirit in my heart. Praise You Lord for doing it all!

"This is even more important than to be held in esteem by good men. This is the root of the matter. If the heart be sound in obedience to God, all is well, or will be well. If right at heart we are right in the main. If we be not sound before God, our name for piety is an empty sound. Mere profession will fail, and undeserved esteem will disappear like a bubble when it bursts; only sincerity and truth will endure in the evil day. [see Ephesians 6:13-17]"[131]

---

131. Spurgeon, Charles Haddon, *Treasury of David*, on Psalm 119:80, e-Sword edition

CHAPTER 11

Kaph: 'Rescued From the Pit'

"Kaph. My soul languishes for Your salvation;
I wait for Your word.
[82] My eyes fail with longing for Your word,
While I say, "When will You comfort me?"
[83] Though I have become like a wineskin in the smoke,
I do not forget Your statutes.
[84] How many are the days of Your servant?
When will You execute judgment on those who persecute me?
[85] The arrogant have dug pits for me,
Men who are not in accord with Your law.
[86] All Your commandments are faithful;
They have persecuted me with a lie; help me!
[87] They almost destroyed me on earth,
But as for me, I did not forsake Your precepts.
[88] Revive me according to Your lovingkindness,
So that I may keep the testimony of Your mouth."

—Psalms 119:81-88

The Psalmist goes from death to life, from hopelessness to hope, from darkness to light. Internally his soul languishes (v. 81), his eyes fail (v. 82), and his flesh suffers (v. 83), and yet he waited for Your word, anticipated Your comfort, and did not forget Your statutes. Externally he was persecuted (v. 84), entrapped (v. 85), and slandered (v. 86) to the point of near destruction (v. 87), yet he knew that Your judgment is sure and he was determined not to be carried away by their evil. His primary concern was to be strengthened for obedience towards You, not for revenge towards them.

"This portion of the gigantic Psalm sees the Psalmist in extremis. His enemies have brought him to the lowest condition of anguish and depression; yet he is faithful to the law and trustful in his God. This octave is the midnight of the Psalm, and very dark and black it is. Stars, however, shine out, and the last verse gives promise of the dawn. The strain will after this become more cheerful; but meanwhile it should minister comfort to us to see so eminent a servant of God so hardly used by the ungodly: evidently in our own persecutions, no strange thing has happened unto us. [1 Peter 4:12]"[132]

Psalm 119:81

"My soul languishes for Your salvation;
I wait for Your word."

Desperate. I am fascinated by this word 'languishes', כָּלָה, kālāh, a verb with the sense of 'to finish, fail, or exhaust'. It is used in a variety of ways, and appears three times just here in Psalm 119 - Kaph: here as 'languishes, v. 82 as 'fail' and v, 87 as 'destroyed'. This is a man who has come to the end of himself. Keil and Delitzsch refer to it as 'earnest desire', and they end their description of this section with 'But he stands in need of fresh grace in order that he may not, however, at last succumb.' What I see here is dryness, deadness, and deep need simply for survival. So it is for us with regard to salvation. Indeed our souls are lifeless

---

132. Spurgeon, Charles Haddon, *Treasury of David*, on Psalm 119 - Kaph, e-Sword edition

without You! Psalm 63:1. Streams in the desert is what I desire (Isaiah 43:19-20), for You will quickly (Psalm 81:13-16) bring life where there was only death.

"Nothing else could satisfy him but deliverance wrought out by the hand of God, his inmost nature yearned and pined for salvation from the God of all grace, and he must have it or utterly fail . . . the fulfilment of his word is near at hand when our hope is firm and our desire fervent . . . We are '*faint* yet pursuing.' Hope sustains when desire exhausts."[133]

Psalm 119:82

> "My eyes fail with longing for Your word,
> While I say, "When will You comfort me?"

Literally, 'my eyes fail for Your word'. Fail is the same word translated as 'languishes' in v.81. We come to the end of ourselves. If I could get but a glimpse of Your word, there is hope. Father, remove all that obscures 'the Light of the knowledge of the glory of God in the face of Christ' (see 2 Corinthians 4:6). Even the godliest of men experience this, here wondering when comfort will come. I notice that my sinful heart seeks comfort everywhere but in You. Exhausted, I cry to You, but I have obscured You by rebelling in my thoughts. There is no true water apart from You, You must answer me (Isaiah 41:17-20)! You give all the life and get all the glory. May I receive it humbly, knowing that You will withhold no good thing, Psalm 84:11. This word for comfort also appears in Psalm 119 in v. 52, v. 76. May I remember more quickly, and be comforted and restored more fully. Thank you for making me hope in this way (Psalm 119:49)!

"To read the word till the eyes can no longer see is but a small thing compared with watching for the fulfilment of the promise till the inner eyes of expectancy begin to grow dim with hope deferred . . . If help does not come from heaven it will never come at all . . . It must be an intense longing which is not satisfied to express itself by the lips, but speaks with

---

133. Spurgeon, Charles Haddon, *Treasury of David*, on Psalm 119:81, e-Sword edition

the eyes, by those eyes failing through intense watching . . . A humble eye lifted up to heaven in silent prayer may flash such flame as shall melt the bolts which bar the entrance of vocal prayer, and so heaven shall be taken by storm with the artillery of tears. Blessed are the eyes that are strained in looking after God. The eyes of the Lord will see to it that such eyes do not actually fail. How much better to watch for the Lord with aching eyes than to have them sparkling at the glitter of vanity."[134]

Psalm 119:83

> "Though I have become like a wineskin in the smoke,
> I do not forget Your statutes."

Like a wineskin in the smoke, I may seem useless and ruined, but my value is not forgetting You! From the previous verses, the soul languishes, the eyes and body fail. I have experienced this despair even as a youth, and as I age it becomes more apparent. Yet Your intent is that we bear fruit even in old age (Psalm 92:14), outwardly moving towards death but inwardly towards life, 2 Corinthians 4:16.

"... we, too, have felt dingy, mean, and worthless, only fit to be cast away ... lackened the man of God might be by falsehood, but the truth was in him, and he never gave it up. He was faithful to his King when he seemed deserted and left to the vilest uses. The promises came to his mind, and, what was a still better evidence of his loyalty, the statutes were there too - he stuck to his duties as well as to his comforts. The worst circumstances cannot destroy the true believer's hold upon his God. Grace is a living power which survives that which would suffocate all other forms of existence. Fire cannot consume it, and smoke cannot smother it. A man may be reduced to skin and bone, and all his comfort may be dried out of him, and yet he may hold fast his integrity and glorify his God."[135]

---

134. Spurgeon, Charles Haddon, *Treasury of David*, on Psalm 119:82, e-Sword edition
135. Spurgeon, Charles Haddon, *Treasury of David*, on Psalm 119:83, e-Sword edition

Psalm 119:84

> "How many are the days of Your servant?
> When will You execute judgment on those who persecute me?"

This is the cry of a man who is struggling to endure persecution day by day, wondering when judgment on persecutors will come. Yet he is Your servant who has something in common with his persecutors: You are Lord of both. Notice the Psalmist asks not if, but when, knowing that You are just.

If we know how long to the end, we can better endure. How much better to know that You are the end of all things. The Great Goal has already been recognized, the end determined, the victory secure. As for my days, they are in Your hands (Psalm 31:15), as are these of Your enemies (Revelation 21:8). The end of both is certain. Your glory reigns. The answer is implied in v.85, Proverbs 26:27, see also Proverbs 1:18. The arrogant who sets a trap for the righteous is setting a trap for himself; such is the blindness of sin. As for Your people, You guide us until death (Psalm 48:14) and receive us into glory, Psalm 73:24.

The Psalmist is putting His hope in You. May I do the same in all circumstances.

"Our life here below is short, so also is the period within which the divine righteousness can reveal itself."[136]

"The brevity of life is a good argument against the length of an affliction . . . He had placed his case in the Lord's hands, and he prayed that sentence might be given and put into execution. He desired nothing but justice."[137]

Psalm 119:85

> "The arrogant have dug pits for me,
> Men who are not in accord with Your law."

---

136. Keil & Delitzsch, *Commentary on the Old Testament*, on Psalm 119:84, e-Sword edition
137. Spurgeon, Charles Haddon, *Treasury of David*, on Psalm 119:84, e-Sword edition

'Live and let live' is not the mantra of the sinner. If we are to understand passages like Romans 1:28 and Psalm 12, we recognize that the god of this world, Satan, demands allegiance, and his followers are quite demanding of others (John 8:44), though often disguised as doing Your will (2 Corinthians 2:11-13, John 16:2). Father, may I see You save such as these! Our battle is not against them (Ephesians 6:13). What we see here is the active works of the arrogant to undermine the righteous. We should not be surprised, but it is to be expected, and a means of Your great blessing to Your faithful people (1 Peter 4:12-14). The sequence of Vanity Fair in John Bunyan's Pilgrim's Progress displays this beautifully. Sinners don't want other sinners to pursue righteousness; victims don't want other victims to be so empowered; in these times of cries for justice, we recognize that this is not to be in our time for the Christian (see Luke 18:7-8, Proverbs 29:26). In the end, we see that the man who digs a pit for others will fall into it (Psalm 57:6), while You specialize in rescue for Your people (Jeremiah 18:22, Jeremiah 38:13, Psalm 40:2)! Surely the cry of the Psalmist for rescue in vv. 87-88 will be answered, for Your sake!

"All God's commandments are an emanation of His faithfulness, and therefore too demand faithfulness; but it is just this faithfulness that makes the poet an object of deadly hatred."[138]

"One would think that such haughty people would not have soiled their fingers with digging; but they swallowed their pride in hopes of swallowing their victim. Whereas they ought to have been ashamed of such meanness, they were conscious of no shame, but, on the contrary, were proud of their cleverness; proud of setting a trap for a godly man . . . It was well for David that his enemies were God's enemies, and that their attacks upon him had no sanction from the Lord. It was also much to his gain that he was not ignorant of their devices, for he was thus put upon his guard, and led to watch his ways lest he should fall into their pits. While he kept to the law of the Lord he was safe, though even then it was an uncomfortable thing to have his path made dangerous by the craft of wanton malice."[139]

138. Keil & Delitzsch, *Commentary on the Old Testament*, on Psalm 119:85, e-Sword edition
139. Spurgeon, Charles Haddon, *Treasury of David*, on Psalm 119:85, e-Sword edition

Psalm 119:86

> "All Your commandments are faithful;
> They have persecuted me with a lie; help me!"

I am coming to grips with the reality of lying. As we see in Psalm 119:69, 78, and 118, lying is common and destructive. I love the contrast in these verses with Your law. I would be in utter despair without Your utter truth, which is utterly active and not passive. All your commandments are faithful! You have commanded in righteousness and exceeding faithfulness, Psalm 119:138. It seems in many cases, the brighter the Light shines, the greater the opposition. Evil men do not understand justice (Proverbs 28:5), and, as stunning as it may seem, the upright are abominable to the wicked (Proverbs 29:27). Men hate the Light because their deeds are evil (John 3:19-20). Psalm 107:10-20 speaks of the salvation of such! Oh Lord, send Your word and heal and deliver many!

"In whatever ways he was afflicted, his mind had not been distracted by various devices, because, trusting in the word of God, he never doubted of his assistance. In the first place, he tells us, that the consideration, by which he was armed for repelling all assaults, was this, That the faithful, under the conduct of God, engage in a prosperous warfare, the salvation which they hope for from his word being absolutely certain."[140]

"Whatever the command might cost him it was worth it; he felt that God's way might be rough, but it was right; it might make him enemies, but still it was his best friend . . . Whoever may hurt us, it matters not so long as the Lord helps us; for if indeed the Lord help us, none can really hurt us. Many a time have these words been groaned out by troubled saints, for they are such as suit a thousand conditions of need, pain, distress, weakness, and sin. 'Help, Lord,' will be a fitting prayer for youth and age, for labour and suffering, for life and death. No other help is sufficient, but God's help is all-sufficient and we cast ourselves upon it without fear."[141]

---

140. John Calvin, *Commentary on the Psalms*
141. Spurgeon, Charles Haddon, *Treasury of David*, on Psalm 119:86, e-Sword edition

Psalm 119:87

> "They almost destroyed me on earth,
> But as for me, I did not forsake Your precepts."

Having reflected in Kaph on pressures within (vv. 81-83) and pressures without (vv. 84-86), the Psalmist had no other place to look than up. Father, what wondrous design! Oh how rebellious I was in my thoughts, directly angry with Adam and indirectly angry with You at the Fall. 'What if . . . ?' But in the Gospel, that gives way to Ephesians 2:7, 'so that in the ages to come He might show the surpassing riches . . . ' There was no better way than that way. And there is no better way for me, O Great Sovereign, than the faithfulness with which You have afflicted me (Psalm 119:75) which brings me to the exceeding faithfulness of Your word (Psalm 119:138). 'Destroyed' has the sense of 'come to an end', and is translated as 'languishes' in v.81, 'fail' in v.82 and v.123. Satan, the prince of this world, certainly seeks to devour (1 John 5:19, 1 Peter 5:8). While the world seeks to make an end of me, I find my supreme End (goal) in Christ and am eternally saved!

"The lions are chained: they can rage no further than our God permits . . . If we are resolved to die sooner than forsake the Lord, we may depend upon it that we shall not die, but shall live to see the overthrow of them that hate us."[142]

"Steadfastness of profession is the evidence of the life of faith: grounded upon this security, the more we are shaken, the more we shall hold fast. Neither long-continued distress, nor determined opposition, will turn us from the ways of God. We would rather forsake all that our heart held dear upon earth, than the precepts of our God . . .

When, therefore, we are tempted to neglect the precepts, or when we fail to live in them, and to delight in them, let us each bring our hearts to this test: 'What would I take in exchange for them? Will the good-will and approbation of the world compensate for the loss of the

---

142. Spurgeon, Charles Haddon, *Treasury of David*, on Psalm 119:87, e-Sword edition

favor of God? Could I be content to forego my greatest comforts, to 'suffer the loss of all things,' yes, of life itself, rather than forsake one of the ways of God? When I meet with such precepts as link me to the daily cross, can I throw myself with simple dependence upon that Savior, who has engaged to supply strength for what He has commanded?"[143]

Psalm 119:88

> "Revive me according to Your lovingkindness,
> So that I may keep the testimony of Your mouth."

While the Psalmist experiences intense pressure within and without, he entrusts those pressures to You for Your response and care. This final prayer in Kaph is that he would be revived and sustained by Your unfailing love so that he would keep Your testimonies. 'Keep' is the Hebrew שָׁמַר, šāmar, a verb with the sense of watch, keep, reserve, guard, be on one's guard.' It reflects the intense focus and purpose in all things, which is to be faithful to Your word. 'Testimony of Your mouth' reminds us that these are not abstract principles, but Your personal, powerful, and perfect words to Your people. The Psalmist's focus was not so much on his circumstances, painful as they were, but on faithfulness to You within those circumstances. How else would any of us know of the power of Your word if we didn't understand our need of them and Your sufficiency in them? So these words provide both an inner testimony and an outer testimony to a hostile, dying world.

"This we must keep, whatever we lose . . . We cannot proceed, nor persevere, in the good way, unless God quicken us and put life into us; we are therefore here taught to depend upon the grace of God for strength to do every good work, and to depend upon it as grace, as purely the fruit of God's favour . . . The surest token of God's good-will toward us is his good work in us."[144]

---

143. Bridges, Charles. *An Exposition Of Psalm 119* (pp. 157-158). Kindle Edition
144. Henry, Matthew, *Commentary on the Whole Bible*, on Psalm 119:88, e-Sword edition

"If we are revived in our own personal piety we shall be out of reach of our assailants. Our best protection from tempters and persecutors is more life. Lovingkindness itself cannot do us greater service than by making us to have life more abundantly. When we are quickened we are able to bear affliction, to baffle cunning, and to conquer sin . . . If quickened by the Holy Ghost we shall be sure to exhibit a holy character . . . We ought greatly to admire the spiritual prudence of the Psalmist, who does not so much pray for freedom from trial as for renewed life that he may be supported under it. When the inner life is vigorous all is well. David prayed for a sound heart in Psalm 119:80, and here he seeks a revived heart; this is going to the root of the matter, by seeking that which is the most needful of all things. Lord let it be heart-work with us, and let our hearts be right with thee."[145]

---

145. Spurgeon, Charles Haddon, *Treasury of David*, on Psalm 119:88, e-Sword edition

CHAPTER 12
Lamedh: 'A Foundation of Perfection'

"Lamedh. Forever, O LORD, Your word is settled in heaven.
[90] Your faithfulness continues throughout all generations;
You established the earth, and it stands.
[91] They stand this day according to Your ordinances,
For all things are Your servants.
[92] If Your law had not been my delight,
Then I would have perished in my affliction.
[93] I will never forget Your precepts,
For by them You have revived me.
[94] I am Yours, save me;
For I have sought Your precepts.
[95] The wicked wait for me to destroy me;
I shall diligently consider Your testimonies.
[96] I have seen a limit to all perfection;
Your commandment is exceedingly broad."

—Psalms 119:89-96

You established Your word (v. 89) and Your world (v. 90) as an eternal, active foundation for all of life (v. 91). It is so sure and so personal that Your active word has both preserved (v. 92) and revived (v. 93) me. Because of this sure foundation, I seek You to save me from this present corruption both within and without (vv. 94-95). All human efforts have extreme limits, but the perfection of Your word is sustaining all things, from the vastness of the universe to the minuteness of my molecules and my very thoughts. Surely You uphold all things by the word of Your power! Colossians 1:16-17, Hebrews 1:3.

"The tone is now more joyful, for experience has given the sweet singer a comfortable knowledge of the Word of the Lord, and this creates a glad theme. After tossing about on a sea of trouble, the psalmist here leaps to shore and stands upon a rock. Jehovah's Word is not fickle or uncertain; it is settled, determined, fixed, sure, and immovable. Man's teachings change so often that there is never time for them to be settled, but the Lord's Word remains the same from days of old, and it will remain unchanged eternally."[146]

Psalm 119:89

> "Forever, O LORD,
> Your word is settled in heaven."

The 'they' of v.90 is the word and the heavens. See Psalm 19. 'Settled' is the Hebrew נָצַב, nāṣab, verb with the sense of station, appoint, erect, take a stand. Lord God, as You have established the boundaries of the earth (Psalm 74:17), You permanently spoke all things into existence (Psalm 33:6-9).

"'*Thy word*, by which the heavens were made, is *settled* there in the abiding products of it;' or the settling of God's word in heaven is opposed to the changes and revolutions that are here upon earth."[147]

---

146. Spurgeon, Charles Haddon. *The Golden Alphabet* (Updated, Annotated): An Exposition of Psalm 119 (pp. 157-158). Aneko Press. Kindle Edition
147. Henry, Matthew, *Commentary on the Whole Bible*, on Psalm 119:89, e-Sword edition

"Man's teachings change so often that there is never time for them to be settled; but the Lord's word is from of old the same, and will remain unchanged eternally. Some men are never happier than when they are unsettling everything and everybody; but God's mind is not with them . . . Covenant settlements will not be removed, however unsettled the thoughts of men may become; let us therefore settle it in our minds that we abide in the faith of our Jehovah as long as we have any being."[148]

Psalm 119:90

"Your faithfulness continues throughout all generations;
You established the earth, and it stands."

'. . . throughout all generations'. A man can scarcely remain faithful in his own generation, and even the best of men cannot determine his legacy for certain (Ecclesiastes 2:16-19), although You have prescribed faithfulness for it (Psalm 78:4-7). Our only hope is that You have been faithful from eternity past and will be faithful to eternity future; only You are God! (Psalm 90:1-2). 'Faithfulness' is the Hebrew נֶהְוּמָא, 'emûnāh, a noun with the sense of truth, faithfulness, describing both Your character and actions, Deuteronomy 32:4. There are three verses which express Your faithfulness to generations: Psalm 89:1, 100:5, and 119:90. Here in Psalm 119, You afflict in faithfulness (v. 75), all Your commandments are faithful (v. 86), here Your faithfulness is throughout all generations, and You have commanded Your testimonies in exceeding faithfulness (v. 138). 'Established' is the Hebrew כּוּן, kûn, a verb with the sense of set up, make firm, establish, prepare, to set in an upright position or make steadfast. As You have established the earth, may my ways be established in Your word (Psalm 119:5, Psalm 119:33), for You have fashioned me for such a purpose (Psalm 119:73). Like the world which You have created with knowledge, understanding, and wisdom (Proverbs 3:19-20), may my life be so established (Proverbs 24:3-4). Psalm 93:1 - surely You have

---

148. Spurgeon, Charles Haddon, *Treasury of David*, on Psalm 119:89, e-Sword edition

established the earth, which will not be moved unless You move it. But You are the same, and Your years will not come to an end, Psalm 102:27.

"God is not affected by the lapse of ages; he is not only faithful to one man throughout his lifetime, but to his children's children after him, yea, and to all generations so long as they keep his covenant and remember his commandments to do them . . . There is an analogy between the word of God and the works of God, and specially in this, that they are both of them constant, fixed, and unchangeable. God's word which established the world is the same as that which he has embodied in the Scriptures; by the word of the Lord were the heavens made, and specially by him who is emphatically THE WORD . . . If the earth abideth the spiritual creation will abide; if God's word suffices to establish the world surely it is enough for the establishment of the individual believer."[149]

Psalm 119:91

"They stand this day according to Your ordinances,
For all things are Your servants."

I have long been exulted by and confused by this verse; exulted by 'all things are Your servants', and confused by 'they' followed by the singular 'the earth, and it stands' in v. 90. The Jamieson-Fausset-Brown Commentary explains it beautifully: 'In all changes God's Word remains firm (1Peter 1:25). Like the heavens, it continually attests God's unfailing power and unchanging care (Psalm 89:2). **is settled in** — that is, stands as firmly as the heaven in which it dwells, and whence it emanated.'

On v.91: '**They** — the heavens (Psalm 119:89) and the earth (Psalm 119:90). Hengstenberg translates, "They stand for thy judgment," that is, ready, as obedient servants, to execute them. The usage of this Psalm favors this view. But see Jer 33:25.'

I think also on Psalm 148:8, where we see the very elements of weather fulfilling Your word. May You give me eyes to see how all things – all things - are Your servants today. May I move according to the flow

---

149. Spurgeon, Charles Haddon, *Treasury of David*, on Psalm 119:90, e-Sword edition

of Your hand. See the 'all things' in Colossians 1:16-17, also Romans 8:28-29. All things are:

- Created by You, through You, for You
- Sustained by You
- Caused to work to the ultimate good: the image of Christ in Your people!

"The word which spake all things into existence has supported them till now, and still supports them both in being and in well-being . . . *'For all are thy servants.'* Created by thy word they obey that word, thus answering the purpose of their existence, and working out the design of their Creator. Both great things and small pay homage to the Lord. No atom escapes his rule, no world avoids his government . . . By that word which is settled may we be settled; by that voice which establishes the earth may we be established; and by that command which all created things obey may we be made the servants of the Lord God Almighty."[150]

Psalm 119:92

"If Your law had not been my delight,
Then I would have perished in my affliction."

Notice it does not say, 'If your law had not been my duty, I would have perished . . .'. Sheer resolve and faithless obedience (as if there were such a thing) will not sustain in affliction. In Psalm 119:77 we see delight as a means of experiencing compassion. We just can't do it in times of ease, how much less in times of affliction! The word for delight is straightforward, our default 'go to' for pleasure. 'Affliction' is the Hebrew עֳנִי, oni, which has the sense of a state of oppression or extreme discomfort, physically, mentally, or spiritually.

"That word which has preserved the heavens and the earth also preserves the people of God in their time of trial. With that word we are charmed; it is a mine of delight to us . . . We should have felt ready to lie

---

150. Spurgeon, Charles Haddon, *Treasury of David*, on Psalm 119:91, e-Sword edition

down and die of our griefs if the spiritual comforts of God's word had not uplifted us; but by their sustaining influence we have been borne above all the depressions and despairs which naturally grow out of severe affliction . . . .That which was our delight in prosperity has been our light in adversity; that which in the day kept us from presuming has in the night kept us from perishing."[151]

"However the believer's real character may be hidden from the world, the hour of trial abundantly proves, both what the law can do for him, and what a lost creature he would have been without it. In affliction, friends mean well; but of themselves they can do nothing. They can only look on, feel, and pray. They cannot 'speak to the heart.' This is God's prerogative: and His law is His voice."[152]

Psalm 119:93

> "I will never forget Your precepts,
> For by them You have revived me."

I note it is You who gives life by means of Your word (see also Luke 8:11, John 4:41-42, Romans 10:17, 1 Peter 1:23). What is man and his word in this spiritual reality? In Your assessment, servants through whom people believe, but in comparison to Your work, essentially nothing (1 Corinthians 3:5-7). You bless Your word; Your work and Your word is where our confidence lies. Praise You Lord! Through these verses You revive me and my confidence in You! When I forget or neglect, I sink; when I remember, I am revived, I am saved.

"We must resolve that we will never, at any time, cast off our religion, and never, upon any occasion, lay aside our religion, but that we will be constant to it and persevere in it."[153]

"If it has once given us life or renewed that life, there is no fear of its falling from our recollection. Experience teaches, and teaches effectually.

---

151. Spurgeon, Charles Haddon, *Treasury of David*, on Psalm 119:92, e-Sword edition
152. Bridges, Charles. *An Exposition Of Psalm 119* (p. 162). Kindle Edition
153. Henry, Matthew, *Commentary on the Whole Bible*, on Psalm 119:93, e-Sword edition

How blessed a thing it is to have the precepts written on the heart with the golden pen of experience, and graven on the memory with the divine stylus of grace. Forgetfulness is a great evil in holy things; we see here the man of God fighting against it, and feeling sure of victory because he knew the life-giving energy of the word in his own soul. That which quickens the heart is sure to quicken the memory. It seems singular that he should ascribe quickening to the precepts, and yet it lies in them and in all the words of the Lord alike. It is to be noted that when the Lord raised the dead he addressed to them the word of command. He said, 'Lazarus, come forth,' or, 'Maid, arise.' We need not fear to address gospel precepts to dead sinners, since by them the Spirit gives them life. Remark that the Psalmist does not say that the precepts quickened him, but that the Lord quickened him by their means"[154]

Psalm 119:94

"I am Yours, save me;
For I have sought Your precepts."

You who have saved Your own will save Your own! 'Sought' is the Hebrew שָׁרַד, dāraš, a verb with the sense of to seek, inquire of, examine, require. It is used of Ezra (perhaps the writer of this Psalm) as 'study' in Ezra 7:10. What is the connection between salvation and the word? It is Your primary means of salvation and sanctification: Psalm 119:41, 81, 123, James 1:21, 1 Peter 1:23, 1 Peter 2:2. So the Psalmist pleads with You to act according to Your promises; may I follow this example.

"Consecration is a good plea for preservation. If we are conscious that we are the Lord's we may be confident that he will save us. We are the Lord's by creation, election, redemption, surrender, and acceptance; and hence our firm hope and assured belief that he will save us. A man will surely save his own child: Lord, save *me* . . . A man may be seeking the doctrines and the promises, and yet be unrenewed in heart; but to

---

154. Spurgeon, Charles Haddon, *Treasury of David*, on Psalm 119:93, e-Sword edition

seek the precepts is a sure sign of grace; no one ever heard of a rebel or a hypocrite seeking the precepts. The Lord had evidently wrought a great work upon the Psalmist, and he besought him to carry it on to completion. Saving is linked with seeking, 'save me, for I have sought'; and when the Lord sets us seeking he will not refuse us the saving. He who seeks holiness is already saved; if we have sought the Lord we may be sure that the Lord has sought us, and will certainly save us."[155]

Psalm 119:95

> "The wicked wait for me to destroy me;
> I shall diligently consider Your testimonies."

Notice the focus. A Godward focus is not merely good and helpful, but it is necessary for survival. It occurs to me what a gift it is to find no satisfaction in the things of this world, which can only deceive and dissatisfy. Truly it is only under Your Word that freedom can be found. Notice the focus of the Psalmist here. The wicked - and we presume they are many - wait to destroy, so the Psalmist focuses not on them - for he surely could not defeat them in his own strength - but on You. He does not anxiously look about him (Isaiah 41:10) but dwells with You inwardly amidst external conflict (Psalm 27:1-4). Having perhaps been surrounded and vigorously opposed, they accuse, but he is in prayer (Psalm 109:3-4). Here the wicked wait to destroy him, but he waits on God. To deliver him? Presumably, but it doesn't say. The Psalmist seems concerned first and foremost with what occurs within and not without. 'Diligently consider' is the Hebrew בִּין, biyn, a verb with the sense of to discern, perceive, observe, pay attention to. It is most often translated as 'understand' or 'understanding' in Psalm 119. It occurs 29 times in Proverbs, notably in Proverbs 2:5. Others may seek me (negatively) but I seek God (positively).

"They were very cruel, and aimed at no less than his destruction; they were very crafty, and sought all opportunities to do him a mischief;

---

155. Spurgeon, Charles Haddon, *Treasury of David*, on Psalm 119:94, e-Sword edition

and they were confident (they expected, so some read it), that they should destroy him; they thought themselves sure of their prey. 2. He comforts himself in the word of God as his protection: 'While they are contriving my destruction, I consider thy testimonies, which secure to me my salvation.'"[156]

"They were like wild beasts crouching by the way, or highwaymen waylaying a defenceless traveller; but the Psalmist went on his way without considering them, for he was considering something better, namely, the witness or testimony which God has borne to the sons of men. He did not allow the malice of the wicked to take him off from his holy study of the divine word, he was so calm that he could 'consider'; so holy that he loved to consider the Lord's 'testimonies'; so victorious over all their plots that he did not allow them to drive him from his pious contemplations. If the enemy cannot cause us to withdraw our thoughts from holy study, or our feet from holy walking, or our hearts from holy aspirations, he has met with poor success in his assaults."[157] [See Proverbs 4:25-27]

Psalm 119:96

> "I have seen a limit to all perfection;
> Your commandment is exceedingly broad."

This is a verse for the perfectionist! Like Ecclesiastes 1:15, it turns our eyes away from looking at the vanity (see Psalm 119:37) of pursuing perfection from men. Only You are perfect (Deuteronomy 32:3-4). Surely there is a limit to all human perfection, but Your perfection is unlimited, too vast to comprehend. 'Limit' is the Hebrew קֵץ, qēṣ, a noun with the sense of an end of time or space, a final point, a completion or consummation. Even Paul's piety was utterly rubbish before You (Galatians 1:14, Philippians 3:4-11), the burden of the law on humans beyond our ability to bear (Acts 15:10). 'Perfection' is the Hebrew תִּכְלָה, tiklāh, a noun indicating perfection, complete without fault, not lacking

---

156. Henry, Matthew, *Commentary on the Whole Bible*, on Psalm 119:95, e-Sword edition
157. Spurgeon, Charles Haddon, *Treasury of David*, on Psalm 119:95, e-Sword edition

in any way. This is the word's only use in Scripture. 'Broad' is the Hebrew רָחָב, rāḥāḇ, an adjective with the sense of broad, wide, spacious, large, translated as 'liberty' in Psalm 119:45. Surely as much as we can explore its depths (e.g. Proverbs 2:1-5), Your word and Your ways are ultimately beyond our full grasp (Romans 11:33).

"God's law is of infinite breadth, reaching to all cases, perfectly meeting what each requires, and to all times (Psa 19:3, Psa 19:6, Psa 19:7-11; Ecc 3:11). It cannot be cramped within any definitions of man's dogmatical systems. Man never outgrows the Word."[158]

"Some men see no end to their own perfection, but this is because they are perfectly blind. The experienced believer has seen an end of all perfection in himself, in his brethren, in the best man's best works . . . When the breadth of the law is known the notion of perfection in the flesh vanishes: that law touches every act, word, and thought, and is of such a spiritual nature that it judges the motives, desires, and emotions of the soul . . . Who would wish to have an imperfect law? Nay, its perfection is its glory; but it is the death of all glorying in our own perfection."[159]

---

158. *Jamieson-Fausset-Brown Commentary*, on Psalm 119:96, e-Sword edition
159. Spurgeon, Charles Haddon, *Treasury of David*, on Psalm 119:96, e-Sword edition

CHAPTER 13
Mem: 'Pure Gold'

"Mem. O how I love Your law!
It is my meditation all the day.
[98] Your commandments make me wiser than my enemies,
For they are ever mine.
[99] I have more insight than all my teachers,
For Your testimonies are my meditation.
[100] I understand more than the aged,
Because I have observed Your precepts.
[101] I have restrained my feet from every evil way,
That I may keep Your word.
[102] I have not turned aside from Your ordinances,
For You Yourself have taught me.
[103] How sweet are Your words to my taste!
Yes, sweeter than honey to my mouth!
[104] From Your precepts I get understanding;
Therefore I hate every false way."

—Psalms 119:97-104

A s one committed to the continual counsel of Your word (see Psalm 119:24), the Psalmist loved it and experienced its immense benefits on earth: 1) Wisdom above his enemies because he held it close (v. 98), 2) Insight above his teachers because of his meditation (v. 99), and 3) Understanding above the aged because of his obedience (v. 99). Of course this was true, because by it You Yourself had taught him (v. 102)! These benefits had gripped his heart to turn from evil (vv. 101-102, love Your word (v. 103), and to hate falsehood (v. 104). This is not abstract, but personal, Psalm 97:10.

"Those who know the power of the gospel perceive an infinite loveliness in the law as they see it fulfilled and embodied in Christ Jesus."[160]

In Hebrews 10:5-9 Jesus reflected the reality of Psalm 40:8:

> *"I delight to do Your will, O my God;*
> *Your Law is within my heart."*

Psalm 119:97

> "O how I love Your law!
> It is my meditation all the day."

'Meditation all the day' reminds us of the blessedness described in Joshua 1:8, Psalm 1:1-3, and Jeremiah 17:7-8. But the delight is not in the success such meditation brings, but in the delight of it itself, and at the root is love, love for the law and the God of it. We do the things which enrapture our affections.

"We love it for its holiness, and pine to be holy; we love it for its wisdom, and study to be wise; we love it for its perfection, and long to be perfect . . . This was both the effect of his love and the cause of it. He

---

160. Spurgeon, Charles Haddon . *The Golden Alphabet* (Updated, Annotated): An Exposition of Psalm 119 (pp. 167-168). Aneko Press. Kindle Edition

meditated in God's word because he loved it, and then loved it the more because he meditated in it . . . Familiarity with the word of God breeds affection, and affection seeks yet greater familiarity."[161]

Psalm 119:98

> "Your commandments make me wiser than my enemies,
> For they are ever mine."

This is the first of three verses that speak to the accelerated wisdom, insight, and understanding that comes from retaining, meditating, and observing Your word. To 'make wiser' is the Hebrew חָכַם, ḥāḵam, a verb with the sense of to be wise, to act according to wisdom. In the Old Testament, wisdom is 'the art of skillful living'. The idea of 'ever mine' is simply 'ever', i.e. they are everlasting and unchanging. They are the rock, the foundation of life (see Matthew 7:24-27). Why is it important to be wiser than enemies? Because for the Christian, the enemies of the world are many and are relentless, and we need energy and skill to endure, thrive, and not fear man. The 'wisdom' of the world can deceive and intimidate, but we must discern its folly, 1 Corinthians 1:18-31.

"The commands were his book, but God was his teacher. The letter can make us knowing, but only the divine Spirit can make us wise. Wisdom is knowledge put to practical use . . . A holy life is the highest wisdom and the surest defence . . . by uprightness we shall baffle fraud, by simple truth we shall vanquish deep-laid scheming, and by open candour we shall defeat slander. A thoroughly straightforward man, devoid of all policy, is a terrible puzzle to diplomatists; they suspect him of a subtle duplicity through which they cannot see, while he, indifferent to their suspicions, holds on the even tenor of his way, and baffles all their arts . . . He was always studying or obeying the commandments; they were his choice and constant companions. If we wish to become proficient we must be indefatigable. If we keep the wise law ever near

---

161. Spurgeon, Charles Haddon, *Treasury of David*, on Psalm 119:97, e-Sword edition

us we shall become wise, and when our adversaries assail us we shall be prepared for them with that ready wit which lies in having the word of God at our fingers' ends. As a soldier in battle must never lay aside his shield, so must we never have the word of God out of our minds; it must be ever with us."[162]

Psalm 119:99

"I have more insight than all my teachers,
For Your testimonies are my meditation."

In this second of the benefits of Your applied word in this section, Mem, the Psalmist speaks of surpassing insight not simply because he meditates on Your precepts, but that they 'are my meditation' (see also v. 97). 'Insight' is the Hebrew שָׂכַל, sāḵal, a verb meaning to act with insight, to be prudent. It appears just this once in Psalm 119. Notice the example of Isaiah 41:20, where the afflicted see, recognize, consider, and gain insight. Is this not a description of meditation, as we think upon Your word and works (see also Psalm 111:2)? 'Teachers' is that classic verb which has the sense of 'training'. 'Testimonies' has a sense of precepts, warnings. 'Meditation' is the Hebrew שִׂיחָה, śiyḥāh, a noun with the sense meditation, reflection, concern of one's thoughts, or musings. These 2 verses along with Job 15:4 are its only Old Testament uses. When something is one's meditation, it is intentional, but it is not forced. It is one's default way of thinking (Psalm 1:2). Such constant immersion cannot help but bring insight, being the perfect counsel from the perfect Counselor (Psalm 119:24).

"Our teachers are not always to be trusted; in fact, we may not follow any of them implicitly, for God holds us to account for our personal judgments. It behooves us then to follow closely the chart of the Word of God, that we may be able to save the vessel when even the pilot errs . . . he teaching of the Lord is better than any teaching which they can

---

162. Spurgeon, Charles Haddon, *Treasury of David*, on Psalm 119:98, e-Sword edition

give us. Disciples of Christ who sit at his feet are often better skilled in divine things than doctors of divinity . . . We may hear the wisest teachers and remain fools, but if we meditate upon the sacred word we must become wise. There is more wisdom in the testimonies of the Lord than in all the teachings of men if they were all gathered into one vast library. The one book outweighs all the rest . . . He who knows the truths taught in the Bible will be guilty of no egotism if he believes himself to be possessed of more important truth than all the agnostic professors buried and unburied."[163]

"The wisdom taught by Scripture is far-reaching and is capable of application to every diversity of case."[164]

Psalm 119:100

"I understand more than the aged,
Because I have observed Your precepts."

This verse speaks of accelerated learning. Since the fear of the Lord is the beginning of knowledge (Proverbs 1:7) and wisdom (Proverbs 9:10), how could this not be so? But notice how the understanding in this case comes: through doing. See also Psalm 111:10, John 14:21. 'Observe' is the Hebrew נָצַר, nāṣar, a verb with the sense of guard, keep, preserve. The word is prominent in Psalm 119, setting the tone with 'how blessed' in Psalm 119:2 and appearing in Psalm 119:22, 33-34, 56 69, 100, 115, 129, and 145. The promise in Proverbs is full life from a heart that keeps Your commandments (Proverbs 3:1-2).

"The men of old age, and the men of old time, were outdone by the holier and more youthful learner . . . He had the word with him, and so outstripped his foes; he meditated on it, and so outran his friends; he practised it, and so outshone his elders. The instruction derived from Holy Scripture is useful in many directions, superior from many points of view, unrivaled everywhere and in every way. As our soul may make

---

163. Spurgeon, Charles Haddon, *Treasury of David*, on Psalm 119:99, e-Sword edition
164. *Studies in the Book of Psalms*, William Swan Plumer (pp. 1920-1923)

her boast in the Lord, so may we boast in his word. 'There is none like it: give it me,' said David as to Goliath's sword, and we may say the same as to the word of the Lord. If men prize antiquity they have it here. The ancients are had in high repute, but what did they all know compared with that which we perceive in the divine precepts? 'The old is better' says one: but the oldest of all is the best of all, and what is that but the word of the Ancient of days."[165]

Psalm 119:101

> "I have restrained my feet from every evil way,
> That I may keep Your word."

We do the things which are most important to us, we clear the way and remove any impediments. I think immediately of the diligence expressed in the highway of the righteous (Proverbs 15:19, Isaiah 35:8), the clarity (Proverbs 4:18-19), the love (Psalm 97:10), and the pursuit (2 Timothy 2:22, Philippians 3:12-14), recognizing our true identity (Colossians 3:1-4). We set aside laziness, falsehood, evil, lust, and the old life to focus directly ahead towards Christ (Proverbs 4:25-27, Hebrews 12:1-2). What joy, energy and focus! 'Keep' is the Hebrew שָׁמַר, šāmar, a verb with the sense of watch, keep, preserve, or guard. It is prominent in Psalm 119, appearing twenty-one times.

"I checked myself and drew back as soon as I was aware that I was entering into temptation. Though it was a broad way, a green way, a pleasant way, and a way that many walked in, yet, being a sinful way, it was an evil way, and he refrained his feet from it, foreseeing the end of that way. And his care was universal; he shunned every evil way."[166]

"There is no treasuring up the holy word unless there is a casting out of all unholiness: if we keep the good word we must let go the evil ... The by-paths were smooth and flowery, but he knew right well that they were evil, and so he turned his feet away, and held on along the

---

165. Spurgeon, Charles Haddon, *Treasury of David*, on Psalm 119:100, e-Sword edition
166. Henry, Matthew, *Commentary on the Whole Bible*, on Psalm 119:101, e-Sword edition

straight and thorny pathway which leads to God . . . How can we keep God's word if we do not keep our own works from becoming vile?"[167]

Psalm 119:102

"I have not turned aside from Your ordinances,
For You Yourself have taught me."

To turn aside from Your ordinances is to turn aside from You, since 'You Yourself have taught me'. 'Ordinances' is the Hebrew מִשְׁפָּט, mišpāṭ, a noun with the sense of a judgment, a legal decision, a proper claim. It is an expression of Your perfect character of justice. 'Taught' isthe Hebrew יָרָה, yārāh, רְהֹוי, a verb with the sense of 'to shoot, throw, or pour'. Here I see You have poured Your word into my soul so that I am immersed in its riches. You are immensely generous! 'Turned aside' is the Hebrew סוֹר, sûr, a verb with the sense of turn away, to remove, to make depart. May I never discard what You have immersed me in, but may I receive it fully! Instead, remove (same word) the false way from me, and graciously grant me Your law (Psalm 119:29)! When I think of turning aside, my mind goes to Deuteronomy 5:32 and 2 Timothy 4:4. To turn aside to falsehood is my natural default; may I be ever diligent in Your judgments, in Your justice.

"A constant adherence to the ways of God in trying times will be a good evidence of our integrity . . . It was divine grace in my heart that enabled me to receive those instructions. All the saints are taught of God, for he it is that gives the understanding; and those, and those only, that are taught of God, will continue to the end in the things that they have learned."[168]

"If we begin to depart a little we can never tell where we shall end. The Lord brings us to persevere in holiness by abstinence from the beginning of sin; but whatever be the method he is the worker of our perseverance, and to him be all the glory."[169]

---

167. Spurgeon, Charles Haddon, *Treasury of David*, on Psalm 119:101, e-Sword edition
168. Henry, Matthew, *Commentary on the Whole Bible*, on Psalm 119:102, e-Sword edition
169. Spurgeon, Charles Haddon, *Treasury of David*, on Psalm 119:102, e-Sword edition

Psalm 119:103

> "How sweet are Your words to my taste!
> Yes, sweeter than honey to my mouth!"

It is only by Your grace that I have an appetite and appreciation for Your word. To Jeremiah, Your words became a joy and the delight of His heart because of Your effectual call on his life (Jeremiah 15:16). My mind goes immediately to Psalm 19:10, more desirable than gold and sweeter than honey. What is interesting is what precedes it in Psalm 19:7-9. The multifaceted word is first experienced, then desired. Which comes first? It is a spiritual mystery, but without You restoring, making wise, rejoicing my heart, enlightening me, I would have no desire. Your word both satisfies and makes me hungry for more. It is not good to each too much honey (Proverbs 25:27), but there is no such dangerous excess with Your word! May my 'sweet tooth' never wane in this regard. Increase my desire, capacity, and overflow of Your word to others.

"Being God's words they were divinely sweet to God's servant; he who put the sweetness into them had prepared the taste of his servant to discern and enjoy it . . . It must be sweet to our taste when we think of it, or it will not be sweet to our mouth when we talk of it [Proverbs 16:21]."[170]

Psalm 119:104

> "From Your precepts I get understanding;
> Therefore I hate every false way."

I am amazed at the reality, the experiential truth of this verse. My desires have truly changed! In so many ways, those things that were appealing to the point of idolatry have lost their grip on my affections. This to the point of, when I seek to return to them - for example, in areas of anxiety, anger, and lust - I find little to no satisfaction. This is not to say that the

---

170. Spurgeon, Charles Haddon, *Treasury of David*, on Psalm 119:103, e-Sword edition

battle is not intense at times and does not require intense diligence, but they are just so empty. Only Your righteousness satisfies (Matthew 5:6), Your presence soothes (Isaiah 26:6, Psalm 17:15) and Your Person delights (1 Peter 1:8-9). 'Get understanding' is the Hebrew בִּין, biyn, a verb with the sense of discern, perceive, observe, pay attention to. 'Way' is the Hebrew אֹרַח, 'ōraḥ, a noun meaning path, way, byway, or highway, figuratively the pathways of one's life. I don't just hate false paths, I perceive where they lead and avoid them, choosing better ones, Proverbs 2:8-9. The thought continues in v.105 as God lights the way by His word.

"From God's laws he acquires the capacity for proving the spirits, therefore he hates every path of falsehood (Psa 119:128), i.e., all the heterodox tendencies which agree with the spirit of the age."[171]

"Every sin is a falsehood; we commit sin because we believe a lie, and in the end the flattering evil turns a liar to us and we find ourselves betrayed. True hearts are not indifferent about falsehood, they grow warm in indignation; as they love the truth, so they hate the lie. Saints have a universal horror of all that is untrue, they tolerate no falsehood or folly, they set their faces against all error of doctrine or wickedness of life . . . This Psa 119:104 marks a great advance in character, and shows that the man of God is growing stronger, bolder, and happier than aforetime. He has been taught of the Lord, so that he discerns between the precious and the vile, and while he loves the truth fervently he hates falsehood intensely. May all of us reach this state of discrimination and determination, so that we may greatly glorify God."[172]

---

171. Keil & Delitzsch, *Commentary on the Old Testament*, on Psalm 119:104, e-Sword edition
172. Spurgeon, Charles Haddon, *Treasury of David*, on Psalm 119:104, e-Sword edition

CHAPTER 14
Nun: 'Incline to Your Inheritance'

"Nun. Your word is a lamp to my feet
And a light to my path.
[106] I have sworn and I will confirm it,
That I will keep Your righteous ordinances.
[107] I am exceedingly afflicted;
Revive me, O LORD, according to Your word.
[108] O accept the freewill offerings of my mouth, O LORD,
And teach me Your ordinances.
[109] My life is continually in my hand,
Yet I do not forget Your law.
[110] The wicked have laid a snare for me,
Yet I have not gone astray from Your precepts.
[111] I have inherited Your testimonies forever,
For they are the joy of my heart.
[112] I have inclined my heart to perform Your statutes
Forever, even to the end."

—Psalm 119:105-112

No sooner had the Psalmist recognized the light of Your word (v. 105) and resolved to follow it (v. 106) than that resolve was severely tested through inner affliction (v. 107) outward danger (v. 109) and the snares of the wicked (v. 110). The light grew dim for him but never went out as he sought revival (v. 107) remembrance (v. 109) and resolve (v. 110). He maintained praise (v. 108) and, as the light grew stronger, he recognized their eternal value and joy (v. 111), becoming eternally resolved in them (v. 112).

"One of the most practical benefits of Holy Scripture is guidance in the actions of daily life. God did not send it to astound us with its brilliant light, but to guide us by its instruction."[173]

Psalm 119:105

"Your word is a lamp to my feet
And a light to my path."

This is the classic, perhaps most familiar verse in Psalm 119. Surely those who walk in darkness have seen a great light (Isaiah 9:2), and that light is Your word. In reinforcement of the fact that You come with Your word, surely You are my light (Psalm 27:1), as You will be for all Your people when Your kingdom comes in its fullness (Revelation 22:5). Surely 'You light my lamp; the LORD illumines my darkness' (Psalm 18:28). 'Lamp to my feet' shows where I am, (see also Hebrews 4:13), and 'light to my path' shows where I am to go. O Father, may I run in this path as You illumine the way (Psalm 119:32). 'Lamp' and 'light' appear again in Proverbs 6:23 in describing the way of life. May I do well by paying full attention to this light (2 Peter 1:19). May I shine Your light on new things and ever follow You in new ways.

"Each man should use the word of God personally, practically, and habitually, that he may see his way and see what lies in it . . . One of the most practical benefits of Holy Writ is guidance in the acts of daily

---

173. Spurgeon, Charles Haddon . *The Golden Alphabet* (Updated, Annotated): An Exposition of Psalm 119 (pp. 177-178). Aneko Press. Kindle Edition.

life; it is not sent to astound us with its brilliance, but to guide us by its instruction. It is true the head needs illumination, but even more the feet need direction, else head and feet may both fall into a ditch . . . He who walks in darkness is sure, sooner or later, to stumble; while he who walks by the light of day, or by the lamp of night, stumbleth not, but keeps his uprightness. Ignorance is painful upon practical subjects; it breeds indecision and suspense, and these are uncomfortable: the word of God, by imparting heavenly knowledge, leads to decision, and when that is followed by determined resolution, as in this case, it brings with it great restfulness of heart."[174]

Psalm 119:106

"I have sworn and I will confirm it,
That I will keep Your righteous ordinances."

The 'modern' man is uncomfortable with vows, and I am no exception. However, I see this as a valid concept in the Scriptures (see Psalm 76:11, Matthew 5:33), yet even Jesus gave a warning against it (Matthew 5:37). Like heavenly rewards, I cannot deny this in Scripture, but I struggle mightily to wrap my mind around them. We see in this verse a strong confirmation that God's ordinances are righteous and worthy of a strong commitment to keep them. What I struggle with is that it seems to smack of confidence in the flesh (Philippians 3:3-4) to follow through, when I have a record of failure, or at least inconsistency, both far short of Your perfect standard, Lord! The meaning of the words 'sworn', 'confirm', and 'keep' are straightforward. But notice the context. Previously the Psalmist confirms Your word as his lamp and light. This would evoke a loving commitment! Following, he expresses his extreme affliction and need for revival. So we are not in a context of self-centered pride.

"Under the influence of the clear light of knowledge he had firmly made up his mind and solemnly declared his resolve in the sight of God. Perhaps mistrusting his own fickle mind, he had pledged himself in

---

174. Spurgeon, Charles Haddon, *Treasury of David*, on Psalm 119:105, e-Sword edition

sacred form to abide faithful to the determinations and decisions of his God . . . righteous men should be resolved to keep them at all hazards, since it must always be right to do right . . . when a man has not vowed in so many words to keep the Lord's judgments, yet is he equally bound to do so by obligations which exist apart from any promise on our part, - obligations founded in the eternal fitness of things, and confirmed by the abounding goodness of the Lord our God. Will not every believer own that he is under bonds to the redeeming Lord to follow his example, and keep his words? Yes, the vows of the Lord are upon us, especially upon such as have made profession of discipleship, have been baptized into the thrice-holy name, have eaten of the consecrated memorials, and have spoken in the name of the Lord Jesus."[175]

Psalm 119:107

"I am exceedingly afflicted;
Revive me, O LORD, according to Your word."

I feel the pain and the hope of this verse. 'Exceedingly' is the Hebrew מְאֹד me'ōḏ, an adverb with the sense of greatly, great, abundance, might, power, and is used just three times in the Psalms, all in Psalm 119: Psalm 119:96 as 'exceedingly broad', Psalm 119:107 as 'exceedingly afflicted', and Psalm 119:167 as 'love them exceedingly'. In its 29 uses in the Old Testament it is never translated as otherwise in the NASB. But there is another word here, a qualifier, the Hebrew עַד, 'aḏ, a preposition and adverb with the sense of as far as, up to, unto. I take this to mean that You know our limits (1 Corinthians 10:13) and sustain our lives. 'According to Your word'. You will not revive merely for my comfort or according to my desires, but for my transformation, for my holiness, for 'in faithfulness You have afflicted me' (Psalm 119:75). You will take me as far as possible for this glorious goal! Regardless of the proximate and efficient causes of affliction, You are its ultimate cause. Revive me

---

175. Spurgeon, Charles Haddon, *Treasury of David*, on Psalm 119:106, e-Sword edition

according to Your word when my soul cleaves to the dust (Psalm 119:25), when I am exceedingly afflicted (Psalm 119:107), when I need You to plead my cause and redeem me (Psalm 119:154). See also Psalm 107; Whether it be sin or circumstances, revive me according to Your word.

"Our service of the Lord does not screen us from trial, but rather secures it for us. The Psalmist was a consecrated man, and yet a chastened man; nor were his chastisements light; for it seemed as if the more he was obedient the more he was afflicted. He evidently felt the rod to be cutting deep, and this he pleads before the Lord. He speaks not by way of murmuring, but by way of pleading; from the very much affliction he argues for very much quickening . . . he soul is raised above the thought of present distress, and is filled with that holy joy which attends all vigorous spiritual life, and so the affliction grows light . . . Frequently the affliction is made the means of the quickening, even as the stirring of a fire promotes the heat of the flame. In their affliction some desire death, let us pray for life. Our forebodings under trial are often very gloomy, let us entreat the Lord to deal with us, not according to our fears, but according to his own word . . . seeing we have more promises, let us offer more prayers."[176]

Psalm 119:108

> "O accept the freewill offerings of my mouth,
> O LORD, And teach me Your ordinances."

Why wouldn't You accept prayers? First, 'accept' is the Hebrew רָצָה, rāṣāh, a verb with the sense of delight, take pleasure, treat favorably, often used in the context of sacrifice. 'Freewill offerings' is the Hebrew נְדָבָה, neḏāḇāh, a noun with the sense of willingness, voluntarily. a freewill offering, a voluntary gift. As an adverb, it means willingly, freely, spontaneously, voluntarily, given without obligation. I read in this a willingness of the heart both to love and to learn. The attitude

---

176. Spurgeon, Charles Haddon, *Treasury of David*, on Psalm 119:107, e-Sword edition

here is above and beyond a mere sense of duty. Having been filled with the word, the Psalmist offers thanks (see Colossians 3:16-17). Certainly this fruit of the heart is from the seeds You have sown, and because it is from, through, and to You, it is acceptable to You. My friend Pastor Mike Riccardi often prays 'get what You are worthy of.' This willingness we see in Psalms also in Psalm 54:6, 110:3. We sacrifice praise to You not to get, but because of what we have been given. Even though You have ordained worship (e.g. see 1 Chronicles 23:31), those done with sinful motives are odious to You (see Isaiah 1:13-15). Certainly no prayer without a regard for Your word will be regarded by You (Nehemiah 9:26, Psalm 50:17, Psalm 66:18, Ezekiel 23:35). May I ever ask from pure motives informed by Your word (Psalm 37:4, John 15:7, James 4:2-3).

"The living praise the living God, and therefore the quickened one presents his sacrifice . . . There can be no value in extorted confessions, God's revenues are not derived from forced taxation, but from freewill donation. There can be no acceptance where there is no willingness; there is no work of free grace where there is no fruit of free will. Acceptance is a favour to be sought from the Lord with all earnestness, for without it our offerings are worse than useless. What a wonder of grace that the Lord will accept anything of such unworthy ones as we are! . . . When we render unto the Lord our best, we become all the more concerned to do better. If, indeed, the Lord shall accept us, we then desire to be further instructed, that we may still be more acceptable . . . Those judgments are not always so clear as to be seen at once; we need to be taught in them till we admire their wisdom and adore their goodness as soon as ever we perceive them."[177]

Psalm 119:109

"My life is continually in my hand,
Yet I do not forget Your law."

---

177. Spurgeon, Charles Haddon, *Treasury of David*, on Psalm 119:108, e-Sword edition

Whose hand is the Psalmist's hands in? v.110 may give the answer: 'the wicked have laid a snare for me'. What is his first inclination? Defending self? Revenge? Human strategy? No. 'I do not forget Your law.' When anything is over our heads we seek the One who is above all things, who is Head over all, 1 Chronicles 29:11.

"This is a very uncomfortable and trying state of affairs, and men are apt to think any expedient justifiable by which they can end such a condition - but David did not turn aside to find safety in sin, for he says, *Yet do I not forget thy law.'* They say that all things are fair in love and war; but the holy man thought not so, while he carried his life in his hand, he also carried the law in his heart. No danger of body should make us endanger our souls by forgetting that which is right . . . In his memory of the Lord's law lay his safety; he was certain not to be forgotten of God, for God was not forgotten of him. It is a special proof of grace when nothing can drive truth out of our thoughts, or holiness out of our lives."[178]

Psalm 119:110

"The wicked have laid a snare for me,
Yet I have not gone astray from Your precepts."

Need I walk through life paranoid? Has anyone laid a snare for me specifically? This I do not know, but I do know this: Satan actively accuses (Romans 8:33-34, Revelation 12:10) and seeks to destroy Your people (1 Peter 5:8-9). He has spiritual powers far stronger than me actively fighting You and Your people (2 Corinthians 10:3-5, Ephesians 6:10-17), physically killing Christians every day (Romans 8:36-37). But I also know that Satan had nothing in Jesus (John 14:30), His powers were neutralized and fate sealed at the cross (Colossians 2:13-14, Revelation 12:9), and that we are more than conquerors through You who loved us (Romans 8:37). So, the path of Your precepts is my protection and

---

178. Spurgeon, Charles Haddon, *Treasury of David*, on Psalm 119:109, e-Sword edition

power. I need not be afraid! Certainly evil men will either be saved or destroyed, while I and Your people pass by safely (Psalm 141:10).

"We shall not find it an easy thing to live the life of the faithful. Wicked spirits and wicked men will leave no stone unturned for our destruction. If all other devices fail, and even hidden pits do not succeed, the wicked still persevere in their treacherous endeavours, and, becoming craftier still, they set snares for the victim of their hate . . . When a man knows that he is thus assailed, he is too apt to become timorous, and rush upon some hasty device for deliverance, not without sin in the endeavour; but David calmly kept his way, and was able to write, 'Yet I erred not from thy precepts.' He was not snared, for he kept his eyes open, and kept near his God. He was not entrapped and robbed for he followed the King's highway of holiness, where God secures safety to every traveller . . . By keeping to the ways of the Lord we shall escape the snares of our adversaries, for his ways are safe and free from treachery."[179]

Psalm 119:111

> "I have inherited Your testimonies forever,
> For they are the joy of my heart."

Like the riches described in Psalm 119:14 and Psalm 119:72, (as also in Psalm 19:10) the Psalmist assesses the eternal value of Your word properly. In particular, Psalm 119:14 - 'all riches' is like receiving an inheritance, being set for life. It is not only endless in present bounty, it is endless in time! What a deep well of joy that will never run dry. Inheritance is a huge concept in the Scriptures. Having not come from relative wealth it is harder for me to grasp this concept, so I feast on these descriptions of a heavenly inheritance in Your word: Ephesians 1:11, 14, Psalm 37:18, 119:111, Acts 20:32, Acts 26:18, Romans 8:17, Galatians 3:18, Colossians 1:12, 3:24, Titus 3:7, James 2:5, 1 Peter 1:4, 3:9. Oh the joy! In the same sense that Your words are my meditation (v.97), they are the

---

179. Spurgeon, Charles Haddon, *Treasury of David*, on Psalm 119:110, e-Sword edition

singular joy of my heart. Stop seeking elsewhere what you already have here. See Psalm 119:56, "This has become mine, That I observe Your precepts." Jeremiah 15:16, by taking them in they become the joy of the heart! The mining of it far exceeds the effort to obtain, Proverbs 2:1-5.

"He has taken and obtained possession of God's testimonies for ever (cf. Psa 119:98); they are his "heritage," for which he willingly gives up everything else, for they (הֵמָּה inexactly for הֵנָּה) it is which bless and entrance him in his inmost soul."[180]

"He chose them as his lot, his portion, his estate; and what is more, he laid hold upon them and made them so, - taking them into possession and enjoyment . . . we have to take our heritage by hard fighting, and, if so, it is worthy of all our labour and suffering; but always it has to be taken by a decided choice of the heart and grip of the will. What God gives we must take . . . That which rejoices the heart is sure to be chosen and treasured. It is not the head-knowledge but the heart-experience which brings the joy . . . Joy fixes the spirit - when once a man's heart rejoices in the divine word, he greatly values it, and is for ever united to it." [181]

Psalm 119:112

"I have inclined my heart to perform Your statutes
Forever, even to the end."

I am reminded of John Maxwell's statement that decision management is more important than decision making. We make important decisions, settle them, and live within them. Christian convictions are - or should be - like that, a settled conviction leading to a stable life.

'Incline' is the Hebrew נָטָה, nāṭāh, verb with the sense of stretch out, extend, give attention. Much of its use in Psalms is that God would incline to the Psalmist to hear and help him (e.g. Psalm 102:2, Psalm 116:2). The Psalmist does not want his heart inclined to evil (Psalm 141:4).

---

180. Keil & Delitzsch, *Commentary on the Old Testament*, on Psalm 119:111, e-Sword edition
181. Spurgeon, Charles Haddon, *Treasury of David*, on Psalm 119:111, e-Sword edition

In Proverbs, the parallel is in Proverbs 2:2, 'incline your heart to understanding'. See also Proverbs 4:20, Proverbs 5:1. In Proverbs 21:1 we see the Lord 'turns' (same word) the heart of the king wherever He wishes.

What is interesting here is the need - following a command - to incline one's heart away from evil and toward God. This is the biblical principle of repentance. But we also see the foundation of God changing the heart so that it is so inclined (Psalm 119:36, Psalm 141:4, Acts 5:31, 2 Timothy 2:25).

Hebrews 6:1 speaks of 'not laying again a foundation of repentance'. This speaks to the earlier thought on decision management. There is a sense in which we enter into a lifelong cycle of repentance and faith, but that is an expression of the foundation of the repentance of salvation. It is a working out of what God has worked in (Philippians 2:12-13).

"He had by prayer, and meditation, and resolution made his whole being lean towards God's commands; or as we should say in other words - the grace of God had inclined him to incline his heart in a sanctified direction. Many are inclined to preach, but the Psalmist was inclined to practise; many are inclined to perform ceremonies, but he was inclined to perform statutes; many are inclined to obey occasionally, but David would obey alway;"[182]

---

182. Spurgeon, Charles Haddon, *Treasury of David*, on Psalm 119:112, e-Sword edition

CHAPTER 15
Samekh: 'Singular Focus'

"Samekh. I hate those who are double-minded,
But I love Your law.
[114] You are my hiding place and my shield;
I wait for Your word.
[115] Depart from me, evildoers,
That I may observe the commandments of my God.
[116] Sustain me according to Your word, that I may live;
And do not let me be ashamed of my hope.
[117] Uphold me that I may be safe,
That I may have regard for Your statutes continually.
[118] You have rejected all those who wander from Your statutes,
For their deceitfulness is useless.
[119] You have removed all the wicked of the earth like dross;
Therefore I love Your testimonies.
[120] My flesh trembles for fear of You,
And I am afraid of Your judgments."

—Psalms 119:113-120

So much distracts within and without: the double-minded (v. 113), evildoers (v. 115), inner shame (v. 116), inner fear (v. 117), the deceitfulness of those who wander (v. 118). Yet this recognition leads to both restraint (see Psalm 119:101) and a focus that grows ever stronger. The Psalmist loves Your law even more (v. 113), takes refuge in You in Your word (v. 114), develops a greater sense of dependency on Your word for very life and living (vv. 116-117). Finally, he recognized the destiny of the wicked (v. 119) which crystalized his focus by fearing You (v. 120), which is the foundation of all knowledge and wisdom (Proverbs 1:7, Proverbs 9:10).

"This octave, whose initial letter is Samech, or S, has been compared to Samson at his death, when he took hold of the pillars of the house and pulled it down on the Philistines. Note how the psalmist grips the pillars of divine power with Uphold me and Hold me up, and see how the house falls down in judgment on the unholy. Thou dost cause all the wicked of the earth to come undone like dross. This section carries the war into the enemy's country and reveals the believer as militant against falsehood and iniquity."[183]

Psalm 119:113

"I hate those who are double-minded,
But I love Your law."

You are consistent and reliable, Your purposes stand forever (Psalm 33:11) and Your lovingkindness to all generations (Psalm 100:5)! Again I am reminded of Isaiah 2:22, having a proper view of man, who is inconsistent, unreliable, wavering in purpose and capricious in character apart from You. Lord, I want to hate double mindedness consistently, not just in others, but starting with myself. I am amazed at, having tasted Your goodness (Psalm 34:8) and taught others, how easily I can waver. My need for You is total, John 15:5. I notice the examples of 1

---

183. Spurgeon, Charles Haddon . *The Golden Alphabet* (Updated, Annotated): An Exposition of Psalm 119 (pp. 187-188). Aneko Press.

Kings 18:21, James 1:8, James 4:8, 2 Peter 3:16. How quick we are to hedge our bets in case You don't come through, or as quickly as we in our impatient impulsiveness would like. As I look back, I am profoundly thankful that You have spared me - with no small pain - from an inauthentic life. 'Double-minded' is the Hebrew סֵעֵף, sē'ēp, a noun with the sense of double-mindedness, vanity of thought, illogical or distorted thought that perverts truth. This is its only use in the Bible. Deception and dissatisfaction cannot help but follow. But - I love Your law! My weakness, inconsistency, and need draws me to You. May I be singular and satisfied in my pursuit (Proverbs 2:1-5).

"... the Psalmist deals with thoughts and things and persons which are the opposite of God's holy thoughts and ways ... The opposite of the fixed and infallible law of God is the wavering, changing opinion of men. David had an utter contempt and abhorrence for this; all his reverence and regard went to the sure word of testimony. In proportion to his love to the law was his hate of men's inventions. The thoughts of men are vanity; but the thoughts of God are verity ... When man thinks his best, his highest thoughts are as far below those of divine revelation as the earth is beneath the heavens [Isaiah 55:8-9]. Some of our thoughts are specially vain in the sense of vain-glory, pride, conceit, and self-trust; others in the sense of bringing disappointment, such as fond ambition, sinful dreaming, and confidence in man; in the sense of emptiness and frivolity, such as the idle thoughts and vacant romancings in which so many indulge; and, yet once more, too many of our thoughts are vain in the sense of being sinful, evil, and foolish."[184]

Psalm 119:114

"You are my hiding place and my shield;
I wait for Your word."

I don't just go to You for help; You are my help. I am reminded of Proverbs 18:10, Deuteronomy 33:29, Psalm 40:17, Psalm 42:5, Psalm

---

184. Spurgeon, Charles Haddon, *Treasury of David*, on Psalm 119:113, e-Sword edition

42:11, Psalm 43:5, and Psalm 71:3. We see also a strong warning in Isaiah 31:1; I am cursed if I look to mankind but blessed if You are my trust (Jeremiah 17:5-8). Surely in any circumstance I can experience the fullness of Your presence and protection (Psalm 27:4-5); in fact, You have orchestrated every circumstance for this very thing. 'Hiding place' is the Hebrew סֵתֶר, sēter, a noun meaning a covering, a hiding place, of God as a refuge (Psalm 32:7, 61:4). 'Shield' is the Hebrew מָגֵן, māgēn, a noun meaning shield, metaphorically as a protection, escape, or refuge, of God in Genesis 15:1, Psalm 3:3. Like Proverbs 30:5, this verse associates Your word with Your protection. Surely You are my strength, my shield, my salvation (Psalm 18:35). You are a sun and a shield, withholding no good thing (Psalm 84:11)! You are my reward (Genesis 15:1)!

"He is their *strength and their shield*, their *help and their shield*, their *sun and their shield*, their *shield and their great reward*, and here their *hiding-place and their shield* . . . Those who depend on God's promise shall have the benefit of his power and be taken under his special protection."

"To his God he ran for shelter from vain thoughts; there he hid himself away from their tormenting intrusions, and in solemn silence of the soul he found God to be his hiding-place. When called into the world, if he could not be alone with God as his hiding-place, he could have the Lord with him as his shield, and by this means he could ward off the attacks of wicked suggestions. This is an experimental verse, and it testifies to that which the writer knew of his own personal knowledge: he could not fight with his own thoughts, or escape from them, till he flew to his God, and then he found deliverance. Observe that he does not speak of God's word as being his double defence, but he ascribes that to God himself . . . It is easy to exercise hope where we have experienced help. Sometimes when gloomy thoughts afflict us, the only thing we can do is to hope, and, happily, the word of God always sets before us objects of hope and reasons for hope, so that it becomes the very sphere and support of hope, and thus tiresome thoughts are overcome. Amid fret and worry a hope of heaven is an effectual quietus."[185]

---

185. Spurgeon, Charles Haddon, *Treasury of David*, on Psalm 119:114, e-Sword edition

Psalm 119:115

> "Depart from me, evildoers,
> That I may observe the commandments of my God."

My mind immediately goes to Psalm 101, where David recognizes that faithfulness requires the decisive removal of and fight against ungodly influences. Certainly while it is possible to experience deep fellowship with You while surrounded by enemies (Psalm 27:1-4), we do not seek this, but rather the company of the godly. This speaks not to the complete avoidance of sinners (1 Corinthians 5:9-11), but rather wisdom as to who most influences our hearts and lives (Proverbs 13:20, Proverbs 2:20, Proverbs 4:23, Psalm 119:74, Psalm 119:79). Surely 'bad company corrupts good morals' (1 Corinthians 15:33). I must avoid the deception that I can have a strong enough inner life that can withstand the consistent influence of evildoers. While corruption comes from within (Mark 7:21-23), it must be guarded against without. Of course the purpose is that I may faithfully observe Your commandments, which is my most treasured possession (Psalm 119:1-2, Psalm 119:56) which I dare not willingly give up.

"If we fly to God from vain thoughts, much more shall we avoid vain men . . . 'Depart from me.' Herein he anticipated the sentence of the last great day, when the Son of David shall say, 'Depart from me, ye workers of iniquity.' [Matthew 7:23] . . . Evildoers make evil counsellors. Those who say unto God, 'Depart from us,' ought to hear the immediate echo of their words from the mouths of God's children, 'Depart from us. We cannot eat bread with traitors.' . . . Because Jehovah is our God therefore we resolve to obey him, and to chase out of our sight those who would hinder us in his service. It is a grand thing for the mind to have come to a point, and to be steadfastly fixed in the holy determination, - 'I will keep the commandments.' God's law is our pleasure when the God of the law is our God."[186]

---

186. Spurgeon, Charles Haddon, *Treasury of David*, on Psalm 119:115, e-Sword edition

Psalm 119:116

> "Sustain me according to Your word, that I may live;
> And do not let me be ashamed of my hope."

With v. 117, when I doubt and fear, what am I saying about Your sustaining power? At least two things. First, how weak I am and how much I need You. Second, if I stay in doubt, I deny Your power and doubt Your word.

How am I sustained? By Your word. Your word is my food (Matthew 4:4, Jeremiah 15:16, Job 23:12). For what purpose? That I may live and not be ashamed of my hope.

'Sustain' is the Hebrew סָמַךְ, sāmak, verb with the sense of lay on, uphold, sustain, of Your support (Psalm 3:5, Isaiah 59:16, 63:5); Isa 63:5). This is the only occurrence of the word in Psalm 119. Lord, You both lay claim on me and sustain me by Your power! I am reminded of Romans 12:1-2. All of this is gained by communion with You; all of this lost by walking in self-will and self-strength. To do the latter would be to be ashamed of my hope, putting hope in self and circumstances and not in You. There is no other hope! Psalm 39:7, Romans 8:24-25.

"He sees himself not only unable to go on in his duty by any strength of his own, but in danger of falling into sin unless he was prevented by divine grace; . . . We stand no longer than God holds us and go no further than he carries us . . . But those that hope in God's word may be sure that the word will not fail them, and therefore their hope will not make them ashamed."[187]

"Our soul would die if the Lord did not continually sustain it, and every grace which makes spiritual life to be truly life would decay if he withdrew his upholding hand . . . We may be ashamed of our thoughts, and our words, and our deeds, for they spring from ourselves; but we never shall be ashamed of our hope, for that springs from the Lord our God. Such is the frailty of our nature that unless we are continually upheld by grace, we shall fall so foully as to be ashamed of ourselves,

---

187. Henry, Matthew, *Commentary on the Whole Bible*, on Psalm 119:116, e-Sword edition

and ashamed of all those glorious hopes which are now the crown and glory of our life . . . David meant to keep the law of the Lord, but he first needed the Lord of the law to keep him."[188]

Psalm 119:117

> "Uphold me that I may be safe,
> That I may have regard for Your statutes continually."

Here the thought continues from v. 116. Why am I upheld? That I may be safe and have regard for Your statutes continually. 'Uphold' is the Hebrew סָעַד, sā`aḏ, a verb with the sense of to support, sustain, or refresh. See Psalm 18:35 - what an unspeakable blessing! The word is otherwise translated as 'refresh' (Genesis 18:5, 1 Kings 13:7, see also Psalm 104:15). Refreshed and energized by You, I am less prone to sin by seeking satisfaction elsewhere. 'Regard' has the sense of to look upon with favor. 'Continually' has the sense of continuity in faithful rituals. His praise shall continually be in my mouth (Psalm 34:1), and I proclaim His salvation continually (Psalm 40:16). It appears elsewhere in Psalm 119 in Psalm 119:44 ('keep Your law continually') and Psalm 119:109 ('my life is continually in my hand'). When I am satisfied in You, I do not deviate from my devotion.

"We are saved by past grace, but we are not safe unless we receive present grace . . . In obedience is safety; in being held up is obedience. No man will outwardly keep the Lord's statutes for long together unless he has an inward respect for them, and this will never be unless the hand of the Lord perpetually upholds the heart in holy love . . . Happy is the man who realizes this verse in his life; upheld through his whole life in a course of unswerving integrity, he becomes a safe and trusted man, and maintains a sacred delicacy of conscience which is unknown to others. He feels a tender respect for the statutes of the Lord, which keeps him clear of inconsistencies and conformities to the world that are so common among others, and hence he is a pillar in the house of the Lord."[189]

---

188. Spurgeon, Charles Haddon, *Treasury of David*, on Psalm 119:116, e-Sword edition
189. Spurgeon, Charles Haddon, *Treasury of David*, on Psalm 119:117, e-Sword edition

Psalm 119:118

> "You have rejected all those who wander from Your statutes,
> For their deceitfulness is useless."

Deceitfulness is not merely useless, it is destructive. May my heart reject what You reject, and may my heart - your dwelling place for Your Holy Spirit - be like the Jerusalem under King David in Psalm 101:6-7, letting the faithful in but keeping the deceitful out. Keep deception and lies far from me (Proverbs 30:8)! Deceitfulness is the default; it comes here merely by wandering from Your statutes (see Romans 3:13). The idea here is an aimlessness, a lack of intentionality. In Psalm 119:119 they will be removed like dross. Remove the dross of my heart that I may be useful to You! Proverbs 25:4.

"Sooner or later God will set his foot on those who turn their foot from his commands: it has always been so, and it always will be so to the end . . . They call it far-seeing policy, but it is absolute falsehood, and it shall be treated as such. Ordinary men call it clever diplomacy, but the man of God calls a spade a spade, and declares it to be falsehood, and nothing less, for he knows that it is so in the sight of God. Men who err from the right road invent pretty excuses with which to deceive themselves and others, and so quiet their consciences and maintain their credits; but their mask of falsehood is too transparent."[190]

Psalm 119:119

> "You have removed all the wicked of the earth like dross;
> Therefore I love Your testimonies."

I find this verse vexing, and I seek Your help, Lord, to understand it. How can it be true? In what sense have the wicked been removed? Psalm 14 speaks of the corruption of mankind, and Psalm 12:8 is explicit in the overtness of evil: 'When vileness is exalted among the sons of men.' Yet,

---

190. Spurgeon, Charles Haddon, *Treasury of David*, on Psalm 119:118, e-Sword edition

when I reflect on biblical history, I recognize that You have done it by a worldwide flood Genesis 7:19-23), and You will do it again at the consummation of all things (2 Peter 3:4-7). What dreadful, marvelous hope! How important it is to understand the flow of history and to not interpret everything from the present. 'Remove' is the Hebrew שָׁבַת, šabat, a verb with the sense of rid of, rest, put away, to leave. Used of the Sabbath day (see Exodus 2:8-11), it is emphatically 'to cease'. What hope the righteous have in Your word, knowing that justice is coming and oppression will cease, what love we have for the promises of Your word! What love we have for the freedom it gives in the present, Psalm 119:45, John 8:31-32. Purify me, Father (Proverbs 25:4)! Even Psalm 14 gives hope because surely the wicked live under dread (Psalm 14:5) and fear (Psalm 28:1), and being in Your presence reminds us of this reality (Psalm 73:17-18 ff). Let terror remain with those for whom it is due, and not for those whose confidence is in You (Proverbs 3:25-26).

"Now see how God deals with them, that you may neither fear them nor envy them. 1. He treads them all down. He brings them to ruin, to utter ruin, to shameful ruin; he makes them his footstool. Though they are ever so high, he can bring them low (Amo 2:9); he has done it many a time, and he will do it, for he resists the proud and will triumph over those that oppose his kingdom . . . There is a day coming which will put them away from among the righteous (Mat 13:49), so that they shall have no place *in their congregation* (Psa 1:5), which will put them away into everlasting fire, the fittest place for the dross."[191]

". . . he treats them accordingly by putting them away. He puts them away from his church, away from their honours, away from the earth, and at last away from himself. 'Depart,' saith he, 'ye cursed.' . . . They looked like precious metal, they were intimately mixed up with it, they were laid up in the same heap; but the Lord is a refiner, and every day he removes some of the wicked from among his people, either by making a shameful discovery of their hypocrisy or by consuming them from off the earth . . . Even the severities of the Lord excite the love of his people.

---

191. Henry, Matthew, *Commentary on the Whole Bible*, on Psalm 119:119, e-Sword edition

If he allowed men to sin with impunity, he would not be so fully the object of our loving admiration; he is glorious in holiness because he thus rids his kingdom of rebels, and his temple of them that defile it."[192]

Psalm 119:120

> "My flesh trembles for fear of You,
> And I am afraid of Your judgments."

A frightening verse. Is this the posture of a faithful believer? I believe the key is in the word 'flesh'. Why would the flesh tremble? Because of my sinfulness, because of my smallness, in the light of Your presence (Psalm 90:8, Isaiah 6:1-7) and in the presence of Your holiness (Psalm 130:3-4), who could stand? Yet notice the connection to forgiveness and fear in Psalm 130:4. Through this we pursue holiness. How utterly loving! The cycle seems to be something like fear-forgiveness-favor-fear. See Psalm 30:5. We live both in favor and fear, in response to lovingkindness and truth, a wonderful tension towards Your glory! 'Tremble' is a bristling or shivering (a physical sensation) that occurs only here and in Job 4:15. 'Fear' here is the Hebrew פַּחַד, paḥaḏ, a noune most often translated as 'terror' or 'dread' (see 'sudden fear' in Proverbs 3:25). It is not the same fear of the Lord that is clean (Psalm 19:9) and is the foundation of wisdom and knowledge (Proverbs 1:7, Proverbs 9:10), a positive quality which acknowledges God's good intentions. The Psalmist had just noted the rejection of the wandering (v.118) and the removal of the wicked (v.119) and did not desire either for himself.

"Alas, poor flesh, this is the highest thing to which thou canst attain . . . we may well cry for cleansed thoughts, and hearts, and ways, lest his judgments should light on us. When we see the great Refiner separating the precious from the vile, we may well feel a godly fear, lest we should be put away by him, and left to be trodden under his feet."[193]

---

192. Spurgeon, Charles Haddon, *Treasury of David*, on Psalm 119:119, e-Sword edition
193. Spurgeon, Charles Haddon, *Treasury of David*, on Psalm 119:113, e-Sword edition

CHAPTER 16
Ayin: 'An Active God'

"Ayin. I have done justice and righteousness;
Do not leave me to my oppressors.
[122] Be surety for Your servant for good;
Do not let the arrogant oppress me.
[123] My eyes fail with longing for Your salvation
And for Your righteous word.
[124] Deal with Your servant according to Your lovingkindness
And teach me Your statutes.
[125] I am Your servant; give me understanding,
That I may know Your testimonies.
[126] It is time for the LORD to act,
For they have broken Your law.
[127] Therefore I love Your commandments
Above gold, yes, above fine gold.
[128] Therefore I esteem right all Your precepts concerning everything,
I hate every false way."

—Psalm 119:121-128

ur doing is all of Your doing through Your word (see also Isaiah 26:12, 1 Corinthians 1:30, James 1:18). The Psalmist has done righteousness and justice, seeking Your protection, knowing that Your enemies are his enemies (vv. 121-122). He knows that he has no righteousness or understanding of His own, so he seeks Your salvation, Your lovingkindness, Your righteousness, Your knowledge (vv. 123-125, see also Psalm 71:16). Because You have acted for him miraculously, the Psalmist is convinced that You will act against Your (and his) enemies, not because they stand against him, but against You (v. 126, see also Psalm 2). Because of this assurance, namely, that Yours are not empty but supremely active words, he treasures them above all earthly treasure (v. 127) and recognized their supreme value, all of them in everything (v. 128)! Any lesser ways are false and worthy of our contempt.

'In this octave, the psalmist first entreats the Lord to intervene on his behalf. He asks for judgment from the great King, just like David had dealt out justice to his own people. He then declares his genuine and unreserved satisfaction with all the Lord's commands and precepts and begs Him to defend His own law. He writes from the standpoint of his official experience. In our public as well as our private position, the Word is precious.'[194]

Psalm 119:121

"I have done justice and righteousness;
Do not leave me to my oppressors."

Justice and righteousness are meant to be done, not simply talked about, Micah 6:8. They are not ethereal, abstract concepts. Don't lie, cheat, or steal - now there's a start. These are foundational to a stable life, Psalm 15:1-5. When you see instability, look no further than to character; inner conflict and instability flow from the hearts of people. 'Justice' is the Hebrew מִשְׁפָּט, mišpāṭ, a noun with the sense of judgment, a legal decision,

194. Spurgeon, Charles Haddon . *The Golden Alphabet* (Updated, Annotated): An Exposition of Psalm 119 (pp. 199-200). Aneko Press. Kindle Edition.

is a foundational attribute of God (Psalm 89:14) often mentioned with His love and faithfulness (Psalm 101:1, 111:7). 'Righteousness' is the Hebrew צֶדֶק, ṣedeq, a noun meaning a right relation to an ethical or legal standard often associated with justice (Psalm 119:106, Isaiah 58:2). As such, it reflects being in alignment and relation with You. Because righteousness and justice are the foundation of the Lord's throne (Psalm 89:14) You love righteousness and justice (Psalm 11:7, Psalm 33:5), and You love the one who pursues it (Proverbs 15:9), then to do righteousness and justice is to live within and promote Your kingdom, i.e. Your rule and reign. 'Do not leave me to my oppressors' - in other words, justice within comes with the expectation of justice without. For the believer, this may not come until eternity - but it will come (see v. 119).

"This was a great thing for an Eastern ruler to say at any time, for these despots mostly cared more for gain than justice . . . If I will not oppress others, I may hopefully pray that others may not oppress me. A course of upright conduct is one which gives us boldness in appealing to the Great Judge for deliverance from the injustice of others. [Proverbs 28:1]"[195]

Psalm 119:122

> "Be surety for Your servant for good;
> Do not let the arrogant oppress me."

An apparently audacious prayer! For who has given anything to You that it should be paid back to him, (Job 41:11)? The idea that You would owe me anything sounds close to blasphemous - until I consider Your nature and Your promises. 'According to Your word' appears 12 times in Psalm 119, e.g. Psalm 119:58. The context is v.121, seeking Your faithfulness to those who faithfully follow You. This is not a barter system, but a faith system based on Your character.

---

195. Spurgeon, Charles Haddon, *Treasury of David*, on Psalm 119:121, e-Sword edition

"He is sensible that he cannot make his part good himself, and therefore begs that God would appear for him. Christ is our surety with God; and, if he be so, Providence shall be our surety against all the world."[196]

"As my Master, undertake thy servants' cause, and represent me before the faces of haughty men till they see what an august ally I have in the Lord my God . . . What a blessing to be able to leave our matters in our Surety's hands, knowing that all will be well, since he has an answer for every accuser, a rebuke for every reviler . . . It seems to be inevitable that proud men should become oppressors, and that they should take most delight in oppressing really gracious men."[197]

Psalm 119:123

"My eyes fail with longing for Your salvation
And for Your righteous word."

'Fail with longing', see the same phrase in Psalm 119:82. Nothing but Your salvation and Your word satisfy. John Piper writes, 'Nothing in this world has a personal worth great enough to meet the deepest longings of our hearts.'[198] Or, as C.S. Lewis put it, "If we find ourselves with a desire that nothing in this world can satisfy, the most probable explanation is that we were made for another world."[199] 'Fail' is the Hebrew כָּלָה, kālāh, a verb with the sense of complete, accomplish, end, finish, fail, exhaust. Its primary meaning is to consummate or to bring to completion. Why must we come to the end of horizontal, earthly seeking before we look up to seek You, the very Source of life? It's not just that nothing in this world can satisfy, it's also that even the most satisfying things are temporary, and my strength limited to enjoy them. I need You to do it for me, to save me, to speak the words of life into my soul. I am reminded that God told the Apostles to speak to those far

---

196. Henry, Matthew, *Commentary on the Whole Bible*, on Psalm 119:122, e-Sword edition
197. Spurgeon, Charles Haddon, *Treasury of David*, on Psalm 119:122, e-Sword edition
198. *https://www.desiringgod.org/articles/when-will-i-be-satisfied*
199. Lewis, C.S., from *Mere Christianity*

from You for that very purpose: "Go, stand and speak to the people in the temple the whole message of this Life." (Acts 5:20) Is the word of God relevant? Is it adequate? Amen and amen! I must be equally confident speaking Your word to others as I am in applying it to my own heart.

"The one chief petition of the poet, however, to which he comes back in Psa 119:124., has reference to the ever deeper knowledge of the word of God; for this knowledge is in itself at once life and blessedness, and the present calls most urgently for it."[200]

"He wept, waited, and watched for God's saving hand, and these exercises tried the eyes of his faith till they were almost ready to give out. He looked to God alone, he looked eagerly, he looked long, he looked till his eyes ached. The mercy is, that if our eyes fail, God does not fail, nor do his eyes fail . . . His eyes as well as his ears waited for the Lord's word: he looked to see the divine word come forth as a flat for his deliverance."[201]

Psalm 119:124

"Deal with Your servant according to Your lovingkindness
And teach me Your statutes."

Your lovingkindness is my life; without it I die. Lamentations 3:22-23. Your lovingkindness sustains all of life and all people who deserve eternal judgment, Psalm 33:5. You have not dealt with us as our sins deserve (Psalm 103:10-12)! Your word to us is the primary expression of it, Psalm 33:4. It could well be stated that You deal with us in Your lovingkindness by teaching us Your statutes . In looking back, let us in all ways see that You have dealt bountifully (Psalm 13:6, Psalm 116:7). 'Deal' is the Hebrew עָשָׂה, `āśāh, a verb with the sense of do, make, accomplish, complete, to perform a distinct purpose and accomplish a goal. Elsewhere in Psalm 119 we see it in Psalm 119:65, a strong parallel to this one, for dealing well with us is according to Your lovingkindness.

---

200. Keil & Delitzsch, *Commentary on the Old Testament*, on Psalm 119:123, e-Sword edition
201. Spurgeon, Charles Haddon, *Treasury of David*, on Psalm 119:123, e-Sword edition

"The ever deeper knowledge of the word of God; for this knowledge is in itself at once life and blessedness,"[202]

"Here he recollects himself: although before men he was so clear that he could challenge the word of righteousness, yet before the Lord, as his servant, he felt that he must appeal to mercy. We feel safest here . . . Yet since our ignorance arises from our own sinful stupidity, it is great mercy on God's part that he condescends to instruct us in his commands."[203]

Psalm 119:125

"I am Your servant; give me understanding,
That I may know Your testimonies."

If I am Your servant, then You set the agenda and I obey You in all things. The term for servant here is the same as the term for slave. The term for understanding has to do with right perception, the word for know, skillful living. I trust Your understanding of things above my own, and Your thoughts, words, and ways above my own (Isaiah 55:7-11). This is not an outward obedience, this is heart obedience of the whole life. You impress on me this singular thought: 'Do You trust Me?' I want to, Lord. Give me understanding, that I may know Your testimonies!

"In the previous verse he sought teaching; but here he goes much further, and craves for understanding. Usually, if the instructor supplies the teaching, the pupil finds the understanding; but in our case we are far more dependent, and must beg for understanding as well as teaching: this the ordinary teacher cannot give, and we are thrice happy that our Divine Tutor can furnish us with it. We are to confess ourselves fools, and then our Lord will make us wise, as well as give us knowledge . . . It is remarkable that the Psalmist does not pray

---

202. Keil & Delitzsch, *Commentary on the Old Testament*, on Psalm 119:124, e-Sword edition
203. Spurgeon, Charles Haddon, *Treasury of David*, on Psalm 119:124, e-Sword edition

for understanding through acquiring knowledge, but begs of the Lord first that he may have the gracious gift of understanding, and then may obtain the desired instruction."[204]

Psalm 119:126

"It is time for the LORD to act,
For they have broken Your law."

How could I know when it is time for You to act? Knowing that Your law is being violated every day, it would seem that the time for You to act is constant. I believe this desire for justice is good, but I also must believe that You are already working all things according to the counsel of Your will (Ephesians 1:11) - and that includes both restraint and overt action designed for people to fear You (Ecclesiastes 3:11-14). Yet, I know that You hear the cry of those who cry out to You for justice and say, 'how long?' (Psalm 90:13, Luke 18:7). May I be sure of Your active sovereignty and Your answering of prayer perfectly. May I rest in this reality.

"Men make void the law of God by denying it to be his law, by promulgating commands and doctrines in opposition to it, by setting up tradition in its place, or by utterly disregarding and scorning the authority of the lawgiver. Then sin becomes fashionable, and a holy walk is regarded as a contemptible puritanism; vice is styled pleasure, and vanity bears the bell. Then the saints sigh for the presence and power of their God: Oh for an hour of the King upon the throne and the rod of iron! Oh for another Pentecost with all its wonders, to reveal the energy of God to gainsayers, and make them see that there is a God in Israel. Man's extremity, whether of need or sin, is God's opportunity. When the earth was without form and void, the Spirit came and moved upon the face of the waters; should he not come when society is returning to a like chaos? When Israel in Egypt

---

204. Spurgeon, Charles Haddon, *Treasury of David*, on Psalm 119:125, e-Sword edition

were reduced to the lowest point, and it seemed that the covenant would be void, then Moses appeared and wrought mighty miracles; so, too, when the church of God is trampled down, and her message is derided, we may expect to see the hand of the Lord stretched out for the revival of religion, the defence of the truth, and the glorifying of the divine name."[205]

Psalm 119:127

"Therefore I love Your commandments
Above gold, yes, above fine gold."

'Therefore' - the Psalmist loves Your commandments because they are active and are not the empty words of men (v. 126). Your blessings and curses apply (Deuteronomy 11:26); surely You will act against those who have broken Your law, either in this life or the next (Revelation 21:8). We love what is truly valuable, and when something fulfills - yes even exceeds - its promises, we seek it above fine gold. We recognize that nothing compares to the value of wisdom (Proverbs 3:15) which comes from knowing You (Jeremiah 9:23-24), and warrants the forsaking of all else (Matthew 13:44-46, Philippians 3:7-14). So - why do I hesitate to trust (1 Kings 18:21)?

"But David saw that the word of God answers all purposes better than money does, for it enriches the soul towards God; and therefore he loved it better than gold, for it had done that for him which gold could not do, and would stand him in stead when the wealth of the world would fail him."[206]

"So far from being swayed by the example of evil men, so as to join them in slighting the Scriptures, he was the rather led into a more vehement love of them . . . It is the mark of a true believer that he does not depend upon others for his religion, but drinks water out of his own

---

205. Spurgeon, Charles Haddon, *Treasury of David*, on Psalm 119:126, e-Sword edition
206. Henry, Matthew, *Commentary on the Whole Bible*, on Psalm 119:127, e-Sword edition

well, which springs up even when the cisterns of earth are all dried . . . God's laws are more enriching, and bring with them more comfort than all the choicest treasures . . . He judged God's holy commands to be better than the best earthly thing, yea, better than the best sort of the best earthly thing; and this esteem was confirmed and forced into expression by those very oppositions of the world which drive hypocrites to forsake the Lord and his ways."[207]

Psalm 119:128

> "Therefore I esteem right all Your precepts concerning everything, I hate every false way."

This is the practical response to the sufficiency of Scripture, a living out of the reality of 1 Thessalonians 2:13. 'All', and 'everything' mean that we cannot and must not be on the 'cafeteria' plan with regard to Scripture; if I love one part and dismiss or despise another, the problem lies with me. Your word is sufficient in its parts and in the whole, Psalm 119:160. 'Esteem' is the Hebrew יָשַׁר, yāšar, a verb with the sense of to be straight, upright, pleasing. Oh, may I transform to be pleasing to You according to Your word, and Your word increasingly pleasing to me as I transform! Because of this new appetite and affection, I hate what is less than, what is false, what is corrupting. Your precepts may at first seem bitter, but they lead to unspeakable life and joy (Proverbs 4:18). False ways may at first seem sweet, but lead to unending death and despair (Proverbs 4:19). 'Therefore' is the second of a two-fold response to Your assured actions against those who have broken Your law (v.126); Your justice is a cause of supreme rejoicing and esteeming.

"The censure of the wicked is a certificate of merit; that which they sanction we may justly suspect, but that which they abominate we may ardently admire. The good man's delight in God's law is unreserved, he believes in all God's precepts concerning all things . . . Love to

---

207. Spurgeon, Charles Haddon, *Treasury of David*, on Psalm 119:127, e-Sword edition

truth begat hatred of falsehood . . . he had not a good word for any practice which would not bear the light of truth. The fact that such large multitudes follow the broad road had no influence upon this holy man, except to make him more determined to avoid every form of error and sin. May the Holy Spirit so rule in our hearts that our affections may be in the same decided condition towards the precepts of the word."[208]

---

208. Spurgeon, Charles Haddon, *Treasury of David*, on Psalm 119:128, e-Sword edition

CHAPTER 17
Pe: 'Filled'

"Pe. Your testimonies are wonderful;
Therefore my soul observes them.
[130] The unfolding of Your words gives light;
It gives understanding to the simple.
[131] I opened my mouth wide and panted,
For I longed for Your commandments.
[132] Turn to me and be gracious to me,
After Your manner with those who love Your name.
[133] Establish my footsteps in Your word,
And do not let any iniquity have dominion over me.
[134] Redeem me from the oppression of man,
That I may keep Your precepts.
[135] Make Your face shine upon Your servant,
And teach me Your statutes.
[136] My eyes shed streams of water,
Because they do not keep Your law."

—Psalm 119:129-136

This is certainly for the overwhelmed. I need understanding, satisfaction, grace, freedom, and favor - and all are found in You. Your word is the only thing we can gorge ourselves on and still be healthy - in fact, the more You fill us, the healthier we are! It is not good to eat much honey nor to search out one's own glory (Proverbs 25:27), yet it is supremely good to feast on Your word and to search out Your glory (Psalm 19:10, Psalm 119:101-104, Proverbs 24:13-14). Your word leaves us both satisfied and hungry for more; what a miracle! Wonderful, I observe them (v. 129), light, I see and walk in them (v. 130), satisfying, I long for them (v. 131). Because this is my very life, which I both know and have experienced, I ask You to turn to me and be gracious (v. 132), establish my steps in Your word (v. 133), redeem me from the oppression of man (v. 134), and shine Your face upon me (v. 135). When I go astray, I am keenly aware of what I have missed, and it is extreme sorrow (v. 136).

"All the verses in this section begin with the seventeenth letter of the Hebrew alphabet, but each verse begins with a different word. This seventeenth letter is the letter P. The section is precious, practical, profitable, and powerful; peculiarly so. Let us pray for a blessing upon the reading of it."[209]

Psalm 119:129

"Your testimonies are wonderful;
Therefore my soul observes them."

How many things can we say are truly wonderful? Inspiring wonder, these things capture our attention and affection. We go back to them again and again for sources of delight and satisfaction. We seemingly can't get enough. How dangerous that is for the affections of this world, but how healthy and strengthening that is when it comes to Your word. 'Wonderful' is the Hebrew פֶּלֶא , pele', a noun with the sense of wonder,

---

209. Spurgeon, Charles Haddon . *The Golden Alphabet* (Updated, Annotated): An Exposition of Psalm 119 (pp. 211-212). Aneko Press. Kindle Edition.

miracle, marvel. Surely Your word is a delightful, life-giving miracle (Jeremiah 15:16, Hebrews 4:12, 1 Peter 1:23). As a result, our observing is no mere outward ritual, but from the soul, having been raised to new life by it (Romans 6:17-18).

"The testimonies of God are פְּלָאוֹת, wonderful and strange (paradoxical) things, exalted above every-day life and the common understanding."[210]

"Those who know them best wonder at them most. It is wonderful that God should have borne testimony at all to sinful men, and more wonderful still that his testimony should be of such a character, so clear, so full, so gracious, so mighty . . . Some men wonder at the words of God, and use them for their speculation; but David was always practical, and the more he wondered the more he obeyed. Note that his religion was soul work; not with head and hand alone did he keep the testimonies; but his soul, his truest and most real self, held fast to them."[211]

Psalm 119:130

"The unfolding of Your words gives light;
It gives understanding to the simple."

This verse reminds me of Psalm 119:18 and Luke 11:34. More light is always needed, for darkness is the default. 'Simple' here can be defined as 'open minded', which I take to be 'undiscerning', which is not a virtue. See John 17:24 - 'that they may see my glory', 2 Corinthians 4:4 - unbelievers do not see the light of the gospel of the glory of Christ, 2 Peter 1:19 - the word of God is like a lamp shining in a dark place. Surely 'in Your light we see light' (Psalm 36:9). Lord, make our spiritual eyes clear so we will be filled with Your light (Matthew 6:22-23).

"If we begin at the beginning, and take it before us, we shall find that the very first verses of the Bible give us surprising and yet satisfying discoveries of the origin of the universe, about which, without that, the

---

210. Keil & Delitzsch, *Commentary on the Old Testament*, on Psalm 119:129, e-Sword edition
211. Spurgeon, Charles Haddon, *Treasury of David*, on Psalm 119:129, e-Sword edition

world is utterly in the dark. As soon as the word of God enters into us, and has a place in us, it enlightens us; we find we begin to see when we begin to study the word of God. The very first principles of the oracles of God, the plainest truths, the milk appointed for the babes, bring a great light into the soul, much more will the soul be illuminated by the sublime mysteries that are found there. 'The exposition or explication of thy word gives light;' then it is most profitable when ministers do their part in giving the sense, Neh 8:8."[212]

"Those whom the world dubs as fools are among the truly wise if they are taught of God. What a divine power rests in the word of God, since it not only bestows light, but gives that very mental eye by which the light is received - 'It giveth understanding.' Hence the value of the words of God to the simple, who cannot receive mysterious truth unless their minds are aided to see it and prepared to grasp it."[213]

Psalm 119:131

> "I opened my mouth wide and panted,
> For I longed for Your commandments."

See also Psalm 81:10. You do not remove, but pour out in abundance. The only question is that of my capacity, which You enlarge by Your Spirit and Your word (Psalm 119:32). As the deer pants, so my soul pants for You (Psalm 42:1-2), and my whole being thirsts for You (Psalm 63:1-2). What does one do with this kind of desire? Proverbs 2:1-5 and Philippians 3:7-11 provide the answer; we subject all other desires to the desire for You, for that has overtaken us. We can pursue without shame or reservation because of the surpassing value of knowing You. Ecclesiastes 1:8 - all earthly desires fulfilled are entirely unsatisfying, and only righteousness satisfies, Matthew 5:6.

"So animated was his desire that he looked into the animal world to find a picture of it. He was filled with an intense longing, and was not

---

212. Henry, Matthew, *Commentary on the Whole Bible*, on Psalm 119:130, e-Sword edition
213. Spurgeon, Charles Haddon, *Treasury of David*, on Psalm 119:130, e-Sword edition

ashamed to describe it by a most expressive, natural, and yet singular symbol. Like a stag that has been hunted in the chase, and is hard pressed, and therefore pants for breath, so did the Psalmist pant for the entrance of God's word into his soul. Nothing else could content him. All that the world could yield him left him still panting with open mouth. *'For I longed for thy commandments.'* Longed to know them, longed to obey them, longed to be conformed to their spirit, longed to teach them to others. He was a servant of God, and his industrious mind longed to receive orders; he was a learner in the school of grace, and his eager spirit longed to be taught of the Lord."[214]

Psalm 119:132

"Turn to me and be gracious to me,
After Your manner with those who love Your name."

'After Your manner'. Grace is entirely of You; You both define it and dispense it. It is mine simply to see and to receive. Oh how my complaining rejects the fullness of grace You have poured and continue to pour out on me! See John 1:16, Ephesians 1:7, Romans 8:32. 'Manner' is the Hebrew 'מִשְׁפָּט, mišpāṭ, a noun with the sense of judgment, legal decision, proper, rectitude', most often translated in Psalm 119 as 'ordinances' or 'judgments'. Your grace comes to us with justice, it is perfectly dispensed, coming to us according to Your word. I think of 1 Samuel 3:18, 'let Him do what seems good in His eyes'. Lord, what seems best to You is best! 'with those who love Your name' - see Psalm 119:74, Psalm 119:79, Psalm 5:11. We rejoice with those who rejoice in You.

"He does not plead merit, but implores mercy. . . . He desires no more, no better, than neighbour's fare, and he will take up with no less; common looks and common mercies will not serve, but such as are reserved for those that love him, which are such as eye has not seen, 1Co 2:9. Note, The dealings of God with those that love him are such that a

---

214. Spurgeon, Charles Haddon, *Treasury of David*, on Psalm 119:131, e-Sword edition

man needs not desire to be any better dealt with, for he will make them truly and eternally happy."[215]

"He would not have the Lord deal better or worse with him than he was accustomed to deal with his saints - worse would not save him, better could not be. In effect he prays, 'I am thy servant; treat me as thou treatest thy servants. I am thy child; deal with me as with a son.'"[216]

Psalm 119:133

"Establish my footsteps in Your word,
And do not let any iniquity have dominion over me."

See also Psalm 19:13, Psalm 114:2. I want to be ruled completely by You, not allowing 'any' iniquity to rule me. 'Establish' is the Hebrew כּוּן, kûn, a verb with the sense of to set up, make firm, establish, prepare, of being fixed or steadfast. Establish my ways in Your word (Psalm 119:5) just as You have established all creation (Psalm 119:90-91). So often my emotions are unstable when I have every reason to be stable in You. May my thoughts and ways be dominated by the peace which reflects this reality (Isaiah 26:3, Isaiah 41:10, Psalm 119:65, Proverbs 3:17). 'Have dominion' ('overpower' LSB) is the Hebrew שָׁלַט, šālaṭ, a verb with the sense of domineer, to be master of, rule. May my heart be ruled by You who have conquered sin and death through the cross, Ephesians 1:15-23.

"Order my steps — *Make firm*, so that there be no halting (Psa 40:2). Any iniquity — Psa 119:34 favors Hengstenberg, 'any iniquitous man,' any 'oppressor.' . . . His hope of deliverance from *external* oppression of man (Psa 119:134) is founded on his deliverance from the *internal* 'dominion of iniquity,' in answer to his prayer (Psa 119:133)."[217]

"This prayer seeks a very choice favour, namely, that every distinct act, every step, might be arranged and governed by the will of God. This does not stop short of perfect holiness, neither will the believer's desires

---

215. Henry, Matthew, *Commentary on the Whole Bible*, on Psalm 119:132, e-Sword edition
216. Spurgeon, Charles Haddon, *Treasury of David*, on Psalm 119:132, e-Sword edition
217. *Jamieson-Fausset-Brown Commentary*, on Psalm 119:133, e-Sword edition

be satisfied with anything beneath that blessed consummation . . . They pant for perfect liberty from the power of evil, and being conscious that they cannot obtain it of themselves, they cry unto God for it."[218]

Psalm 119:134

"Redeem me from the oppression of man,
That I may keep Your precepts."

The oppression of man seems unrelenting (Psalm 56:1) and utterly destructive (Psalm 119:87). 'Redeem' is the Hebrew פָּדָה, pādāh, a verb with the sense of ransom, redeem, deliver (Deuteronomy 7:8; Micah 6:4). 'Oppression' is the Hebrew עֹשֶׁק, `ōšeq, a noun with the sense of oppression, extortion, defrauding, robbing, denying justice. It seems like an overly strong word for just living this life under the sun, but in You we recognize the danger of those far from You. Man's sin is such that it is not content to indulge selfish desires (Psalm 17:14, Philippians 3:18-19) but is such slavery that it demands approval and participation from others (Proverbs 1:10 ff, Romans 1:32). It is not content to be merely internal, and is shown to be 'utterly sinful' (Romans 7:13). Surely it is nothing to be toyed with, but to be freed from! Oh that I may walk in the liberty of Your word (Psalm 119:45), having been brought into a broad place of freedom (Psalm 18:19). Oh to stay in that freedom of keeping Your precepts! How blessed (Psalm 119:1-2)! May I not be overcome by evil, but overcome evil with good (Romans 12:21), from the inside out.

"It is said that oppression makes a wise man mad [see Ecclesiastes 7:7], and no doubt it has made many a righteous man sinful. Oppression is in itself wicked, and it drives men to wickedness. We little know how much of our virtue is due to our liberty; . . . Although we ought not to yield to the threatenings of men, yet many do so; . . . it usually pleases God ere long to overthrow those powers and dominions which compel men to do evil. The worst of it is that some persons, when the

---

218. Spurgeon, Charles Haddon, *Treasury of David*, on Psalm 119:133, e-Sword edition

pressure is taken off from them, follow after unrighteousness of their own accord . . . When saints are freed from the tyrant they joyfully pay homage to their king."[219]

Psalm 119:135

> "Make Your face shine upon Your servant,
> And teach me Your statutes."

I am reminded immediately of Aaron's blessing in Numbers 6:24-26. 'In Your light we see light' (Psalm 36:9). The light of Your presence is our salvation and favor (Psalm 44:3). Life, warmth, security, and peace are all found in Your presence, as is fullness of joy (Psalm 16:11). As we look to You, we are radiant with Your glory, our faces never ashamed (Psalm 34:5). Moses' face shone with Your glory in such a way that the Israelites could not bear without a veil (Exodus 34:33-35). In Christ, we are seeing, savoring, and reflecting Jesus (2 Corinthians 3:7-18). We have this in our hearts, 'the Light of the knowledge of the glory of God in the face of Christ' (2 Corinthians 4:6). No subjective or merely emotional thing, we seek and savor Your face by a hunger to know and obey Your word. I want to be fully with You, to hear all that You have for me today.

"Oppressors frown, but do thou smile. They darken my life, but do thou shine upon me, and all will be bright. The Psalmist again declares that he is God's servant, and he seeks for no favour from others, but only from his own Lord and Master. 'And teach me thy statutes.' This is the favour which he considers to be the shining of the face of God upon him. If the Lord will be exceeding gracious, and make him his favourite, he will ask no higher blessing than still to be taught the royal statutes . . . he most favoured believer needs teaching; even when he walks in the light of God's countenance he has still to be taught the divine statutes or he will transgress."[220]

219. Spurgeon, Charles Haddon, *Treasury of David*, on Psalm 119:134, e-Sword edition
220. Spurgeon, Charles Haddon, *Treasury of David*, on Psalm 119:135, e-Sword edition

Psalm 119:136

> "My eyes shed streams of water,
> Because they do not keep Your law."

I am reminded of Proverbs 28:4, having a soft heart and a clean conscience, sensitive to sin and not hardened by my flesh. How amazing it is that we, having stone hearts replaced with flesh (Ezekiel 36:26), desire the opposite too often! May not hardness make me harder when reproved! Notice the 'they' here - my eyes! In what way do they not keep Your law? By wandering (Proverbs 17:24), by lusting (Job 31:1, 1 John 2:16), by self-deception (Proverbs 12:15), by pride (Proverbs 26:12). These things blind me from seeing the greatness of Your glory (Psalm 63:1-2), Your law (Psalm 119:18), and the depths of my sin (Proverbs 21:4, Matthew 6:23). This is certainly grievous, and even as I write this I feel I should be weeping, but I am not. May it come to me, emotions in line with reality! As I look at this, may I have misinterpreted? 'They' could also be the men of v.134; both interpretations are appropriate.

"He wept in sympathy with God to see the holy law despised and broken. He wept in pity for men who were thus drawing down upon themselves the fiery wrath of God. His grief was such that he could scarcely give it vent; his tears were not mere drops of sorrow, but torrents of woe. In this he became like the Lord Jesus who beheld the city, and wept over it; and like unto Jehovah himself, who hath no pleasure in the death of him that dieth, but that he turn unto him and live. The experience of this verse indicates a great advance upon anything we have had before: the Psalm and the Psalmist are both growing. That man is a ripe believer who sorrows because of the sins of others. In Psa 119:120 his flesh trembled at the presence of God, and here it seems to melt and flow away in floods of tears. None are so affected by heavenly things as those who are much in the study of the word, and are thereby taught the truth and essence of things,"[221]

---

221. Spurgeon, Charles Haddon, *Treasury of David*, on Psalm 119:136, e-Sword edition

CHAPTER 18
Tsadhe: 'Exceeding Faithfulness'

"Tsadhe. Righteous are You, O LORD,
And upright are Your judgments.
[138] You have commanded Your testimonies in
righteousness
And exceeding faithfulness.
[139] My zeal has consumed me,
Because my adversaries have forgotten Your words.
[140] Your word is very pure,
Therefore Your servant loves it.
[141] I am small and despised,
Yet I do not forget Your precepts.
[142] Your righteousness is an everlasting righteousness,
And Your law is truth.
[143] Trouble and anguish have come upon me,
Yet Your commandments are my delight.
[144] Your testimonies are righteous forever;
Give me understanding that I may live."

—Psalm 119:137-144

Righteous (vv. 137-138, 142, 144), exceedingly faithful (v. 138), pure (v. 140), everlasting (vv. 142, 144), truth (v. 142), a delight (v. 143) are You and Your word. As You are, so is Your word (Psalm 138:2), so is Your praise (Psalm 48:10, Psalm 119:48). Because of this reality, zeal overtakes at its neglect (v. 139) yet assuring strength bathes me in my weakness (v. 141). It creates in me love (v. 140), delight in affliction (v. 143), and understanding in all things (v. 144).

"This passage deals with the perfect righteousness of Jehovah and his word, and expresses the struggles of a holy soul in reference to that righteousness. The initial letter with which every verse commences sounds like the Hebrew word for righteousness: our keynote is righteousness."[222]

Psalm 119:137

> "Righteous are You, O LORD,
> And upright are Your judgments."

Because of Your righteous character, Your judgments can be nothing but upright. 'Righteous' is the Hebrew צַדִּיק ṣaddiyq, an adjective with the sense of just, righteous. 'Upright' is the Hebrew יָשָׁר, yāšār, an adjective with the sense of straight, just, right. 'Judgments' is the Hebrew מִשְׁפָּט, mišpāṭ, a noun with the sense of judgment, legal decision, claim, proper, rectitude. These are not merely good recommendations; they are perfect standards, the rule of life for a God follower. I must start here as the source of knowledge, understanding, and wisdom, i.e. to see things rightly, to know what to do, and to have the power and skill to do it. All come from Your word! The world, by contrast, will seek to actively punish such an approach (Proverbs 17:26), and this is becoming increasingly common even among professing Christians.

"God is always right, and he is always actively right, that is, righteous ... That which comes from the righteous God is itself righteous. Jehovah

---

222. Spurgeon, Charles Haddon, *Treasury of David*, Psalm 119 - Tsadhe, e-Sword edition

both saith and doth that which is right, and that alone. This is a great stay to the soul in time of trouble. When we are most sorely afflicted, and cannot see the reason for the dispensation, we may fall back upon this most sure and certain fact, that God is righteous, and his dealings with us are righteous too. It should be our glory to sing this brave confession when all things around us appear to suggest the contrary. This is the richest adoration - this which rises from the lips of faith when carnal reason utters about undue severity, and the like."[223]

Psalm 119:138

> "You have commanded Your testimonies in righteousness
> And exceeding faithfulness."

'Commanded' is the Hebrew צִוָּה, ṣāwāh, a verb with the sense of order, direct, appoint, command. Your word is not merely good advice, the best wisdom, but commands! Righteousness – there is no higher standard. Faithfulness – there is no greater assurance. You command and You accomplish. Your word always achieves its intended result (Isaiah 55:10-11) as it has from the beginning (Psalm 33:8-9). See also Psalm 107:20, Isaiah 25:1. We see God's righteousness and faithfulness together in Deuteronomy 32:4, 1 Samuel 26:23, Psalm 40:10, Psalm 96:13, Psalm 119:75, Psalm 119:138, Psalm 143:1, Isaiah 11:5, Isaiah 16:5. Your testimonies exceed all expectations of faithfulness; You always fulfill Your promises, and we have yet to exceed them in our faith.

"It is righteous, and may be relied upon for the present; it is faithful, and may be trusted in for the future . . . Not only the precepts but the promises also are commanded of the Lord, and so are all the teachings of Scripture. It is not left to our choice whether we will accept them or no; they are issued by royal command, and are not to be questioned. Their characteristic is that they are like the Lord who has proclaimed them, they are the essence of justice and the soul of truth."[224]

---

223. Spurgeon, Charles Haddon, *Treasury of David*, on Psalm 119:137, e-Sword edition
224. Spurgeon, Charles Haddon, *Treasury of David*, on Psalm 119:138, e-Sword edition

Psalm 119:139

> "My zeal has consumed me,
> Because my adversaries have forgotten Your words."

Zeal overwhelms us at times. Sometimes it is wrong, sometimes it starts out with righteous anger and quickly turns to unrighteous anger, and less often it stays righteous to the end. As those who fear You, it still amazes us that the blind and hardened seemingly have no fear of You before their eyes (Psalm 36:1, Romans 3:18). The only person whose response was righteous beginning to end was Jesus, and this verse is quoted in reference to it in John 2:17. It has particular strength in this context, where the Psalmist has just reflected on the righteousness and exceeding faithfulness of Your words. Who wouldn't want that? Hence the strong emotional reaction. Are the culpable to be recipients of compassion? Certainly my salvation has required it! May I be as angry when I forget Your words and go rogue, as I do in small ways every day.

"This was no doubt occasioned by his having so clear a sense of the admirable character of God's word. His zeal was like a fire burning within his soul. The sight of man's forgetfulness of God acted as a fierce blast to excite the fire to a more vehement flame, and it blazed until it was ready to consume him . . . These men had gone so far in iniquity that they not only violated and neglected the commands of God, but they appeared actually to have forgotten them. This put David into a great heat; he burned with indignation. How dare they trample on sacred things! How could they utterly ignore the commands of God himself! He was astonished, and filled with holy anger."[225]

Psalm 119:140

> "Your word is very pure,
> Therefore Your servant loves it."

---

225. Spurgeon, Charles Haddon, *Treasury of David*, on Psalm 119:139, e-Sword edition

'Very pure'. 'Pure' is the Hebrew צָרַף, ṣārap, a verb with the sense of refine, test, of refining precious metal, Proverbs 25:4. It is in Psalm 12:6 as 'tried' and in 2 Samuel 22:31 and Proverbs 30:5 as 'tested'. The Living Bible paraphrases Proverbs 30:5 as 'every word of God proves true', ESV 'well tried', and HCSB 'completely pure'. Of course we love it! When we see its perfection and beauty, we are drawn to it and can scarcely look away. There is nothing equal to it, Psalm 119:96.

"It is truth distilled, holiness in its quintessence. In the word of God there is no admixture of error or sin. It is pure in its sense, pure in its language, pure in its spirit, pure in its influence, and all this to the very highest degree - 'very pure.' *Therefore thy servant loveth it,'* which is a proof that he himself was pure in heart, for only those who are pure love God's word because of its purity. His heart was knit to the word because of its glorious holiness and truth. He admired it, delighted in it, sought to practise it, and longed to come under its purifying power."[226]

Psalm 119:141

> "I am small and despised,
> Yet I do not forget Your precepts."

'Yet' is so important here. My stature before the world and my unworthiness before You are more than overcome by the power of Your word in my life. Oh, that I might be a living demonstration of this! 1 Samuel 16:7 - You see not as man sees; physical stature is nothing to You. Proverbs 12:9 - how much better to be lightly esteemed than to honor oneself. What freedom and power there is in exalting God and not self! Isaiah 66:1-2, Proverbs 16:18-19. The word 'despise' is also used here in Psalm 51:17; a broken and contrite heart may be despised by men, but it is precious to You. The surpassing greatness of power is surely of You and not from ourselves, 2 Corinthians 4:6-7, 1 Corinthians 4:7, Ephesians 1:18-19. Whom God has chosen is not whom the world has chosen. Boast in God! 1 Corinthians 1:26-31.

---

226. Spurgeon, Charles Haddon, *Treasury of David*, on Psalm 119:140, e-Sword edition

"When we are small and despised we have the more need to remember God's precepts, that we may have them to support us under the pressures of a low condition."[227]

"How many a man has been driven to do some ill action in order to reply to the contempt of his enemies: to make himself conspicuous he has either spoken or acted in a manner which he could not justify. The beauty of the Psalmist's piety was that it was calm and well-balanced, and as he was not carried away by flattery, so was he not overcome by shame. If small, he the more jealously attended to the smaller duties; and if despised, he was the more in earnest to keep the despised commandments of God."[228]

Psalm 119:142

"Your righteousness is an everlasting righteousness,
And Your law is truth."

As You are everlasting righteousness, so is Your word (Isaiah 40:8, Hebrews 13:8). 'Truth' is the Hebrew אֱמֶת 'emet, a noun with the sense of truth, faithfulness. Truth is a barometer, a means of measurement. You are the God of truth, Exodus 34:6, 2 Chronicles 15:3, Psalm 31:5. Your words are not simply true, they are truth, that is «God's words are 'truth' in the sense that they are the final standard by which truthfulness is to be judged: whatever conforms to God's own words is also true, and what fails to conform to his words is not true." (Grudem, Systematic Theology, p. 196) See also 2 Samuel 7:28, 1 Kings 17:24, Psalm 119:151, 160, and John 17:17. Let Your righteousness come to me according to Your word (Psalm 119:41), for You desire truth in the innermost being (Psalm 51:6). May I be true, through and through! I think on the glorious example of Jesus (1 Peter 2:21-22).

"Both the righteousnesses and the un-righteousnesses of man come to an end, but the righteousness of God is without end . . . Note, that

---

227. Henry, Matthew, *Commentary on the Whole Bible*, on Psalm 119:141, e-Sword edition
228. Spurgeon, Charles Haddon, *Treasury of David*, on Psalm 119:141, e-Sword edition

they are not only true, but the truth itself. We may not say of them that they contain the truth, but that they are the truth: 'thy law is the truth.' There is nothing false about the law or preceptory part of Scripture. Those who are obedient thereto shall find that they are walking in a way consistent with fact, while those who act contrary thereto are walking in a vain show."[229]

Psalm 119:143

> "Trouble and anguish have come upon me,
> Yet Your commandments are my delight."

I read this as 'trouble and anguish have come upon me, so that Your commandments would be my delight.' I think of Psalm 119:67, Psalm 119:71, namely, that afflictions are necessary for me to truly delight in Your commandments, which is a sure indication of learning. 'Trouble' is the Hebrew צַר, tsar, a noun which has the sense of affliction, anguish, restriction, distress, misery. 'Anguish' is the Hebrew מָצוֹק, māṣôq, noun with the sense distress, anguish, hardship, anxiety, whether as the result of sin or circumstances. Delight is often associated with following Your word (Psalm 119:24, 77, 92, 143, 174). Relief can only come from delight in Your word. As I read this I am reminded that You rescue and bring to a broad place because of Your delight in us (Psalm 18:19), and that You are my exceeding joy in oppression, Psalm 43. Think inner freedom in all circumstances; the circumstances without may be oppressive, but within are a broad place through Your word.

"*Trouble and anguish have taken hold on me* - trouble without, anguish within; they surprised him, they seized him, they held him . . . All this trouble and anguish did not put his mouth out of taste for the comforts of the word of God, but he could still relish them and find that peace and pleasure in them which all the calamities of this present time could not deprive him of. There are delights, variety of delights, in the

---

229. Spurgeon, Charles Haddon, *Treasury of David*, on Psalm 119:142, e-Sword edition

word of God, which the saints have often the sweetest enjoyment of when they are in trouble and anguish, 2Co 1:5."[230]

"His griefs, like fierce dogs, had taken hold upon him; he felt their teeth. He had double trouble: trouble without and anguish within, as the apostle Paul put it, 'without were rightings and within were fears.' *'Yet thy commandments are my delights.'* Thus he became a riddle; troubled, and yet delighted; in anguish, and yet in pleasure. The child of God can understand this enigma, for well he knows that while he is cast down on account of what he sees within himself he is all the more lifted up by what he sees in the word . . . Does he find more joy in being sanctified than sorrow in being chastised? Then the spot of God's children is upon him."[231]

Psalm 119: 144

> "Your testimonies are righteous forever;
> Give me understanding that I may live."

The Psalmist ends this section of exalting Your word and lamenting how his adversaries have forgotten it, how small and despised he is, and how trouble and anguish have come upon him. He lands on the eternal righteousness of Your testimonies and that his very life requires an understanding of them. Certainly implied here is that Your word is needed for both fullness of life here and now, as well as eternal life and bliss with You. Surely Deuteronomy 8:3 and Matthew 4:4 are true, we live on Your word more even than 'necessary' food (Job 23:12). With Your word in my heart, I shall never go hungry again, and am only famished to the extent that I turn away from You (Psalm 68:6). May I have a continual feast (Proverbs 15:14-15) in Your word, never feeding on folly!

"God's testimonies to man cannot be assailed, they are righteous from beginning to end; and though ungodly men have opposed the divine justice, especially in the plan of salvation, they have always

---

230. Henry, Matthew, *Commentary on the Whole Bible*, on Psalm 119:143, e-Sword edition
231. Spurgeon, Charles Haddon, *Treasury of David*, on Psalm 119:143, e-Sword edition

failed to establish any charge against the Most High . . . To live without understanding is not to live the life of a man, but to be dead while we live. Only as we know and apprehend the things of God can we be said to enter into life. [John 17:3] . . . As we love life, and seek many days that we may see good [Psalm 34:12], it behoves us to seek immortality [Romans 2:7] in the everlasting word which liveth and abideth for ever, and to seek good in that renewal of our entire nature which begins with the enlightenment of the understanding and passes on to the regeneration of the entire man."[232]

---

232. Spurgeon, Charles Haddon, *Treasury of David*, on Psalm 119:144, e-Sword edition

CHAPTER 19
Qoph: 'Heart Cry'

"Qoph. I cried with all my heart; answer me, O LORD!
I will observe Your statutes.
[146] I cried to You; save me
And I shall keep Your testimonies.
[147] I rise before dawn and cry for help;
I wait for Your words.
[148] My eyes anticipate the night watches,
That I may meditate on Your word.
[149] Hear my voice according to Your lovingkindness;
Revive me, O LORD, according to Your ordinances.
[150] Those who follow after wickedness draw near;
They are far from Your law.
[151] You are near, O LORD,
And all Your commandments are truth.
[152] Of old I have known from Your testimonies
That You have founded them forever."

—Psalm 119:145-152

The sacrificial cry here is echoed in Proverbs 2:1-5, particularly v.3. Note the sacrifice of heart (v. 145), desperate need (v. 146), and sleep (v. 147) due to the anticipated benefit (v. 148). The Psalmist would be revived (v. 149), protected (vv. 150-151), and grounded (v. 152). Reflecting on v. 151, since Your nearness is the ultimate good (Psalm 73:28), and there is no truth apart from You (Psalm 31:5), we are strong and secure.

"This section is given up to memories of prayer. The Psalmist describes the time and the manner of his devotions, and pleads with God for deliverance from his troubles. He who has been with God in the closet will find God with him in the furnace. If we have cried we shall be answered. Delayed answers may drive us to importunity; but we need not fear the ultimate result, since God's promises are not uncertain, but are 'founded for ever.' The whole passage shows us: How he prayed (Psa 119:145). What he prayed for (Psa 119:146). When he prayed (Psa 119:147). How long he prayed (Psa 119:148). What he pleaded (Psa 119:149). What happened (Psa 119:150). How he was rescued (Psa 119:151). What was his witness as to the whole matter (Psa 119:152)."[233]

Psalm 119:145

> "I cried with all my heart; answer me, O LORD!
> I will observe Your statutes."

The 'all my heart' phrases are difficult. Who can say they are so wholehearted? Yet that is the goal, all in love for (Deuteronomy 6:5) and fear of (Psalm 86:11) You. Am I this desperate for You? Reality dictates that I should be. The answer, as always, comes from Your word. Have I plumbed its depths for the answer? Proverbs 2:1-5. What an inestimable privilege to commune with You, to receive such perfect truth.

"Lip-labour, if that be all, is lost labour . . . all the powers of his soul were not only engaged and employed, but exerted to the utmost,

---

233. Spurgeon, Charles Haddon, *Treasury of David*, on Psalm 119 - Qoph, e-Sword edition

in his prayers. *Then* we are likely to speed when we thus strive and wrestle in prayer."[234]

"He mentions the unity of his heart in this holy engagement. His whole soul pleaded with God, his entire affections, his united desires all went out towards the living God . . . There may be no beauty of elocution about such prayers, no length of expression, no depth of doctrine, nor accuracy of diction; but if the whole heart be in them they will find their way to the heart of God. . . . He could not expect the Lord to hear him if he did not hear the Lord [see John 15:7], neither would it be true that he prayed with his whole heart unless it was manifest that he laboured with all his might to be obedient to the divine will. His object in seeking deliverance was that he might be free to fulfil his religion and carry out every ordinance of the Lord. He would be a free man that he might be at liberty to serve the Lord."[235]

Psalm 119:146

"I cried to You; save me
And I shall keep Your testimonies."

This is an echo and an emphasis of the sentiment in v. 145. Here, the Psalmist pleads for the answer of salvation, with a promise to keep Your testimonies. 'Answer me' is now 'save me', and 'I will observe Your statutes' is now 'I shall keep Your testimonies'. The Psalmist is to be saved for God's benefit and glory, not his own, yet this is of consummate blessedness to the Psalmist! We notice in the verses that follow the priority of this obedience to the point of sacrificing sleep.

"'Not only rescue me from ruin, but make me happy.' We need desire no more than God's salvation (Psa 50:23) and the things that accompany it, Heb 6:9."[236]

---

234. Henry, Matthew, *Commentary on the Whole Bible*, on Psalm 119:145, e-Sword edition
235. Spurgeon, Charles Haddon, *Treasury of David*, on Psalm 119:145, e-Sword edition
236. Henry, Matthew, *Commentary on the Whole Bible*, on Psalm 119:146, e-Sword edition

"This was his great object in desiring salvation, that he might be able to continue in a blameless life of obedience to God, that he might be able to believe the witness of God, and also to become himself a witness for God. It is a great thing when men seek salvation for so high an end. He did not ask to be delivered that he might sin with impunity; his cry was to be delivered from sin itself. He had vowed to keep the statutes or laws, here he resolves to keep the testimonies or doctrines, and so to be sound of head as well as clean of hand. Salvation brings all these good things in its train. David had no idea of a salvation which would allow him to live in sin, or abide in error: he knew right well that there is no saving a man while he abides in disobedience and ignorance."[237]

Psalm 119:147

"I rise before dawn and cry for help;
I wait for Your words."

With v. 148, this reflects the Psalmist's commitment to Your word. It is truly worth losing sleep over, and it is the minimal sacrifice of the Christian under 'normal' circumstances, that is, not overtly under a trial. Jesus certainly exemplified this in His earthly life (Mark 1:35, Luke 6:12). Why does the Psalmist do it? His need for Your help was obvious, and he could not wait until sunrise to seek it. In v. 128 we see the anticipation of waking up, not the fear of it! So often for me my thoughts stray to the point where I can't make it through the night without seeking Your help. It is clear to me that my very survival depends on this. We also see this sentiment in Psalm 130:5-6, an anticipation greater than the watchmen for the morning!

"Whatever is worth doing is worth doing speedily. This is the third time that he mentions that he cried. He cried, and cried, and cried again. His supplications had become so frequent, fervent, and intense, that he might hardly be said to be doing anything else from morning to night

---

237. Spurgeon, Charles Haddon, *Treasury of David*, on Psalm 119:146, e-Sword edition

but crying unto his God. So strong was his desire after salvation that he could not rest in his bed; so eagerly did he seek it that at the first possible moment he was on his knees . . . He who is diligent in prayer will never be destitute of hope."[238]

Psalm 119:148

"My eyes anticipate the night watches,
That I may meditate on Your word."

Continuing the thought from v. 147, this further explains the 'why' of losing sleep to hear from You. Each verse in Kaph that precedes is an intense cry for help, and the Psalmist anticipates that help to come through the meditation on Your word. This is primarily how You answer. As Peter said, "Lord, to whom shall we go? You have words of eternal life." (from John 6:68). I am amazed at how prone I am to look everywhere else before I dive into Your word! Perhaps my sinful pride wants to solve problems apart from You and to avoid the realization that the problems lie within my own heart. 'Anticipate' is the Hebrew קָדַם, qādam, a verb with the sense to come before, meet, engage, and is the same as 'rise' in the previous verse, both as 'eagerly greet' in the LSB. Surely I am to put Your word front and center in my thinking and to meet it fully and submit to Your full intent for me in it. There is always more than I expect! 'Mediate' in this case is the Hebrew שִׂיחַ, śiyaḥ, a verb with the sense of ponder, converse, meditate, pray, speak. It is to always go deeper. I hear echoes of Psalm 16:7 and Psalm 42:8, that in the night my thoughts and prayers will be directed towards You. David gave himself no rest without putting You first (Psalm 132:3-5).

"He was none of those that say, Yet a little sleep [Proverbs 6:10, Proverbs 24:33]. 2. That he began the day with God. The first thing he did in the morning, before he admitted any business, was to pray, when his mind was most fresh and in the best frame. If our first thoughts in

---

238. Spurgeon, Charles Haddon, *Treasury of David*, on Psalm 119:147, e-Sword edition

the morning be of God they will help to keep us in his fear all the day long. 3. That his mind was so full of God, and the cares and delights of his religion, that a little sleep served his turn . . . He was full of business all day, but that will excuse no man from secret devotion; it is better to take time from sleep, as David did, than not to find time for prayer."[239]

"He did not need to be informed as to how the hours were flying, for every hour his heart was flying towards heaven . . . Meditation was the food of his hope, and the solace of his sorrow: the one theme upon which his thoughts ran was that blessed 'word' which he continually mentions, and in which his heart rejoices. He preferred study to slumber; and he learned to forego his necessary sleep for much more necessary devotion. It is instructive to find meditation so constantly connected with fervent prayer, it is the fuel which sustains the flame. How rare an article is it in these days."[240]

Psalm 119:149

"Hear my voice according to Your lovingkindness;
Revive me, O LORD, according to Your ordinances."

'Nothing in my hands I bring / Simply to the cross I cling' (from the hymn 'Rock of Ages, Cleft for Me'). I have done nothing of my own to incline Your ear to me, nothing to warrant Your attention, save humble desperation, and even that is from You (Isaiah 66:1-2, Deuteronomy 8:2-3, Ezekiel 36:27, 2 Timothy 2:25). How great is Your lovingkindness (Psalm 57:10, Psalm 103:11), so how great is Your hearing (Psalm 65:2, Psalm 116:2), Your inclination towards us! May that form our expectation that the greatness of Your hearing be met with the greatness of Your revival according to the greatness of Your word (Ezekiel 11:19, Ezekiel 36:26, Ezekiel 37:13-14, Psalm 119:25, Psalm 119:88, Psalm 119:107, Psalm 119:154, Psalm 119:156, Psalm 119:159). May this revival be marvelous (Psalm 118:23, Isaiah 29:14)

---

239. Henry, Matthew, *Commentary on the Whole Bible*, on Psalm 119:148, e-Sword edition
240. Spurgeon, Charles Haddon, *Treasury of David*, on Psalm 119:148, e-Sword edition

and a marvel to many (Psalm 71:7). You hear and answer perfectly, according to Your character and not my desires. Father, praise You for not giving me what I want per se, but what You want, which is infinitely better, Proverbs 16:1.

"Note, that he does not plead his own deservings, nor for a moment appeal for payment of a debt on account of merit; he takes the free-grace way, and puts it, 'according unto thy lovingkindness.' When God hears prayer according to his lovingkindness he overlooks all the imperfections of the prayer, he forgets the sinfulness of the offerer, and in pitying love he grants the desire though the suppliant be unworthy. It is according to God's lovingkindness to answer speedily, to answer frequently, to answer abundantly, yea, exceeding abundantly above all that we ask or even think [Ephesians 3:20] . . . . 'Quicken me.' This is often the very best way of delivering us from trouble, - to give us more life that we may escape from death; and to add more strength to that life that we may not be overloaded with its burdens . . . it will be our wisdom to wish to receive grace, not according to our notion of how it should come to us, but according to God's heavenly method of bestowing it. It is his prerogative to make alive as well as to kill, and that sovereign act is best left to his infallible judgment. Hath he not already given us to have life more and more abundantly [John 10:10]?"[241]

Psalm 119:150

> "Those who follow after wickedness draw near;
> They are far from Your law."

In this section of crying after You, we get from the Psalmist a sense of why, namely, the nearness of those who are far from You. Because He wished to follow You and not wickedness, this was of great concern to him. In v.151 He would proclaim Your nearness and Your truth to counteract this. To 'follow after' has the sense of 'chase' or 'pursue'; it is

---

241. Spurgeon, Charles Haddon, *Treasury of David*, on Psalm 119:149, e-Sword edition

not casual. We recognize that those who follow after wickedness are not content to follow alone, but desire many companions. The 'wickedness' described here has the sense of evil purposes or counsel. 'Draw near' has the sense of imminence, so we conclude here that the Psalmist sensed imminent danger. He did not want to participate in or be carried away from Your law. I think of the contrast of Ephesians 5:5-12, how we are not to participate in but rather expose evil. We must play defense against the sinfulness of the heart and those who would stir it up. Surely folly cries out (Proverbs 9:13-16) along with wisdom (Proverbs 9:1-4), and we must choose our companions wisely (Proverbs 13:20), starting with the Lord Himself and those who love His word (Psalm 119:74, Psalm 119:79). Psalm 1:1-2 is ever apt!

"They are not prosecuting a good object, but persecuting a good man. As if they had not enough mischief in their own hearts, they are hunting after more . . . David mentions this to the Lord in prayer, feeling some kind of comfort in the fact that those who hated him hated God also, and found it needful to get away from God before they could be free to act their cruel parts towards himself. When we know that our enemies are God's enemies, and ours because they are his, we may well take comfort to ourselves."[242]

Psalm 119:151

> "You are near, O LORD,
> And all Your commandments are truth."

Perhaps more than any other, this verse reminds me that You are not separate from Your word, and has inspired the title of this volume. Your nearness is my good, that goodness come to me through Your word, and that word comes to me personally as Your good Spirit leads me on level ground (Psalm 143:10) through it. By wondrous contrast, we see in v. 150 that those who are far from Your law draw near, but they cannot

---

242. Spurgeon, Charles Haddon, *Treasury of David*, on Psalm 119:150, e-Sword edition

be nearly as near as You are; they are near, but You are ever nearer. You have never abandoned me nor forsaken me. Psalm 27:9, Psalm 94:14, Hebrews 13:5, Isaiah 41:17. 'Your commandments are truth' - see also Psalm 119:142, Psalm 119:160. Utterly and ultimately reliable, You are the only God of truth (Psalm 31:5 , Isaiah 65:16). Your words are not simply true, they are truth, that is 'the final standard by which truthfulness is to be judged' (Grudem, Systematic Theology, p. 196).

"Near as the enemy might be, God was nearer: this is one of the choicest comforts of the persecuted child of God . . . God neither commands a lie, nor lies in his commands . . . This sentence will be the persecuted man's protection from the false hearts that seek to do him mischief, God is near and God is true, therefore his people are safe. If at any time we fall into danger through keeping the commands of God we need not suppose that we have acted unwisely.: we may, on the contrary, be quite sure that we are in the right way; for God's precepts are right and true. It is for this very reason that wicked men assail us: they hate the truth, and therefore hate those who do the truth. Their opposition may be our consolation; while God's presence upon our side is our glory and delight."[243]

Psalm 119:152

"Of old I have known from Your testimonies
That You have founded them forever."

'Your word is not only the foundation of my life (1 Peter 1:23), but it is the foundation of all creation (Proverbs 3:19-20) and of all creativity (Proverbs 24:3-4). 'Of old' is echoed in Psalm 102:25. The phrase 'of old' appears 42 times in the NASB Bible, 14 in the Psalms, 2 in Psalm 119; see also Psalm 119:52, where remembrance of Your ordinances of old is a great comfort. Why? Because You never change, Your word never changes, it is a sure foundation beyond me and my times and

---

243. Spurgeon, Charles Haddon, *Treasury of David*, on Psalm 119:151, e-Sword edition

circumstances. 'Founded' in the Hebrew ' יָסַד, yāsaḏ, a verb meaning to establish, to found, to fix.' Oh, to live upon the rock of Your word and upon the Rock of Christ (Isaiah 28:16, Romans 9:33, 1 Peter 2:6, 1 Corinthians 10:4). Following v.151, I rejoice that You are near and will always be near (Hebrews 13:5, Hebrews 13:18).

"David found of old that God had founded them of old, and that they would stand firm throughout all ages ... He had begun by building on a rock, by seeing that God's testimonies were 'founded,' that is, grounded, laid as foundations, settled and established; and that with a view to all the ages that should come, during all the changes that should intervene ... a man cannot have much expectation from a changing friend, but he may well have confidence in a God who cannot change ... Let those who choose follow at the heels of the modern school and look for fresh light to break forth which will put the old light out of countenance; we are satisfied with the truth which is old as the hills and as fixed as the great mountains. Let 'cultured intellects' invent another god, more gentle and effeminate than the God of Abraham; we are well content to worship Jehovah, who is eternally the same. Things everlastingly established are the joy of established saints. Bubbles please boys, but men prize those things which are solid and substantial, with a foundation and a bottom to them which will bear the test of ages."[244]

---

244. Spurgeon, Charles Haddon, *Treasury of David*, on Psalm 119:152, e-Sword edition

CHAPTER 20
Resh: 'Nearness in Affliction'

"Resh. Look upon my affliction and rescue me,
For I do not forget Your law.
[154] Plead my cause and redeem me;
Revive me according to Your word.
[155] Salvation is far from the wicked,
For they do not seek Your statutes.
[156] Great are Your mercies, O LORD;
Revive me according to Your ordinances.
[157] Many are my persecutors and my adversaries,
Yet I do not turn aside from Your testimonies.
[158] I behold the treacherous and loathe them,
Because they do not keep Your word.
[159] Consider how I love Your precepts;
Revive me, O LORD, according to Your lovingkindness.
[160] The sum of Your word is truth,
And every one of Your righteous ordinances is everlasting."

—Psalm 119:153-160

If Your nearness is my good (Psalm 73:28), then distance from You is an unbearable terror (Psalm 27:9). Here we see the Psalmist relish Your attention (v. 153), advocacy and revival (v. 154, 156, 159), lovingkindness (v. 159) and complete and everlasting truth (v. 160). This stands in sharp contrast with the wicked who do not seek Your statutes (v. 155), many persecutors and adversaries who can take comfort only in one another (v. 157, see also Psalm 2:2-4, Psalm 25:19), and the treacherous who are worthy of godly loathing, rejecting the riches of Your word (v. 158, see also Psalm 139:21, Proverbs 13:13). How miraculous, Father, that You would use the affliction of those who are far from You to bring Your people near to You.

"In this section the Psalmist seems to draw still nearer to God in prayer, and to state his case and to invoke the divine help with more of boldness and expectation. It is a pleading passage, and the key-word of it is, 'Consider.' With much boldness he pleads his intimate union with the Lord's cause as a reason why he should be aided. The special aid that he seeks is personal quickening, for which he cries to the Lord again and again."[245]

Psalm 119:153

> "Look upon my affliction and rescue me,
> For I do not forget Your law."

Look upon my affliction, and that I do not forget Your law. Surely You see and hear according to the promise of Your word, Psalm 33:13-22. I don't merely need direction, I need rescue. 'Affliction' is the Hebrew עֳנִי, oni which also has the sense of poverty. 'Rescue' is the Hebrew חָלַץ, ḥālaṣ, a verb with the sense of draw out, prepare, deliver, equip for war, to strengthen or fortify (Isaiah 58:11). Like David in Psalm 40:1-3, I need you to draw me up out of the miry clay, the pit of destruction, to cleanse me, to set me on solid ground, and strengthen me to live above ground.

---

245. Spurgeon, Charles Haddon, *Treasury of David*, on Psalm 119 - Resh, e-Sword edition

May I not forget; in other words, let my remembrance and focus on Your word be permanently sharpened for any circumstance. Let each affliction draw me permanently closer to You so that I don't shrink back again (Philippians 3:16, Hebrews 10:39).

"It should be the desire of every gracious man who is in adversity that the Lord should look upon his need, and relieve it in such a way as shall be most for the divine glory, and for his own benefit . . . His prayer is eminently practical, for he seeks to be delivered; that is, brought out of the trouble and preserved from sustaining any serious damage by it. For God to consider is to act in due season, men consider and do nothing; but such is never the case with our God . . . He forgot prosperity, but he did not forget obedience . . . If we do not forget his law the Lord will not forget us. He will not long leave that man in trouble whose only fear in trouble is lest he should leave the way of right."[246]

Psalm 119:154

> "Plead my cause and redeem me;
> Revive me according to Your word."

I am wholly inadequate as an advocate. My spirit leaps at the truth of 1 John 2:1, which Job foresaw in Job 16:19. 'Jesus Christ the righteous.' 1 Peter 3:18, 2 Corinthians 5:21 - what an unfair and glorious exchange! 'Revive' as we have discovered has the sense of granting and sustaining life.

"Plead, etc. — Hengstenberg translates, 'Fight my fight.' (See Psa 35:1; Psa 43:1; Mic 7:9)."[247]

"Alexander reads it, 'Strive my strife, and redeem me' - that is, stand in my stead, bear my burden, fight my fight, pay my price, and bring me out to liberty. When we feel ourselves dumb before the foe, here is a prayer made to our hand. What a comfort that if we sin we have an advocate, and if we do not sin the same pleader is engaged on our side."[248]

---

246. Spurgeon, Charles Haddon, *Treasury of David*, on Psalm 119:153, e-Sword edition
247. *Jamieson-Fausset-Brown Commentary*, on Psalm 119:154, e-Sword edition
248. Spurgeon, Charles Haddon, *Treasury of David*, on Psalm 119:154, e-Sword edition

Psalm 119:155

> "Salvation is far from the wicked,
> For they do not seek Your statutes."

This is both just and tragic. It is also common, Romans 3:11ff. For salvation to come to the unrepentant rebel when the riches of Your grace is offered would be utterly unjust. To reward the seeking of one's own way above Yours would be entirely corrupt. Mercy beyond measure, incalculable grace, You have laid our iniquities on Christ (Isaiah 53:6) that we would be saved from what we deserve (Romans 6:23) and bring us to the proper place of fear and worship (Psalm 130:4, Psalm 40:16). You save sinners, save them even today. For those who remain in sin, may I not fret over them (Psalm 37:5-8), but rather pray that You would grant repentance leading to the knowledge of the truth (1 Peter 2:25, 2 Timothy 2:25-26). Because Your nearness is the ultimate good, how terrifying it must be ultimately to be far from You (Psalm 73:27-28, Psalm 14:4-5)!

"How can those expect to seek God's favour with success, when they are in adversity, who never sought his statutes when they were in prosperity? But eternal salvation is certainly far from them."[249]

"Every step they have taken in the path of evil has removed them further from the kingdom of grace: they go from one degree of hardness to another till their hearts become as stone . . . they seek themselves, they seek evil, and therefore they never find the way of peace and righteousness. When men have broken the statutes of the Lord their wisest course is by repentance to seek forgiveth, and by faith to seek salvation . . . Salvation and God's statutes go together: those who are saved by the King of grace love the statutes of the King of glory."[250]

---

249. Henry, Matthew, *Commentary on the Whole Bible*, on Psalm 119:155, e-Sword edition
250. Spurgeon, Charles Haddon, *Treasury of David*, on Psalm 119:155, e-Sword edition

Psalm 119:156

"Great are Your mercies, O LORD;
Revive me according to Your ordinances."

See also Psalm 119:149. We plead on the basis of Your character and Your word. If it was on the basis of self, I would have no ground at all. Your compassion, mercy, affection abound. Cause me to live according to Your standards for life! 'Revive' again has the sense of to grant and sustain life. I think of Job 33:4, where it is used as 'gives me life' and Psalm 22:29, Psalm 30:3 as to keep my soul alive, but most commonly in Psalm 119 as 'revive'. And of course we know the word itself brings life (Luke 8:11, 1 Peter 1:23, Hebrews 4:12), healing (Psalm 107:20), and provision (Matthew 24:45, Matthew 11:5).

"In the first case he mentions his prayer, but leaves the method of its accomplishment with the wisdom or judgment of God; while here he pleads no prayer of his own, but simply the mercies of the Lord, and begs to be quickened by judgments rather than to be left to spiritual lethargy . . . 'Great are thy tender mercies, O Lord.' Here the Psalmist pleads the largeness of God's mercy, the immensity of his tender love; yea, he speaks of mercies - mercies many, mercies tender, mercies great; and with the glorious Jehovah he makes this a plea for his one leading prayer, the prayer for quickening . . . We shall never be short of arguments if we draw them from God himself, and urge both his mercies and his judgments as reasons for our quickening."[251]

Psalm 119:157

"Many are my persecutors and my adversaries,
Yet I do not turn aside from Your testimonies."

'Many'. How important it is to be free from the fear of man (Proverbs 29:25), for 'let God be found true, though every man be found a liar'

---

251. Spurgeon, Charles Haddon, *Treasury of David*, on Psalm 119:156, e-Sword edition

(Romans 3:4). May I not say in despair, "All men are liars." (Psalm 116:11) and then be distracted from Your word. May all things cause me to turn to You for the right character and wisdom. The litmus test is the filling of the Spirit.

" . . . multitudes will follow the pernicious ways of abused authority. David, being a public person, had many enemies, but withal he had many friends, who loved him and wished him well; let him set the one over-against the other. In this David was a type both of Christ and his church. The enemies, the persecutors, of both, are many, very many . . . A man who is steady in the way of his duty, though he may have many enemies, needs fear none."[252]

"The disciple cannot be loved where his Master is hated. The seed of the serpent must oppose the seed of the woman: it is their nature . . . There is enough in the testimonies of God to recompense us for pushing forward against all the hosts that may combine against us. So long as they cannot drive or draw us into a spiritual decline our foes have done us no great harm, and they have accomplished nothing by their malice. If we do not decline they are defeated. If they cannot make us sin they have missed their mark. Faithfulness to the truth is victory over our enemies."[253]

Psalm 119:158

> "I behold the treacherous and loathe them,
> Because they do not keep Your word."

Something impresses my heart that is both very right and very wrong at the same time. It is right to loathe treachery and essential not to participate in it. It is right to view it primarily as an offense to You and not to me, Lord. Yet, at the same time, I must not dwell with or focus on such treachery (Psalm 1:1, Psalm 101:3-8), and I must not live in hatred (Luke 6:27, Luke 6:35) or bitterness (Ephesians 4:31, Hebrews 12:15). It is

---

252. Henry, Matthew, *Commentary on the Whole Bible*, on Psalm 119:157, e-Sword edition
253. Spurgeon, Charles Haddon, *Treasury of David*, on Psalm 119:157, e-Sword edition

interesting how Psalm 139:21-24 ends. David hates those who hate You 'with the utmost hatred' as his enemies, then asks you to search and know his heart, to lead him away from any hurtful ways. Is this hatred one of them? This 'loathing' is the Hebrew קוט, qûṭ, a verb with the sense of to loathe, to abhor. This loathing seems appropriate and short of hatred, both in terms of its intensity and duration.

"It *grieved* him to see them dishonour God, serve Satan, debauch the world, and ruin their own souls, to see the transgressors so numerous, so daring, so very impudent, and so industrious to draw unstable souls into their snares. All this cannot but be a grief to those who have any regard to the glory of God and the welfare of mankind. . . . He was grieved, not because they were vexatious to him, but because they were provoking to God: *They kept not thy word.*"[254]

"I was sorry to see such sinners. I was sick of them, disgusted with them, I could not endure them. I found no pleasure in them, they were a sad sight to me, however fine their clothing or witty their chattering. Even when they were most mirthful a sight of them made my heart heavy; I could not tolerate either them or their doings. 'Because they kept not thy word.' My grief was occasioned more by their sin against God than by their enmity against myself . . . I cannot keep the company of those who keep not God's word."[255]

Psalm 119:159

"Consider how I love Your precepts;
Revive me, O LORD, according to Your lovingkindness."

Can you love something and still not fully experience it? This would seem to be the case for the Psalmist here. He loves the word but his current experience does not match his love. Feeling the deadness of sin, he desires the liveliness of righteousness. So often that is the case for me, as I ask You to revive me each morning! I seek You in the morning

---

254. Henry, Matthew, *Commentary on the Whole Bible*, on Psalm 119:158, e-Sword edition
255. Spurgeon, Charles Haddon, *Treasury of David*, on Psalm 119:158, e-Sword edition

because I love You and Your word more than anything! (Psalm 119:147-148) But my emotions are slow to follow. Previously the Psalmist had asked that You revive him according to Your lovingkindness (Psalm 119:88), underserved for sure, but utterly necessary to please and glorify You! 'Get what You are worthy of.' (Mike Riccardi summarizing Augustine). Considering the love You have already produced in me for Your word, may that blossom into fulness!

"He does not say, 'Consider how I fulfil thy precepts;' he was conscious to himself that in many things he came short; but, "Consider how I love them." Our obedience is pleasing to God, and pleasant to ourselves, only when it comes from a principle of love."[256]

"He loved the precepts of God - loved them unspeakably - loved them so as to be grieved with those who did not love them . . . The Psalmist so loved everything that was good and excellent that he loved all God had commanded. The precepts are all of them wise and holy, therefore the man of God loved them extremely, loved to know them, to think of them, to proclaim them, and principally to practise them . . . We may understand that David felt like one who was half stunned with the assaults of his foes, ready to faint under their incessant malice. What he wanted was revival, restoration, renewal; therefore he pleaded for more life, O thou who didst quicken me when I was dead, quicken me again that I may not return to the dead! Quicken me that I may outlive the blows of my enemies, the faintness of my faith, and the swooning of my sorrow . . . Because God is love he will give us life; because he is kind he will again kindle the heavenly flame within us."[257]

Psalm 119:160

"The sum of Your word is truth,
And every one of Your righteous ordinances is everlasting."

---

256. Henry, Matthew, *Commentary on the Whole Bible*, on Psalm 119:159, e-Sword edition
257. Spurgeon, Charles Haddon, *Treasury of David*, on Psalm 119:159, e-Sword edition

In part and in whole, Your word is eternal truth. Isaiah 40:8, Psalm 119:89. You are true though every man be found a liar (Romans 3:4). Your words are not simply true, they are truth, that is 'the final standard by which truthfulness is to be judged' (Grudem, Systematic Theology, p. 196). 'Sum' is the Hebrew שׁאר, rōʾš, a noun with the sense of head, best, lead, complete, entire. The meaning of 'every one' is straightforward, effectively 'each and every'. Not just each ordinance, but 'every word' (see Deuteronomy 8:3, Matthew 4:4). 'Everything' in Deuteronomy 8:3 is the same word. For both breadth and depth, nothing compares! While I am profoundly thankful for the small amount of living water I have acquired, I swim in a veritable ocean of it! Safe, alive, strong, and true. All praise to You, Father, for this unspeakable gift!

"The ungodly are false, but God's word is true. They charge us with being false, but our solace is that God's true word will clear us. 'From the beginning.' God's word has been true from the first moment in which it was spoken, true throughout the whole of history, true to us from the instant in which we believed it, ay, true to us before we were true to it. Some read it, 'Thy word is true from the head;' true as a whole, true from top to bottom . . . Against the decisions of the Lord no writ of error can be demanded; neither will there ever be a repealing of any of the acts of his sovereignty. There is not one single mistake either in the word of God or in the providential dealings of God. Neither in the book of revelation nor of providence will there be any need to put a single note of errata. The Lord has nothing to regret or to retract, nothing to amend or to reverse. All God's judgments, decrees, commands, and purposes are righteous, and as righteous things are lasting things, every one of them will outlive the stars."[258]

---

258. Spurgeon, Charles Haddon, *Treasury of David*, on Psalm 119:160, e-Sword edition

CHAPTER 21
Shin: 'Peace'

"Shin. Princes persecute me without cause,
But my heart stands in awe of Your words.
[162] I rejoice at Your word,
As one who finds great spoil.
[163] I hate and despise falsehood,
But I love Your law.
[164] Seven times a day I praise You,
Because of Your righteous ordinances.
[165] Those who love Your law have great peace,
And nothing causes them to stumble.
[166] I hope for Your salvation, O LORD,
And do Your commandments.
[167] My soul keeps Your testimonies,
And I love them exceedingly.
[168] I keep Your precepts and Your testimonies,
For all my ways are before You."

—Psalm 119:161-168

The treasure is secure. Unjust persecution (v. 161) and falsehood (v. 163) could not keep the Psalmist from it, for he had found great spoil (v. 162) in Your word, and praised You unceasingly for it (v. 164). The peace is beyond compare, enduring any circumstance (v. 165). But the real benefit comes in the doing, which is the Psalmist's most precious possession (see Psalm 119:60). In his hope he does Your commandments (v. 166), in love he keeps them (v. 167), and he obeys in the light of Your presence (v. 168, see also Psalm 44:3, Psalm 90:8, Hebrews 4:12-13).

"We are drawing near to the end. The pulse of Psalm 119 beats more quickly than usual. The sentences are shorter, the sense is more vivid, the tone is more full and deep. The veteran of a thousand battles and the receiver of ten thousand mercies rehearses his experience and again declares his loyalty to the Lord and His law. Oh, that when we come to the close of life we might be able to speak like David does as he closes his life-psalm! Not boastfully, but still boldly, he places himself among the obedient servants of the Lord. Oh, to be clear in conscience when life's sun is setting!"[259]

Psalm 119:161

"Princes persecute me without cause,
But my heart stands in awe of Your words."

The awesome of the earth may persecute me, but I know Whose I am and Who speaks to me, and my awe is directed properly! 'Stop regarding man', Isaiah 2:22. 'Stands in awe' is the Hebrew פָּחַד, pāḥaḏ, a verb with the sense of dread, be in awe. Who holds sway in my life? It should not even be close. One might say that princes may persecute without cause, and God has grace without cause. I read from this that I gain no true comfort or strength from great men, but I gain it from Almighty God.

---

259. Spurgeon, Charles Haddon . *The Golden Alphabet* (Updated, Annotated): An Exposition of Psalm 119 (pp. 249-250). Aneko Press. Kindle Edition.

The fear of man vanishes with the awe (LSB 'dread') of God, and we see how that plays out in the rest of Shin (vvv. 161-168). Moses was most humble (Numbers 12:3) because he had seen You (Exodus 33:18-34:9). We see this also with Isaiah (Isaiah 6:1-7). The Apostles' boldness (Acts 4:19-20) was not simply in what that had seen in the past (1 John 1:1-4), but the stronger reality they were experiencing in the present (John 16:7, Acts 2:43, Acts 7:55-56, 1 Peter 1:9). 'Knowing the fear of God, we persuade men' (2 Corinthians 5:11), bowing not to them, but to You with whom we have to do (Hebrews 4:13).

"In the midst of persecution God's word was still his fear, his joy, and his love, the object of his thanksgiving, and the ground of his hope."[260]

Psalm 119:162

"I rejoice at Your word,
As one who finds great spoil."

See also Psalm 119:14, Psalm 119:72, Psalm 119:111. Surely Your wisdom from Your mouth (Proverbs 2:6) is beyond anything I can desire (Proverbs 3:15, Proverbs 8:11), Your power and ability beyond anything I can conceive (Ephesians 3:20), as is Your knowledge (Romans 11:33). Surely this is a cause of awe (see v. 161), of indescribable rejoicing. I know about all of this from the revelation of Your word (Psalm 119:130), which is the very origin and sustainer of my life (James 1:18, Matthew 4:4). There is no receiving what we need and walking away, 'taking it from here'. You sustain all things by the word of Your power (Hebrews 1:3), and Your word is my very life (Deuteronomy 32:47). You both wound and heal through Your word (Job 5:17-18), and I can't live a moment without it, for to live without it is to live without You because I have ceased listening to You - what coldness, what utter darkness! May my rejoicing multiply, even today, as You lift me up to the heights by Your word (Habakkuk 3:19).

---

260. Keil & Delitzsch, *Commentary on the Old Testament*, on Psalm 119:161, e-Sword edition

"He trembled at the word of the Lord, and yet rejoiced at it. He compares his joy to that of one who has been long in battle, and has at last won the victory and is dividing the spoil . . . The profits made in searching the Scriptures were greater than the trophies of war. We too have to fight for divine truth; every doctrine costs us a battle, but when we gain a full understanding of it by personal struggles it becomes doubly precious to us . . . Whether we come by the truth as finders or as warriors fighting for it, the heavenly treasure should be equally dear to us. With what quiet joy does the ploughman steal home with his golden find! How victors shout as they share the plunder! How glad should that man be who has discovered his portion in the promises of holy writ, and is able to enjoy it for himself, knowing by the witness of the Holy Spirit that it is all his own."[261]

Psalm 119:163

"I hate and despise falsehood,
But I love Your law."

It is human nature to go speck hunting and let logs lie (see Matthew 7:3-5, Luke 6:41-42). The only way I can control its outside influence is to make the good word (Psalm 119:104) and good men (Proverbs 2:20) the things that primary influence my heart, knowing that the mouths of liars will eventually be stopped (Psalm 63:11). The only way I can control its inside influence is by the repentance that follows. Show me the falsehood in my own heart and the fruit of discontent (Psalm 119:165) and of the flesh (Galatians 5:19-21, James 3:15-16) that result. Lead me on to the better path of repentance and faith. May love of Your law wash away angst of lies. Whenever I seek to present an image that is inconsistent with my thoughts and character, I am loving falsehood. Make me true, through and through! Psalm 51:6. Proverbs 21:28. A sure future comes from listening to the truth.

---

261. Spurgeon, Charles Haddon, *Treasury of David*, on Psalm 119:162, e-Sword edition

"Love and hatred are the leading affections of the soul; if those be fixed aright, the rest move accordingly . . . Hypocrisy is lying; false doctrine is lying; breach of faith is lying. Lying, in commerce or conversation, is a sin which every good man hates and abhors, hates and doubly hates, because of the seven things which the Lord hates one is a lying tongue and another is a false witness that speaks lies, Pro 6:16. Every man hates to have a lie told him; but we should more hate telling a lie because by the former we only receive an affront from men, by the latter we give an affront to God . . . The more we see of the amiable beauty of truth the more we shall see of the detestable deformity of a lie."[262]

"This was a remarkable state for an Oriental, for generally lying is the delight of Easterns, and the only wrong they see in it is a want of skill in its exercise so that the liar is found out . . . He set down all opposition to the God of truth as lying, and then he turned his whole soul against it in the intensest form of indignation. Godly men should detest false doctrine even as they abhor a lie. 'But thy law do I love,' because it is all truth. His love was as ardent as his hate. True men love truth, and hate lying . . . Both love and hate are contagious, and when they are sanctified the wider their influence the better."[263]

Psalm 119:164

> "Seven times a day I praise You,
> Because of Your righteous ordinances."

As a Protestant Christian, my immediate reaction to verse like this is to resist legalism. As a recovering perfectionist, this is doubly my reaction. When shall I schedule these 7 times, and how will I track my progress? But then I think of Psalm 34:1-3, how can Your praise not be continually in my mouth? If the goal of my life is to magnify You, seven times seems light duty.

---

262. Henry, Matthew, *Commentary on the Whole Bible*, on Psalm 119:163, e-Sword edition
263. Spurgeon, Charles Haddon, *Treasury of David*, on Psalm 119:163, e-Sword edition

'At the sight of the oppressive princes, and at the hearing of the abounding falsehood around him, he felt all the more bound to adore and magnify God - who in all things is truth and righteousness. When others rob us of our praise it should be a caution to us not to fall into the same conduct towards our God, who is so much more worthy of honour.'[264]

Psalm 119:165

> "Those who love Your law have great peace,
> And nothing causes them to stumble."

I am slayed by this verse. How greatly I would say that I love Your law, but how greatly I have striven to find peace. So I would say that I have often not loved Your law as I ought. What does it truly mean to love Your law? Well, my initial thought is that I must love it above my own thoughts. This is often not true! I must also love its ways above my own default ways; again, often not true! Now we are getting past the mind and into the affections.

Peace here is shalom, utter well-being. This is eagerly sought but elusive. This means that the sufficiency of Your word must be appropriated in new ways. 'When my anxious thoughts multiply within me, Your consolations delight my soul.' (Psalm 94:19). Multiplication of anxiety must be met with multiplication of consolations, a bathing in Your attributes and promises. Perfect peace awaits those whose mind is 'stayed on Thee' (Isaiah 26:3 RSV); Your peace guards those who entrust all to You (Philippians 4:7).

"He gives thanks to God for His word, which so righteously decides and so correctly guides, is a source of transcendent peace to all who love it . . . "[265]

"But with those who love it, whose hearts and hands are made to square with its precepts and demands. These men are ever striving, with

---

264. Spurgeon, Charles Haddon, *Treasury of David*, on Psalm 119:164, e-Sword edition
265. Keil & Delitzsch, *Commentary on the Old Testament*, on Psalm 119:165, e-Sword edition

all their hearts, to walk in obedience to the law, and though they are often persecuted they have peace, yea, great peace; . . . They have many troubles, and are likely to be persecuted by the proud, but their usual condition is that of deep calm - a peace too great for this little world to break . . . That peace which is founded upon conformity to God's will is a living and lasting one, worth writing of with enthusiasm,"[266]

Psalm 119:66

"I hope for Your salvation, O LORD,
And do Your commandments."

This is an expression of 'in His word do I hope' in Psalm 130:5. Surely You have done it, Lord, causing me to hope in Your word (Psalm 119:49). Your word truly is my hope! Psalm 119:116. May my expectations be properly placed. I think of Proverbs 10:28; may I live in the gladness of a true hope and not act like the wicked whose expectation perishes. Notice how this hope works itself out. The Psalmist does the commandments (this verse), and he keeps the testimonies and precepts with love and awareness of Your presence (vv. 167-168). 'Hope' here is the Hebrew שָׂבַר, sabar, a verb with the sense of to wait, hope. We see it as 'wait' or 'look to' in Psalm 104:27 and Psalm 145:15, to give food in due season/time. The sense is in Psalm 123:2, looking to you as our great Master to graciously provide. Because Your provision is in Your word, I proceed with hope in that path. I don't look to others, I don't look to circumstances or systems. I look to You. How important that it be an exclusive hope for it to be real! Psalm 62:5-6. Surely I entrust myself to You in doing what is right, 1 Peter 4:19.

"Those who place least reliance upon good works are very frequently those who have the most of them; that same divine teaching which delivers us from confidence in our own doings leads us to abound in every good work to the glory of God."[267]

---

266. Spurgeon, Charles Haddon, *Treasury of David*, on Psalm 119:165, e-Sword edition
267. Spurgeon, Charles Haddon, *Treasury of David*, on Psalm 119:166, e-Sword edition

Psalm 119:167

> "My soul keeps Your testimonies,
> And I love them exceedingly."

I have no interest in an outward appearance of righteousness without a soul reality. The cultural moment we are in (2023 does not value faithfulness to Your word, often even in professing Christianity. 'I have come to an empty place, to the wilderness of my soul / The selfish life that I once embraced seldom satisfies me anymore' (Steve Camp, from 'After God's Own Heart'). All this to say, I am thankful for the lack of external motivation to obey You. It must be deep, in the soul, 'exceedingly', above all other desires, including reputation and the approval of men. In fact, it so much needs to be against that. I keep coming back to Psalm 51:6, 'truth in the innermost being'. I see other uses of the word 'innermost' in Job 38:36, Proverbs 20:27, and John 7:38. May my integrity be disarming - both of sin in my own heart and externally as I interact with others (Proverbs 20:8). 'How blessed' are we in this full heart engagement (Psalm 119:1-2)!

"As they keep God's law from motives of love for it, and are free from slavish fear, they are ready to subject their lives to His inspection."[268]

"He felt that he could sooner die than give up any part of the revelation of God. The more we store our minds with heavenly truth, the more deeply shall we be in love with it: the more we see the exceeding riches of the Bible the more will our love exceed measure, and exceed expression."[269]

Psalm 119:168

> "I keep Your precepts and Your testimonies,
> For all my ways are before You."

---

268. *Jamieson-Fausset-Brown Commentary*, on Psalm 119:167, e-Sword edition
269. Spurgeon, Charles Haddon, *Treasury of David*, on Psalm 119:167, e-Sword edition

Like Proverbs 5:21, this verse seems to emphasize the 'negative' of the fear of God. Father, You see everything! Because You are full of lovingkindness and truth (Deuteronomy 34:6), I want to receive the 'all my ways are before You' as an indescribable gift! You see, You hear, You understand, You draw near to be gracious (Psalm 33:13-18). You know everything about me, yet Your love is infinite (Psalm 103:1-5). Because I will have to give an account to You (Romans 14:12), keeping on the straight and narrow is a safeguard against sure destruction to self and others (Proverbs 1:32-33, 1 Peter 2:11). Precepts are your instructions, testimonies are Your proclamations of truth. The context of Shin is great love and rejoicing in Your word! Because I love them exceedingly (v. 167), my heart keeps Your commandments (Proverbs 3:1-2), and this is no outward facade (Matthew 6:5-6, Colossians 3:22).

"Both the practical and the doctrinal parts of God's word he had stored up, and preserved, and followed. It is a blessed thing to see the two forms of the divine word, equally known, equally valued, equally confessed: there should be no picking and choosing as to the mind of God . . . Before God we may be clear of open fault and yet at the same time mourn over a thousand heart-wanderings which need his restoring hand."[270]

---

270. Spurgeon, Charles Haddon, *Treasury of David*, on Psalm 119:168, e-Sword edition

CHAPTER 22
Tav: 'Let It Be'

"Tav. Let my cry come before You, O LORD;
Give me understanding according to Your word.
[170] Let my supplication come before You;
Deliver me according to Your word.
[171] Let my lips utter praise,
For You teach me Your statutes.
[172] Let my tongue sing of Your word,
For all Your commandments are righteousness.
[173] Let Your hand be ready to help me,
For I have chosen Your precepts.
[174] I long for Your salvation, O LORD,
And Your law is my delight.
[175] Let my soul live that it may praise You,
And let Your ordinances help me.
[176] I have gone astray like a lost sheep; seek Your servant,
For I do not forget Your commandments."

—Psalm 119:169-176

'Let' my cry come before You (v. 169), my supplication come before You (v. 170), my lips utter praise (v. 171), my tongue sing of Your word (v. 172), Your hand be ready to help me (v. 173), my soul live (v. 175), and Your ordinances help me (v. 175). Like one being lifted out of the pit, the Psalmist is revived and delivered (vv. 169-170) to the place of worship from seeing and learning Your word (vv. 171-172), resolve in them (v. 173), longing and delight (v. 174), and a life assured that is sustained by Your active, seeking word (vv. 175-176).

"The psalmist is now at the last section of the psalm, and his petitions gather still more force and fervency. He seems to break into the inner circle of divine fellowship and to even come to the feet of the great God for whose help He is pleading. This nearness creates the lowliest view of himself and leads him to close the psalm, prostrate in the dust, in deepest self-humiliation, begging to be sought out like a lost sheep."[271]

Psalm 119:169

"Let my cry come before You, O LORD;
Give me understanding according to Your word."

This is yet another cry of desperation for You to grant me what I could not gain alone: understanding according to Your word. Confusion and frustration abound. We were not made to live in it.

"He desires spiritual light and understanding as it is promised in God's word, as it proceeds from God's word, and as it produces obedience to God's word. He pleads as though he had no understanding whatever of his own, and asks to have one given to him. 'Give me understanding.' In truth, he had an understanding according to the judgment of men, but what he sought was an understanding according to God's word, which is quite another thing. To understand spiritual things is the gift of God. To have a judgment enlightened by heavenly light and conformed

---

271. Spurgeon, Charles Haddon . *The Golden Alphabet* (Updated, Annotated): An Exposition of Psalm 119 (pp. 259-260). Aneko Press. Kindle Edition.

to divine truth is a privilege which only grace can give. Many a man who is accounted wise after the manner of this world is a fool according to the word of the Lord. May we be among those happy children who shall all be taught of the Lord."[272]

Psalm 119:170

"Let my supplication come before You;
Deliver me according to Your word."

Where is my faith? I am short in thankfulness for all the prayers answered, short in faith for future deliverance. Yet, mustard size is all that is required (Matthew 17:20)! Lord, You know my faith and what is best. The words here are straightforward. I am reminded of Psalm 65:2 and Psalm 102:1, asking that You would hear according to Your word. I am reminded also of John 15:7, 1 John 5:14-15, that confidence comes in knowing Your will through Your word, and praying accordingly. This is exactly the spirit of Psalm 119:169-170.

"The prayer for understanding of the truth precedes that for deliverance. The fulfillment of the first is the basis of the fulfillment of the second (Psa 90:11-17). On the terms 'cry' and 'supplication' (compare Psa 6:9; Psa 17:1)."[273]

"Rid me of mine adversaries, clear me of my slanderers, preserve me from my tempters, and bring me up out of all my afflictions even as thy word has led me to expect thou wilt do. It is for this that he seeks understanding."[274]

Psalm 119:171

"Let my lips utter praise,
For You teach me Your statutes."

---

272. Spurgeon, Charles Haddon, *Treasury of David*, on Psalm 119:169, e-Sword edition
273. *Jamieson-Fausset-Brown Commentary*, on Psalm 119:170, e-Sword edition
274. Spurgeon, Charles Haddon, *Treasury of David*, on Psalm 119:170, e-Sword edition

'Let' - my cry come before You for understanding (v. 169), my supplication come before You for deliverance (v.170), and now my lips to utter praise. Through Your word I get understanding and deliverance, and those beyond measure! See Psalm 119:47-48. Depths of knowledge lead to heights of worship. Oh the depths (Romans 11:33)! Oh the sweetness (Psalm 19:10, Psalm 119:103)! Oh the satisfaction (Psalm 36:8)! Oh the joy (Jeremiah 15:16)! Oh the eternal pleasure (Psalm 16:11)! Have You not taught me, even lowly me (Proverbs 22:17-19)?

"We have learned nothing to purpose if we have not learned to praise God."[275]

"He will not always be pleading for himself, he will rise above all selfishness, and render thanks for the benefit received . . . The best possible praise is that which proceeds from men who honour God, not only with their lips, but in their lives . . . he would express that gratitude in appropriate terms: his lips would utter what his life had practised. Eminent disciples are wont to speak well of the master who instructed them, and this holy man, when taught the statutes of the Lord, promises to give all the glory to him to whom it is due."[276]

Psalm 119:172

"Let my tongue sing of Your word,
For all Your commandments are righteousness."

Worship and the word cannot be separated. When you experience something this good, this perfect, one cannot help but worship, Psalm 138:8. I notice also in Jeremiah 7:2 and Jeremiah 26:2 that Your word is the fuel of Your worship. We must worship with knowledge (John 4:21-24), in spirit and in truth.

"The worst of us is that for the most part we are full of our own words, and speak but little of God's word . . . We may extol its truth,

---

275. Henry, Matthew, *Commentary on the Whole Bible*, on Psalm 119:171, e-Sword edition
276. Spurgeon, Charles Haddon, *Treasury of David*, on Psalm 119:171, e-Sword edition

its wisdom, its preciousness, its grace, its power; and then we may tell of all it has revealed, all it has promised, all it has commanded, all it has effected."[277]

Psalm 119:173

"Let Your hand be ready to help me,
For I have chosen Your precepts."

While this may sound like a bargain or something of a 'quid pro quo', I am reminded of Romans 11:36, from Job 41:11, namely, that I warrant no blessing from You, only judgment from Your hand. Ah, but Your word is full of gracious promises, what Spurgeon calls 'faith's checkbook'. 'Be gracious to me according to Your word' (Psalm 119:58) for if You were to mark iniquities, who would stand? (Psalm 130:3). I have chosen my trust, I lean into Your promises. An Ebeneezer is a 'stone of help' (1 Samuel 7:2), and here I raise it (see the hymn 'Come Thou Fount of Every Blessing'). Surely when I look to the only true Source of help, I will be helped on the grounds of the precious blood of Christ, Hebrews 4:16. Help is needed and justice sought, but true help and true justice can only come from You, Psalm 60:11-12, Proverbs 29:26. It is You Lord, it is always You! May You strongly support a heart of mine that is whole towards You, 2 Chronicles 16:9, and may you make it so.

"A man may fitly ask help from God's hand when he has dedicated his own hand entirely to the obedience of the faith . . . In reference to all earthly rules and ways, in preference even to his own will, he had chosen to be obedient to the divine commands . . . If grace has given us the heart with which to will, it will also give us the hand with which to perform. Whenever, under the constraints of a divine call, we are engaged in any high and lofty enterprise, and feel it to be too much for our strength, we may always invoke the right hand of God in words like these."[278]

---

277. Spurgeon, Charles Haddon, *Treasury of David*, on Psalm 119:172, e-Sword edition
278. Spurgeon, Charles Haddon, *Treasury of David*, on Psalm 119:173, e-Sword edition

Psalm 119:174

"I long for Your salvation, O LORD,
And Your law is my delight."

What one longs for is what one seeks delight in. Rescue me from the futility of my thoughts, words, and works! Isaiah 55:7-11. May I actively forsake mine for Yours, finding only futility within self but delight in You.

"Not only I delight in it, but it is my delight, the greatest delight I have in this world."[279]

"God's law, contained in the ten commandments, gives joy to believers. God's law, that is, the entire Bible, is a well-spring of consolation and enjoyment to all who receive it. Though we have not yet reached the fulness of our salvation, yet we find in God's word so much concerning a present salvation that we are even now delighted."[280]

Psalm 119:175

"Let my soul live that it may praise You,
And let Your ordinances help me."

Teach me the path of life (Psalm 16:11) that I may run it (Psalm 119:32) and see more light (Proverbs 4:18). Tav is full of 'let', the idea being simply 'may it come to be'. The Psalmist wants His desperate cry to come before You (v. 169-170), his lips to express praise based on Your word (vv. 171-172), Your hand to help him (v. 173), and now a quickened soul to praise You. 'Help' seems so understated regarding what I desperately need for my survival. This speaks not only of eternal life (see Psalm 30:3), but a plea for extended life to give You praise (Psalm 30:9). I remember my Mom praying this, a selfless prayer for an extended life. Yet, in Your providence, You have ordained that in life or death we may glorify You (John 21:19, 2 Corinthians 5:6-9).

---

279. Henry, Matthew, *Commentary on the Whole Bible*, on Psalm 119:174, e-Sword edition
280. Spurgeon, Charles Haddon, *Treasury of David*, on Psalm 119:174, e-Sword edition

"Fill it full of life, preserve it from wandering into the ways of death, give it to enjoy the indwelling of the Holy Ghost, let it live to the fulness of life, to the utmost possibilities of its new-created being . . . The more it shall live, the more it shall praise, and when it shall live in perfection it shall praise thee in perfection . . . let me be quickened and developed . . . Let all thy deeds in providence instruct me, and aid me in the struggle to overcome sin and to practise holiness."[281]

Psalm 119:176

"I have gone astray like a lost sheep; seek Your servant,
For I do not forget Your commandments."

The Psalmist acknowledges in the end that, in spite of Your wondrous word, He still wanders. Like a sheep, he both wanders and cannot save himself. This is true of all of us (Isaiah 53:6), and we need the Great Savior who became a lamb like us to pay the price, redeem us (John 1:29), and become the great Shepherd of the sheep (Hebrews 13:20). May we both join You in seeking and saving the lost (Luke 19:10) and in following You as our Great Shepherd. 'I do not forget Your commandments' - the Psalmist realizes that Your word is the means of the redemption, 'for by them You have revived me' (Psalm 119:93). So powerful and perfect is Your word! As I have come to You in faith and repentance, may I continue to live in it. 'Seek' is the Hebrew שַׁקֵּב, bāqaš, a verb with the sense of seek, require. This is the only occurrence in Psalms where it is used of You. You have redeemed me; may I live in that redemption!

"'I went astray' from the practical precepts, from the instructive doctrines, and from the heavenly experiences which thou hadst set before me. I lost my road, and I lost myself. Even now I am apt to wander, and, in fact, have roamed already; therefore, Lord, restore me. 'Seek thy servant.' He was not like a dog, that somehow or other can find its way back; but he was like a lost sheep, which goes further and further away

---

281. Spurgeon, Charles Haddon, *Treasury of David*, on Psalm 119:175, e-Sword edition

from home; yet still he was a sheep, and the Lord's sheep, his property, and precious in his sight, and therefore he hoped to be sought in order to be restored. However far he might have wandered he was still not only a sheep, but God's 'servant,' and therefore he desired to be in his Master's house again, and once more honoured with commissions for his Lord . . . I have a homesickness after my God, I pine after the ways of peace; I do not and I cannot forget thy commandments, nor cease to know that I am always happiest and safest when I scrupulously obey them, and find all my joy in doing so . . . Yet let the reader remember Psa 119:1 while he reads Psa 119:176, the major blessedness lies not in being restored from wandering, but in being upheld In a blameless way even to the end."[282]

---

282. Spurgeon, Charles Haddon, *Treasury of David*, on Psalm 119:176, e-Sword edition

ABOUT THE AUTHOR

Mark Daniel Twombly is fueled by the desire to know Christ, proclaim Him, and 'present every man complete in Christ' (Colossians 1:28-29) as God's transcendent purpose for him. Having come to faith in Christ as a child, God has built into him a love for His word as the foundation for all of life. He lives in central New Jersey as a husband to Betty, father of 6, and grandfather to 4. He has been blessed to serve in local church ministry in formal leadership for most of his adult life and continues to be active in teaching, leading, and discipleship. A graduate of Rutgers College, vocationally he is a Senior Manager of Program Management in the Telecommunications industry. He has written for Well Thought magazine and is author of the blog 'In His Grip' (http://mdtwombly.blogspot.com/).